MICROECONOMICS

Also by Mike Rosser

Women and the Economy: A Comparative Study of Britain and the USA
(with A. T. Mallier)

MICROECONOMICS
THE FIRM AND THE MARKET ECONOMY

Mike Rosser
Principal Lecturer, Coventry Polytechnic

MACMILLAN

First published 1988 by
THE MACMILLAN PRESS LTD
Houndmills, Basingstoke, Hampshire RG21 2XS
and London
Companies and representatives
throughout the world

ISBN 0–333–42309–7 hardcover
ISBN 0–333–46297–1 paperback

A catalogue record for this book is available
from the British Library.

Printed in Hong Kong

Reprinted 1993

Contents

Preface

Typically, on the first year of many undergraduate economics degree courses the majority of students have already studied economics at A level and microeconomics is taught at a level that goes beyond basic introductory economics but does not involve the depth of analysis presented in most standard intermediate microeconomics texts. The same applies to many second year microeconomics courses on degrees which include economics as a subsidiary subject, such as business studies and modular degree courses, where most students will have followed a first year introductory economics course and where the depth of theoretical analysis required is less than that expected on intermediate microeconomics courses on specialist economics degrees. It is for these courses that this book is mainly intended. However, for the benefit of any students who have not studied the subject before, Chapter 1 does provide an introduction to some basic economic concepts which can also profitably be used for revision by other students.

As well as covering the standard topics taught on most microeconomics courses, including the theory of production and costs, market structures, consumer theory, factor markets and welfare economics, this book also considers some other approaches to the study of the firm and the market economy. It examines some alternatives to the profit maximising theory of the firm, including the Marxian explanation of firms' behaviour in market economies, and looks at the relatively recent development of the theory of contestable markets.

Throughout the book the relationship between economic theory and practice is always kept in mind. Although there is not room for detailed case studies in this concise text, examples of the relevance of microeconomic theory to the real world are presented where appropriate. For example, there is a section devoted to linear production theory as well as an explanation of the conventional economic theory of production based on the assumption of perfect substitutability of inputs. With respect to welfare economics,

ix

Chapter 12 provides a critical appraisal of the policy guidelines that economists have put forward rather than just the arid technical analysis that is conveyed in some presentations of this topic.

The treatment of the material is mainly in terms of graphical analysis and requires no more than a knowledge of basic algebra and geometry. There are, however, certain sections which require an understanding of more advanced quantitative techniques, in particular the differential calculus. These sections have been kept to a minimum and are marked*. It is not necessary to cover them in order to follow the rest of the book, but students who are also following a quantitative methods course may find that these sections help them to relate the mathematical techniques that they have learned to economic concepts.

Each chapter is followed by a set of problems. Some are straightforward tests to see if the chapter has been properly understood and many of the calculation problems can be solved either algebraically or graphically. Other questions are of the 'discussion' type where there is no one correct response. In some cases there may appear to be one obvious answer, but students should always try to think carefully of any other possibilities, bearing in mind what they have learned from the chapter.

Lastly, in the examples presented in this book it is not implicitly assumed that all managers, investors, consumers, and so on are male. As can be seen from the biographical note on the author, one of my research interests is the female labour force. There are many ways in which sex discrimination permeates society and one small way in which lecturers and students can help to change the biased stereotyped attitudes towards the economic position of women that are still relatively widespread is through the references that they make with respect to the gender of the individuals, such as company managers, who perform different economic roles. Given that in most other texts the usual assumption is that they are all male, in most of the examples in this book they are assumed to be female in order to try to restore the balance.

Coventry   MIKE ROSSER

Acknowledgements

The author would like to acknowledge the use of material from the following sources and to express his thanks for permissions granted to reproduce copyright material. Cambridge University Press for material from C. F. Pratten, *Economies of Scale in Manufacturing Industry*; The Econometrics Society for material from A. A. Walters, *Econometrica*, vol. 31, 1963; the Controller of Her Majesty's Stationery Office for material from the *Annual Abstract of Statistics, The UK National Accounts* and the *Census of Population* (1971 and 1981); *The Journal of Industrial Affairs* for material from A. Cockerill, *JIA*, vol. 4, 1976; Philip Allan Publishers Limited for material from G. Rhys, *The Economic Review*, vol. 3, 1986; The Society of Motor Manufacturers and Traders for material from their yearbook.

I would also like to thank Mrs M. W. Fyvie and Mrs M. Lloyd for their invaluable assistance in typing the tables, diagrams and problem sheets, and my colleague Shinder Thandi for his constructive criticisms and useful suggestions with respect to Chapter 11. Last, but not least, I would like to thank my students who have, over the years, contributed to the way that this book has developed. In particular I would like to thank the part-time students on the BA Applied Economics Degree at Coventry Polytechnic who helped to highlight the errors, deficiencies and ambiguities in earlier versions of the material used in this book. I, of course, remain responsible for any remaining errors or omissions.

M. R.

CHAPTER 1

The market economy

This chapter outlines the main features of a market economy and provides an introduction to some basic concepts used in economics. It is mainly intended for students who are studying the subject for the first time. Many of those using this book will have already studied economics at A level, or will have followed some other introductory economics course, and should be familiar with this material. These students can proceed straight to Chapter 2, although it would still be a useful revision exercise for them to begin by working through this chapter, particularly if they have had a long summer vacation since last opening an economics textbook!

WHAT IS ECONOMICS?

Economists rarely all agree on an issue and the problem of defining the subject of economics is no exception. The most widely accepted definition is that economics is the study of how resources are allocated. This problem of resource allocation applies to consumers, firms, industries, the government and the economy as a whole. Although this book is mainly concerned with the allocation of resources at the level of individual firms and industries, or 'microeconomics', it is first necessary to understand how these different components fit into the economic system. Microeconomics does not just study how individual firms behave in isolation but how they behave in relation to other firms, other industries, consumers, the government and other features of an economic system.

Resources

The resources of an economy can be grouped into three broad categories:

1.   Land

This includes all the natural resources of an economy, such as mineral reserves, the amount of cultivable land, water sources.

2.   Labour

The potential labour power of an economy depends not just on the total number of people who are able and willing to work, but also on the skills that they can offer and their health and strength.

3.   Capital

This category covers those products of industry that are used in the production of other goods and services. The capital resources of an economy can include a wide range of items, varying from a multi-million pound steel mill to the ladder and bucket used by a window-cleaner. At a national level there are some capital items which may contribute to the production process of many different firms as well as directly satisfying consumers' needs; for example, a road system allows firms to have inputs delivered and output distributed and can also be used by private motorists driving for pleasure. It should be noted that the word 'capital' can be used in other senses, such as funds available for investment. This is just one of several terms that economists use in a sense different from their usual meaning in everyday language and the different definitions should not be confused.

The economic problem

Although the total resources of an economy can change naturally, for instance, through population growth or climatic change, or by design (which may involve foregoing a certain amount of current consumption), for example, by building factories or increasing education provision, at any given moment in time there exists a finite amount of resources that can be used for production. In other words, resources are limited.

On the other hand, the needs and desires of the population are unlimited. Most people would like to have more than they currently have of at least one good. There are not enough resources to supply every individual with the amount of every good that they would like to have and hence the basic economic problem arises of how to allocate limited resources, to satisfy unlimited wants.

This basic problem can be subdivided into three main questions:

1.   Which goods and services should be produced, and in what quantities?

2. How are they to be produced? Different production methods will draw differently on resources; for example, manual production methods obviously use more labour than automated systems.
3. How are the goods and services that are produced to be shared out among different members of the population? In a market economy this allocation is usually made according to what people are prepared to pay, but there are other methods; for example, hospital treatment can be given freely to those who need it.

It is important here to distinguish the terms 'needs' and 'desires' from the word 'demand', which is frequently used in economics. The demand for a good is defined as the amount of the good that consumers are willing and able (that is, can afford) to buy. Thus although there are some people in parts of the third world who need food, in other words, who are starving, because they cannot afford to buy it they have no demand for food in the economic sense of the word. The basic economic problem of unlimited wants and limited resources is concerned with 'needs and desires' in the wider senses of these words.

ECONOMIC SYSTEMS

The market economy solution, which only involves the satisfaction of those wants that can be backed up by purchasing power, is not the only way of tackling the problem of the allocation of resources. The other main system is the state-planned economy. Neither system actually exists in its pure form and all economies in the real world contain elements of both planned and market economic systems to a greater or lesser degree. The state-planned (or command) economy is exactly what the name suggests. The government plans and controls all production and the distribution of what is produced. The USSR and some other communist countries come closest to this theoretical model, although even there not everything is centrally planned. The state may decide on the total amount of most goods and services that are produced, but workers are paid wages and have some choice as to what they spend them on even if the range of goods available may not be as great as in some market economies. Services like education and health care, though, are usually supplied according to criteria other than ability to pay. There are different methods of organising production and of taking the population's wishes into account in a state-planned economy, but these are not examined here as this book's concern is the firm and the market economy.

Economies such as the United Kingdom and the USA are often described as free market economies. Although in these countries most goods and services may be produced by private enterprise through the market system, there are still many ways in which the government affects the allocation of resources. The state restricts what private firms may do, for instance, through monopoly control. The state itself produces goods and services, such as defence, road systems, and education, and collects taxes to pay for them, and it redistributes income through the tax and social security systems.

THE FREE MARKET ECONOMIC SYSTEM

In a pure free market economy decision making is decentralised. Individuals own resources, including their own labour, which they sell to firms in order to get income. They then use this income to buy the goods and services that they want. Firms produce those goods and services that can be sold at a profit. This system is based on the principles of private ownership and self-interest. Individuals must own resources before they can sell them to firms, and firms must own the goods they produce before they can sell them to consumers. People only voluntarily engage in trade if they expect to gain from a transaction. The concept of the firm is central to this process (see Figure 1.1).

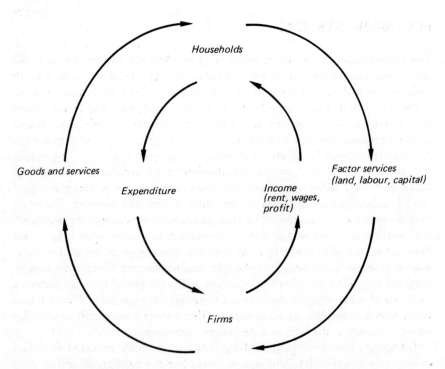

FIGURE 1.1   The operation of a market economy

Economists usually talk about consumers as individuals, but in fact people usually live in households where income is pooled and goods bought collectively. (The number of single person households has increased substantially in the last few decades, however.) How resources are allocated within households is an interesting question but for the purposes of this analysis intra-household resource allocation is ignored and the usual assumption is made that the terms 'households' and 'consumers' can be treated synonymously. (Although it is worth pointing out that the interdependence of labour supply of different members of a household is one aspect of intra-household resource allocation that has received more attention in recent years.)

Households allow firms to use the resources of land, labour and capital that they own and in return receive income in the form of rent, wages and profits, with most households obtaining their major source of income from selling their labour, that is, working for firms. Although not many people rely entirely on income from capital, a large number receive a proportion of their income from capital, often indirectly via the financial system. Anyone who earns interest on a bank account or contributes to a pension fund or has a life assurance policy indirectly owns shares in firms and receives income from their profits.

Firms pay for the use of resources and sell what they produce to households, but what is their reason for doing this? Households clearly take part in the system because it allows them to obtain goods and services for consumption, but who benefits from what firms do? The answer is that in a free market economy the objective of a firm is to make profits. Thus firms will try to maximise the third of the income flows indicated in Figure 1.1, that is, the income to capital. In other words, firms try to maximise the income going to those individuals who own the means of production.

The profit incentive is a crucial factor in determining the allocation of resources in a market economy. If people wish to buy more of a particular good then, if it is profitable, firms will produce more. Conversely, if people wish to buy less of a particular good then firms will move resources out of the industry that produces it because there will be less profits available.

The amounts of goods and services that flow from firms to households in return for expenditure, and the amounts of factor services that flow from households to firms in return for income, are determined by the market mechanism. In competitive markets the higher the price of a good then the greater the amount that firms will be willing to supply and the less households will wish to buy. Price will adjust until the amount of a good offered for sale equals the amount that consumers wish to buy. Similarly, in markets for factors of production it will usually be the case that the higher the price of a factor of production the more households will be willing to supply and the less firms will wish to purchase and, again, adjustments in prices will tend to bring about the equality of these two variables.

This simplified model of a free market economy obviously ignores many features of a real economy. There is no mention of foreign trade, of saving and investment for the future, or of government expenditure and taxation. It also ignores the fact that some firms sell intermediate products to other firms, as opposed to selling finished products directly to consumers. Economists have devised more complex economic models that take these, and other, factors into account, but it is first necessary to understand the basic principles on which a free market economy is based before considering these other issues.

Consumer sovereignty and competition

One sometimes hears the term 'consumer sovereignty' used to imply that it is consumers, by their spending patterns, who determine what is produced, but this is only half the story. Firms will only produce goods that will make profits, and they will choose to produce those goods that make the greatest profit when faced with a choice between alternative production possibilities. People cannot express a preference through the market for something that is not on sale and sometimes firms will not produce what consumers want because the profits they earn from selling another good might be diminished. This is most likely to occur where there is some degree of monopoly power, but not always. For example, off the peg clothes are usually only sold in a number of standard sizes. People who are in between these standard sizes would prefer to buy clothes that fitted them. However, although manufacturers could produce a wider range of sizes this would probably cost them more, and it would be more difficult to plan production, and so their profits would fall. As long as the in between size people continue to buy ill-fitting standard size clothes, a situation which they may have no choice over if no other clothes are available, the clothing manufacturers continue to make their profits. This situation is summed up in the response 'Sorry, the manufacturers don't make them because there's no demand for them' one sometimes gets when trying to buy a particular product. What the retailer really means is that the demand is not sufficient for manufacturers to increase their profits by making this product. The fact that you have just asked for it is evidence that some demand exists!

The word 'monopoly' was used in the last paragraph. When asked to explain what a free market economy is, students frequently say that one feature of a free market economy is that in all markets there are always a large number of firms competing with one another, sometimes known as 'perfect competition' (see Chapter 5). This is not true, however. A free market economy is one that is not state-planned and in which resources are allocated by a system of trade and exchange based on the principles of private property rights and self-interest. Uncompetitive monopolies can, and do, exist in a free market economy. Free enterprise does not necessarily mean competition. It can mean private monopoly.

Another common misconception that students often have is that a competitive free market economy will efficiently allocate an economy's resources and is the 'best' solution to the economic problem of resource allocation. This also is not necessarily true. Although different ways of tackling the economic problem have been mentioned, nothing has yet been said about the criteria by which the successfulness of these different methods might be judged.

POSITIVE AND NORMATIVE STATEMENTS

Although ways do exist of trying to assess the efficiency of an economic system and to measure welfare (see Chapter 12) it must be realised that there can be no scientific 'proof' that one system is 'better' than another. This sort of comparison involves value-judgements about what 'ought' to be, whereas economics is usually concerned with what 'is'. To understand this point the distinction between positive and normative statements needs to be made clear.

Positive statements are statements that can be tested against evidence to see if they are true or false. They may be correct, for example, 'The country with the largest population in the world is China' or incorrect, for example, 'The country with the largest population in the world is the United Kingdom'. The point is that they can be proved to be either true or false. Some positive statements may be in the form of predictions, such as 'It will rain tomorrow', that can be tested by waiting to see if the predicted event takes place. It may be difficult actually to test some positive statements, such as 'The nearest star is four light years away from the earth', but the practicality of testing a statement does not affect its categorisation as positive.

Normative statements are based on value-judgements that cannot be proved to be true or false. A value-judgement is a belief in the rights or wrongs of something, which may be based on ethical or religious grounds, or sometimes just on blind prejudice. Normative statements can never be 'proved' true or false by evidence; for example, 'Men and women should get equal pay for equal work' or 'Capital punishment is wrong'.

Normative statements about the moral rights and wrongs of issues should be clearly distinguished from positive statements on the same subject. For example, the statement 'Paying women the same as men will encourage more married women to seek employment' is a positive statement that can be tested, but the question of whether or not men and women 'ought' to get the same pay is a normative one.

Economists try to base their explanations of the way the economy works on positive statements. It is generally considered that it is the responsibility of the government, representing the wishes of the electorate, to decide what policy objectives should be and that economists, in their professional role, should explain how the government can achieve these objectives and should not decide for themselves what the objectives of economic policies ought to be. As individuals, of course, economists still have their own normative views on how the economy should operate. This distinction helps explain why economists are often derided by public opinion for frequently disagreeing amongst themselves over different issues. Economists can disagree on the normative issue of what policy objectives should be, given their own personal views, and they can also disagree over positive statements of fact about how the economy operates. Positive statements are often disputed because it is not always easy to test against evidence the type of predictions that are made in the social science of economics, as explained later.

The difference between positive statements and normative statements is not always obvious. The statement 'If you wish to use this machine you should first ensure that the electricity is switched on' is a positive statement. Even though it contains the word 'should' it is still a statement of fact because it can be proved that the machine will only work if the electricity is switched on. On the other hand the statement 'If the government wishes to bring down the rate of inflation it should reduce the rate of growth of the money supply' is a normative statement even though it is of the same 'if/should' type as the previous example. The reason for this is that when alternative possibilities exist for doing something – for example, the government could try bringing down inflation by wage and price controls – then to say that one particular course course of action should be followed is to make a normative statement. Different individuals will be affected in different ways by the alternative policies and deciding whether or not one set of events is preferable to another set will obviously involve normative judgements.

MARKET FAILURE

In relation to this distinction between positive and normative statements, some of the criticisms that have been made about the free market economy's ability to allocate resources can briefly be considered here. Some of these points are explored more fully in Chapter 12. No definite answer can be given to the questions of whether these shortcomings mean that the free market economy is not the best economic system, or whether they justify government intervention in the market, because all the arguments rest on normative propositions. It must be stressed, though, that the fact that normative statements are involved is not necessarily a reason for trying to avoid an issue. All actual economic policies are based on value-judgements and it is relevant to take into account some of the basic policy issues that arise from the free market economic system. The main areas of criticism are:

1. Monopoly

If one producer, or a group of producers, can control output and price in a market to their own advantage this may be the detriment of consumers. In the absence of competition monopolies can increase their profits by charging high prices. Similarly one large buyer in a market may be able to exploit suppliers by driving down the price.

2. Externalities and public goods

Some resources fall outside the property rights system. An externality occurs when one party's use of these resources affects another party and there is no payment involved. Pollution is an obvious example. There is no market for resources such as air, for example, because no one 'owns' it. One obvious reason for this is that it is difficult to measure the quantity of air that individuals consume and to identify the extent to which different firms may have polluted any given portion of air. Even if the measurement problem could be overcome there would still remain the normative issue of who should be allocated the ownership of this resource. Thus, although firms may adversely affect consumers' welfare by discharging unpleasant substances into the air, there is no market where the individuals affected can buy clean air even if they are prepared to pay for it.

Linked to the problem of externalities is the issue of public goods. These are goods that one cannot exclude anyone from enjoying the benefits of and that one person can consume without affecting the benefits that anyone else gets from the good. Examples of public goods are pollution control and road gritting in icy weather. Individuals are usually reluctant to pay for public goods because others will enjoy the benefits without contributing towards their cost and so the free market system will not ensure their provision. Consequently, in practice public goods are usually provided by the state and paid for from taxation.

3. Income distribution

An argument sometimes put forward in support of the free market economy is that it reflects the wishes of the population with respect to which goods and services should be produced. People 'vote' for different goods by spending money on them. One reply to this argument is that these 'votes' are not evenly distributed. Income is not evenly distributed because the ownership of resources that are sold to earn income are not evenly distributed. Opinions differ on how egalitarian the distribution of income should be, but most people would agree that something should be done to reduce extreme inequalities. For example, a handicapped person may be unable to work and so in a pure free market economy would receive no income and starve. In practice, however, such individuals usually receive assistance through their family, if they have one, and from the state.

4. Imperfect information and bounded rationality

People can only make the best use of their income if they have full knowledge of all the possibilities for spending it, including the qualities of the goods that are available for purchase. It can be argued that in some cases consumer protection by the state is needed because some producers may give incorrect or misleading information about their products. This is particularly relevant when it is difficult for consumers to find out the true qualities of products for themselves, for example, the effect of food additives. Even if full information about different product choices was available, consumers might still need assistance from the state in deciding which goods would best satisfy their needs because the ability of individuals to take in information and use it to their best advantage is limited; that is, they have 'bounded rationality'. For example, how many people would be able to make sense out of all the scientific literature that exists on the effects of food additives?

5. Paternalism

In many market economies consumers are not allowed to buy certain goods that they may wish to, such as drugs, explosives or pornography, or to buy certain goods at particular times, for example, a pint of lager after eleven o'clock at night or a set of tables and chairs on a Sunday. In some cases it can be argued that this restriction is warranted because people do not have full information about the product. This is particularly relevant where children are concerned, as evidenced by age restrictions on the sale of alcohol and tobacco. In other cases the use of the product may be likely to cause an externality and adversely affect an innocent third party. For example, cars must have safe brakes, steering and the rest by law, even though some individuals would be prepared to (and do) buy and use an unsafe car. In the case of restrictions on the Sunday opening of shops, the government may wish to protect shopworkers who want to spend the day with their families from being forced to work on Sundays by their employers.

There are other cases, though, where it could be argued that none of these reasons apply and the reason for the ban is that most people's, or the government's, opinion is that it is just 'wrong' to consume specified products. Book and film censorship can sometimes be cited as examples of this. Whether this sort of paternalism is something that is desirable or not is a normative question.

ECONOMIC MODELS

One of the purposes of economics is to try to explain and predict the behaviour of firms and consumers in a market economy. In a completely planned economy this sort of economics is redundant because (in theory at least) the economy operates according to what the government decides and so there is nothing to predict. Economists use theoretical economic models to explain behaviour and it is important to understand the basic philosophy behind this approach before studying any of these models. Many students who complain that the economic theories that they are studying 'bear no relation to what goes on in the real world' have not understood the methodology that economists use.

The methodology of economics

Sciences try to explain and predict behaviour. The social sciences, such as economics, are different from the physical sciences, such as physics and chemistry, because they attempt to explain the actions of people, who are all different and can all behave differently at different times. For this reason, in economics predictions are made about the behaviour of large groups and not about individuals. For example, an economist might predict that if the price of apples goes down by 20 per cent the amount of apples bought will rise by 5 per cent. All that this means is that the total consumption of apples is expected to increase by 5 per cent if the price falls by 20 per cent. Some individuals may buy the same amount of apples as before, others may buy less, and some may stop buying apples altogether. However, as long as, on average, consumers buy 5 per cent more apples this prediction will be correct. This contrasts with the physical sciences where predictions are meant to apply in every instance. In physics, for example, every physical body moving through space is assumed to obey Newton's laws of motion. It would be awkward to build, say, an aeroplane if the different pieces of metal used in its construction did not all obey the same set of physical laws.

All the sciences, both physical and social, use theories, which are simplified pictures of what goes on in the real world. The reason theories are used is that the real world is a complex place and a simplified model is much easier to understand. Depending on what it is that one is trying to explain, one can leave out of an economic model:

1. Factors that are irrelevant, such as the price of soap if one is analysing the market for carrots. Sometimes the relevance or irrelevance of a

particular factor is immediately obvious, but in other cases it can only be discovered by statistical analysis.

2. Factors that do not change; for example, the total population of the United Kingdom has hadly changed over the last decade and so, although the size of the population will affect the demand for many products, it need not be taken into consideration when trying to explain the short-term demand for most goods.

Assumptions and predictions

One should never lose sight of the fact that the purpose of an economic model is to make general predictions about the behaviour of large groups. The simplifying assumptions that are sometimes made in order to arrive at workable economic models can mean that these models may appear to be rather unrealistic. This may be so, but the crucial factor is not the apparent realism of the model but whether or not it can be used to predict behaviour, and the only way to find this out is to test the predictions against empirical evidence. If an economic model can correctly predict behaviour, within reasonable margins of error, then it fulfills the purpose for which it is designed. As explained in Chapter 4, with respect to theories of the firm, it is often the case that, as a model of the firm becomes more realistic, the incorporation of features that are specific to certain firms makes it less useful for making predictions about firms in general.

The same methodological approach underlies the physical sciences as well as the social sciences. For example, a chemist might predict that water and iron will produce rust. Today this chemical reaction might be explained in terms of the way that the atoms of different natural elements combine, but no one is a hundred per cent sure that these assumptions about the way these substances combine are completely correct and that there is nothing more to learn on the subject. For the purposes of prediction, though, the present body of knowledge predicts that water and iron will produce rust, and if tested this will be found to be correct. If in a hundred years' time scientists discover that there are other factors that explain how elements combine this does not invalidate the predictions made today, even though the reasons for these predictions may be wrong. The usefulness of a theory is determined by empirically testing the accuracy of its predictions.

Testing economic models

There are two important differences between the social sciences and the physical sciences which mean that different approaches to testing must be used:

1. In the physical sciences predictions regarding the effect of a change

in a specific variable can often be tested in laboratory conditions where all other factors are held constant. However, in the social sciences this is not possible. The nearest equivalent of a laboratory experiment in economics might be a questionnaire. Although they may give a rough guide as to what consumers' intentions are, questionnaires which ask hypothetical questions about what one might do in certain specified circumstances can be inaccurate and cannot properly be used to test predictions. If you were asked how many more apples you would buy in a typical month if the price fell by 20 per cent, assuming all other factors were held constant, would you be able to give an accurate answer? Instead, economists use observations of what actually happens in the real world to test their predictions. For example, in order to test the prediction that a fall in the price of apples will cause an increase in sales economists would examine figures for apple sales at different prices.

One problem with this approach is that if one is investigating the effect of a price fall on the amount of apples sold then one has to make sure that any observed changes in apple sales have not been the result of changes in other variables, such as incomes.

2.   As has already been pointed out, in the physical sciences predictions are meant to apply in every instant. Thus if a chemist wishes to test what happens when two substances are combined at a certain temperature then she need only perform an experiment a few times with different samples to establish the result. (More than one experiment is usually conducted to ensure that change circumstances have not caused a particular result.) In economics, however, because all people are different one cannot just observe the behaviour of one or two individuals to test a theory. Because economics only predicts the behaviour of large groups a large number of observations are needed to test predictions. The use of statistical analysis to test economic predictions against empirical data is called 'econometrics'. The basic approach used is to try to find which mathematical equation best explains a set of data.[1] If only two variables are involved then this can be illustrated graphically.

Assume that one is testing the relationship between the price of apples and the amount bought. The points plotted in Figure 1.2 represent different observations of the price of apples and the corresponding quantity bought by consumers. The 'line of best fit' is then drawn through these points. (In practice the parameters of this line would be estimated by statistical analysis, but this is just an intuitive pictorial explanation to convey the main principles involved.)

In this case the equation that best describes the data is

$$Q = 30 - 0.5P$$

---

1.   For further explanation of how economic predictions can be statistically tested see any text on introductory econometrics, for example, B. Haines, *An Introduction to Quantitative Economics* (London: George Allen & Unwin, 1978).

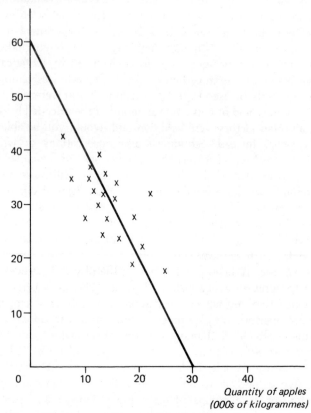

FIGURE 1.2   The line of best fit

where *p* is price per kilogramme and *Q* is quantity bought, measured in metric tonnes per month. This can then be used to predict sales at any price. For example, if price is 40p per kilogramme then predicted sales would be 10 tonnes,

Note that this approach allows predictions to be quantified as well as qualified, that is, the amount by which sales are expected to change in response to a price change can be predicted as well as the direction of the change.

MANAGERIAL ECONOMICS

Although the main purpose of economics is to explain and predict behaviour in different sectors of the economy, one exception is the branch of economics known as managerial economics or, sometimes, business economics. This entails the application of economic analysis to the sort of internal resource allocation problems faced by managers of firms, such as deciding on which input mix to use, choosing the best price to sell their product at, and planning for future production. The ideas developed in the simplified economic models constructed mainly for predictive purposes can sometimes be used for this sort of real world problem solving. Students must realise, though that, having mastered the basic economic principles explained in a book such as this one, they cannot then simply apply them directly to the decision-making problems that a real firm faces. Economic principles can only be applied to certain types of managerial decision-making problems and in each case other relevant factors that may have a bearing on the outcome of the decision will also need to be taken into account.

THE PRICE SYSTEM

In a market economy the quantity of a good that is sold by producers to consumers, and the price that it is sold at, are determined by the interaction of demand and supply.

Demand

The demand for a good is defined as the amount that consumers are willing to buy at any given price. It should be noted that:

1. What people are willing to buy and what they would like to have are not always the same thing. To be willing to buy something a consumer must also be able to afford it.
2. The amount of a good that consumers demand is not necessarily the amount that they may actually purchase. For example, it is possible that at certain prices consumers may wish to buy more of a good than firms are willing to sell.
3. The demand for a good is a *flow* and must be expressed as a quantity per time period: for example, the average demand for shoes is two pairs per year. If the words 'per year' were missing the sentence would be meaningless. The time dimension is not relevant only if one is talking about *stocks*: for example, the average person owns five pairs of shoes.

Having said this, it can be cumbersome to specify the time period every time a quantity demanded is mentioned, and so the time period is often omitted when it is not crucial to the analysis. (In the same way the relevant time period for other flows, such as the quantity supplied by firms, is not always spelled out.)

Determinants of Demand

The total demand for a good, or the 'market' demand, is the sum of individuals' demands and will be influenced by the following factors:

1. Price. As its own price rises it is expected that less of a good will be demanded, and vice versa. This is a reasonable proposition that can be accepted at this stage without further explanation. (Further analysis of the relationship between consumer demand and price is presented in Chapter 9, where some possible exceptions to this rule are also considered.)
2. Income. As consumers' incomes rise the demand for many goods will increase. These are known as *normal* goods. In some cases, though, when incomes rise consumers can afford to buy another product which is a superior substitute and consequently demand for the original good may fall. For example, if incomes rise consumers may be able to afford to switch from black and white televisions to colour televisions (and the higher licence fee!) A good whose demand falls when incomes rise is known as an *inferior* good. It should be noted that the demand for these goods only falls as incomes rise over a certain range, when a preferred alternative becomes available, and at lower income levels they may be normal goods.
3. Prices of other goods. There are several ways in which the demand for one good may be affected by changes in the prices of other goods:

    (a)   Substitutes. Goods that are substitutes can be used as alternatives and so if the price of a substitute rises the demand for the first good will increase; for example, if the price of bus journeys rises then the demand for private cars will increase.
    (b)   Complements. Goods are complements if they are used together. If the price of a complement rises the demand for the first good will fall; for example, if the price of petrol rises the demand for cars will fall.
    (c)   Changes in real income. A change in the price of one good may have no effect on the demand for another; for example, a rise in the price of peanuts will not significantly affect the demand for economics textbooks. However, if the price of a good that takes up a large proportion of a consumer's total expenditure rises, or the prices of a number of different goods rise, then the demand for the original good may still be affected even if these other goods are neither substitutes nor complements. This is because these price rises have the same effect as a reduction in income. Although money income may not have changed, the consumer's *real income*, or spending power, has dropped. Consequently demand for the original good will fall (if it is a normal good) or rise (if it is an inferior good).

4. Tastes. All the other non-measurable factors that can influence the demand for a product are included under this heading. Sometimes the causes of changes in tastes can be identified. They may, for example, be the result of advertising campaigns by producers, or health warnings, or climatic factors, such as the increased demand for ice cream when the weather is hot. However, other changes in consumers' tastes cannot always be so easily explained.
5. Population. If the total population increases then demand for most products will rise, given that market demand is just the sum of individuals' demands. Aggregate demand will also be affected by the distribution of the population with respect to various characteristics, such as age, which will influence 'tastes', and income.

Ceteris paribus

It is rather difficult to analyse at the same time the effects of all the different factors which influence demand and so economists make the assumption of *ceteris paribus*, which is Latin for 'other things being equal'. The effect of changes in each influencing factor can then be looked at separately.

The most common way of analysing the demand for a good is to first assume that only its price alters and that all other factors, that is to say, those mentioned in (2) to (5) above, do not change. A graph of the relationship between price and the quantity demanded can then be drawn. This is usually known as a 'demand curve' (even though it may be a straight line!) or a 'demand schedule'. Because more is demanded as price falls the demand curve slopes down from left to right. (Assuming that quantity is measured on the horizontal axis. Note that this is the reverse of the usual mathematical convention where the dependent variable in a relationship is usually measured on the vertical axis.)

At any given price the amount of a good that consumers are willing to buy can be found by simply reading the corresponding quantity off the horizontal axis. In Figure 1.3, for example, if price is £3 then the quantity demanded (per time period) is 40 units. If the price rises to £4 then the quantity demanded falls to 30 units.

Changes in demand

It is important to distinguish a movement of the whole demand curve from a movement along a given demand curve. The whole demand curve moves when something which affects demand, other than price, alters, that is, any of the factors (2) to (5) above. This is because the *ceteris paribus* assumption no longer holds and so the relationship between price and quantity demanded

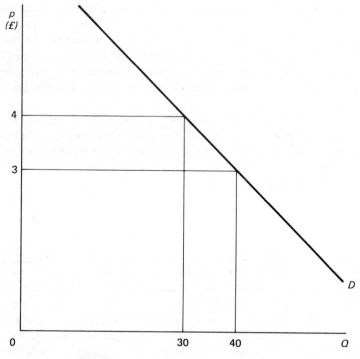

FIGURE 1.3   The demand schedule

will alter and a new demand curve must be drawn to illustrate the new relationship.

Economists use the phrase 'an increase in demand' to describe an outward shift of the whole demand curve, such as that shown in Figure 1.4. The movement of the demand curve from D_1 to D_2 may be caused, for example, by the price of a substitute rising. This movement means that at any given price the quantity demanded increases. For example, if price is P_1 then quantity demanded increases from Q_1 to Q_2.

If only price alters then the position of the demand curve does not change and there is just a movement along it. For example, in Figure 1.3 when price falls from £4 to £3 there is an increase in the quantity demanded from 30 to 40 units. The phrase 'an increase in the quantity demanded' is used to describe this movement in order to distinguish it from the phrase 'an increase in demand', which describes a shift outward of the whole demand curve.

Similarly, a 'fall in demand' means a leftward shift of the whole demand curve whereas a rise in price causes a movement along a demand curve and consequently a 'fall in the quantity demanded'. For example, if the price of petrol rises less petrol will probably be bought, but this price rise will not

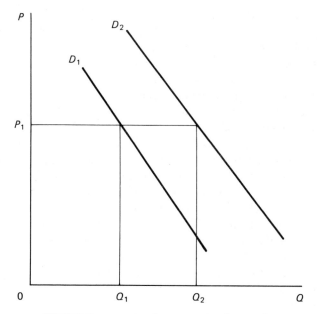

FIGURE 1.4   An increase in demand

cause the demand curve for petrol to change. All that will happen is that there will be a movement along the demand curve and thus a fall in the quantity demanded.

Supply

The supply of a good is the quantity that producers are willing to sell at any given price. Like demand, it is a flow per time period, and producers may not necessarily be able to sell the quantity that they would like to.

Determinants of supply

1. Price. As price rises the quantity that firms wish to sell will usually increase. Existing firms may find it profitable to expand their output and new firms may be attracted into the industry. These adjustments to the quantity supplied will depend on the time period involved, firms' cost structures and the state of competition in the industry, which are analysed more fully in later chapters. At this stage it is just assumed that more of a good will be supplied as price rises.
2. Firms' objectives. It is usually assumed that firms try to maximise profits, and this is the assumption that underlies the basic analysis of the price

system explained in this chapter. Firms may pursue other objectives, though, and in Chapter 4 the implications for supply of some non-profit maximising theories of the firm are considered.

3. Prices of other goods. If the price of another good changes it may cause a shift in resource usage and alter supply of the original good. For example, a farmer with a fixed amount of land may switch production from cabbages to carrots if the price of carrots increases, even though the price of cabbages does not alter.

4. Prices of inputs. An increase in the price of an input, such as a rise in energy costs, will usually cause the quantity of the good supplied at any given price to fall. The amount of the adjustment will depend on various factors, such as the time period involved and the ease with which different inputs can be substituted for each other.

5. The state of technology. This is rather like the influence of 'tastes' on demand, in that it is not something that can be easily measured or predicted. Changes in the state of technology do occur, though, and they usually bring down the cost of production and hence increase supply.

The supply curve

Assuming *ceteris paribus*, the relationship between quantity supplied and price can be plotted on a graph. The supply curve which illustrates this relationship is expected to be upward sloping, such as S in Figure 1.5.

Changes in supply

As with the analysis of demand, one must be careful to distinguish 'a change in supply', which is a shift of the whole supply curve due to something other than price changing, from 'a change in the quantity supplied', which may result from a change in price causing a movement along a given supply curve. An increase in supply is shown by the movement of the supply curve from S_1 to S_2 in Figure 1.6. This might be caused by, for example, a fall in input prices. An increase in the quantity supplied is shown in Figure 1.5, where the rise in price from P_1 to P_2 causes quantity supplied to increase from Q_1 to Q_2.

PRICE DETERMINATION

When a supply and a demand curve are shown on the same diagram then the market price can be determined, assuming that there are no restrictions on the movement of resources in or out of the industry and that there is a

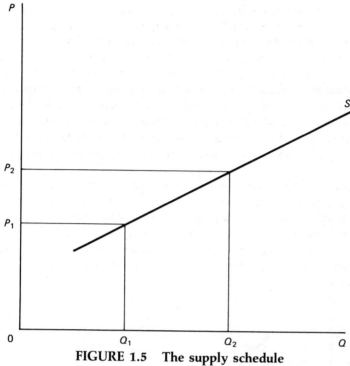

FIGURE 1.5   The supply schedule

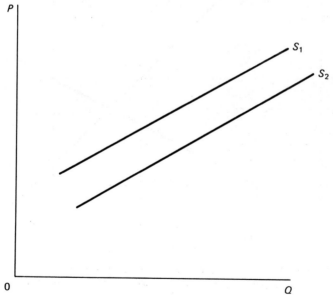

FIGURE 1.6   An increase in supply

competitive market and price flexibility. Consider what would happen in Figure 1.7 if price was initially £3.50. Firms would wish to supply 100 units of good Q, but consumers would only wish to buy 68 units. Firms would not wish to produce goods that they could not sell and so they might lower price in order to sell off this over-production. Consumers may also indicate to firms that they would be willing to buy more if price was lower. As price falls the quantity supplied decreases and the quantity demanded increases until at a price of £2.90 quantity supplied equals quantity demanded. If price was initially below £2.90, at £1.50, then quantity demanded would exceed quantity supplied and price would be bid up until the excess demand was eliminated.

The price at which quantity demanded equals quantity supplied is known as the *equilibrium price* because once this price is reached it will stay there unless something causes the supply or demand curve to move. It is also a stable equilibrium because market forces will always cause price to move towards this equilibrium value if it is initially at some other value. The demand and supply curves only interesect once and so there is only one possible equilibrium price in a market.

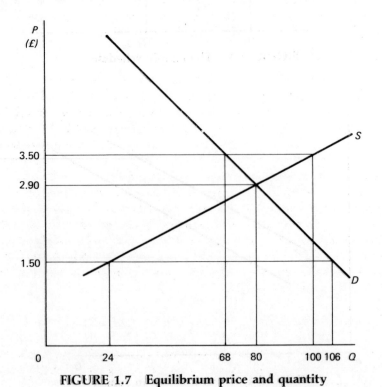

FIGURE 1.7   Equilibrium price and quantity

Although in this simple model equilibrium price is easily determined where the supply and demand curves intersect, it should not be assumed that in all competitive markets price will always be at this intersection point. The exact process by which price is adjusted and the time taken for it to change will vary across industries. In some highly organised markets, such as commodity exchanges, where buyers and sellers are constantly revising prices, adjustment to the equilibrium price may only take a matter of minutes. In other industries price adjustment may be a slow trial and error process and it may take years for price to get close to its equilibrium level. Given that over time numerous factors may cause both the supply and demand curves to shift about, the equilibrium price may change before the adjustment process causes the actual market price to reach it. Thus in some markets price may never actually be at its equilibrium level.

Changes in supply and demand

The expected changes in equilibrium price and output in response to changes in supply and demand can now be predicted. Because different equilibrium situations are compared this is known as comparative static analysis.

An increase in demand

Assume that a market's supply and demand schedules are initially as shown by S and D_1 in Figure 1.8. Equilibrium price and output will then be P_1 and Q_1. If demand then increases to D_2 equilibrium price and output will both increase, to P_2 and Q_2 respectively. With the information available from this diagram only the direction of the expected changes in price and quantity can be predicted. The amounts by which these variables change will depend on the slopes of the two curves, which will be different for each market and will have to be determined by empirical testing, and the magnitude of the movement in the demand curve. The predictions about the expected direction of the changes in price and output, however, will be the same for all markets which have an upward sloping supply curve and a downward sloping demand curve. Obviously the reverse happens when there is a fall in demand. If the demand curve falls from D_2 to D_1 then equilibrium price and output fall back to P_1 and Q_1 respectively.

An Increase in Supply

The effect of an increase in supply is shown in Figure 1.9. If the supply curve shifts from S_1 to S_2 then equilibrium price falls from P_1 to P_2 and equilibrium quantity increases from Q_1 to Q_2.

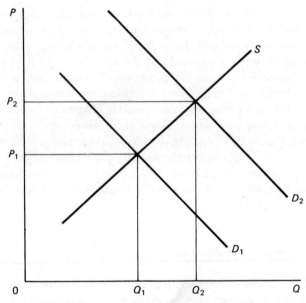

FIGURE 1.8   An increase in demand

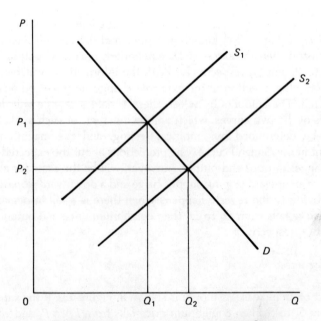

FIGURE 1.9   An increase in supply

Increases in Supply and Demand

If both supply and demand curves shift outward simultaneously then the equilibrium output will increase, but the change in the equilibrium price cannot be predicted without further information. In Figure 1.10 a shift in supply from S_1 to S_2, and three possible positions for the new demand curve which represent a shift from D_1, are shown. If the new demand curve is D_2 then the new equilibrium price is P_2, which is lower than the original price P_1. However, if the new demand curve is D_4 then the equilibrium price increases to P_4. Another possibility is that the new demand curve is D_3, in which case the equilibrium price will remain unchanged at P_1. The change in the equilibrium price could only be predicted if more information was made available about the magnitudes of the shifts in supply and demand and the slopes of the two curves.

It is important to realise that there are limits to what can be predicted by supply and demand analysis. There are other combinations of movements in the two curves where the direction of the change in equilibrium price, or quantity, cannot be unambiguously predicted. It should not be assumed that if there are two forces working in opposite directions they will necessarily cancel each other out. The net effect will depend on the relative strengths of the two forces.

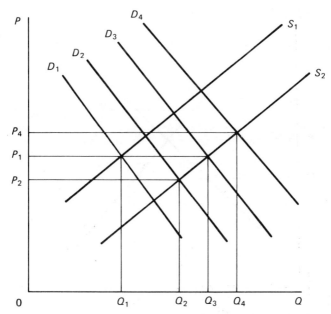

FIGURE 1.10   Increases in both supply and demand

APPLICATIONS OF PRICE THEORY

Price controls

Maximum Prices

Governments sometimes impose a maximum price at which a particular product may be sold, usually with the aim of trying to help consumers. For example, during the Second World War it was difficult to import food into Britain. Given that the country had previously relied heavily on imported food, this meant that the supply curves for different types of food shifted inwards. Without government intervention this would have meant that the market price of food would have risen sharply and poorer people might not have been able to buy enough food to live on. To try to ensure that everyone received at least a certain minimum quota of food the government therefore decided to hold down food prices.

The effect of this policy is shown in Figure 1.11. A maximum price of P_2, which is below the equilibrium price P_1, would mean that the quantity demanded, Q_D, would be greater than the quantity supplied, Q_S, that is to say, there would be a shortage equal to the quantity $Q_S Q_D$. How will the

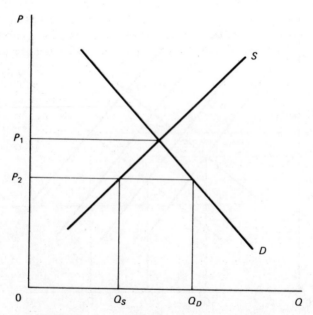

FIGURE 1.11   Maximum price controls

quantity Q_S that is supplied be allocated? There are various possibilities. The government may introduce a rationing scheme so that consumers are allocated a given quota, which may not necessarily be the same for each consumer. This was the system adopted for food during the Second World War. If a rationing system is not introduced then the product may simply be distributed on a first come first served basis, with consumers having to queue. There will also be some distribution on a personal contact basis; for example, if there is a shortage of bread and your aunt runs a bakery then you will probably get your bread without having to queue. Even if rationing is introduced, a shortage is also likely to result in a black market, that is, some illegal trading at prices above the official maximum. As there are some consumers who would be willing to pay more than the official maximum price, suppliers who are willing to break the law would find it profitable to meet this demand.

Although maximum price controls can cause disruption in a market, the decision of whether or not to implement them is a normative one. Most actual instances of maximum price controls have been with respect to basic goods, such as food or housing, which the government has decided are necessities that everyone should have and which the free market would have priced out of the range of some poorer people.

Minimum Prices

A minimum price such as P_2 in Figure 1.12, which is above the market equilibrium price P_1, would result in quantity supplied exceeding quantity demanded. Suppliers would then try to unload their unsold stocks below the official minimum price. To maintain a minimum price above the equilibrium price the government would either have to buy up the surplus, $Q_D Q_S$, or enforce production quotas that ensured that total quantity supplied did not exceed Q_D. The food 'mountains' created by the EEC's Common Agricultural Policy are basically the result of farmers being paid a minimum price above the free market equilibrium price, which is maintained by the buying up of unsold produce. There is pressure being applied, though, for more use to be made of production quotas.

A sales tax

Assume that the government imposes a sales tax of 15 per cent on each unit of a good that firms sell. The effect of this is shown in Figure 1.13 by the movement of the supply curve from S to S_t. Because the price that firms will require from consumers in order to supply any given quantity increases by 15 per cent the supply schedule shifts vertically upward by the amount of this price increase. For example, before the imposition of the tax firms would have required a price of £60 to supply 400 units and so with the tax they

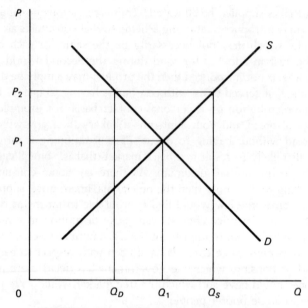

FIGURE 1.12   Minimum price controls

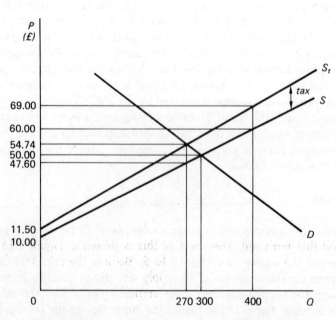

FIGURE 1.13   The effect of a 15 % sales tax

would require consumers to pay £69. This is a proportional tax and so the actual amount paid in tax will rise with price as will the vertical distance between S_t and S.

The upward shift of the supply schedule causes the equilibrium price to rise, from £50.00 to £54.74, and the equilibrium quantity to fall, from 300 to 270 units. Price does not rise by 15 per cent, however. The fall in quantity means that the net price received by firms decreases from £50 to £47.60, and so when the 15 per cent tax is added the gross price paid by consumers of £54.74 is less than it would have been had there been no decrease in quantity supplied, that is, £57.50, which is the original price of £50 plus 15 per cent. In this particular example the gross price paid by consumers rises by £4.74 and the net price received by firms falls by £2.40 and the burden of the tax is shared between consumers and firms. The actual distribution of the effect of a tax depends on the elasticities of the demand and supply schedules. If the demand schedule was vertical then the whole of the tax could be passed on to consumers and if it was horizontal then suppliers would have to bear all the cost of the tax, but most cases will lie between these two extremes.

PRICE ELASTICITY OF DEMAND

Consider the two demand curves D_1 and D_2 in Figure 1.14 (a) and (b). If price is initially £2 then the quantity demanded is 300 units in both cases. When price is increased to £3 the quantity demanded falls to 100 units in case (a) and only to 250 in case (b). Clearly demand curve D_1 shows a much stronger response to the price change than does D_2. It can also be seen that

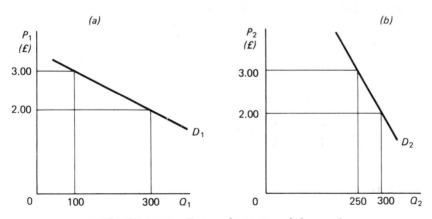

FIGURE 1.14   Price elasticity of demand

in case (a) total sales revenue falls from £600 to £300 while in case (b) it rises to £750.

In this example it is obvious that the flatter demand curve (a) is the more responsive to price charges. The slope of a demand curve, however, is not a satisfactory measure of the responsiveness of demand to price changes because it will depend on the units that are measured along the axes. In this case, for example, if price was measured in pence instead of pounds then the absolute values of the slopes of both curves would be increased a hundredfold. To overcome this problem the concept of *elasticity* is used to measure the response of demand to price.

The price elasticity of demand (e) is defined as

$$e = (-1)\frac{\text{proportional change in quantity demanded}}{\text{proportional change in price}}$$

The (-1) is used to ensure that the measure of price elasticity of demand takes a positive value. (The change in quantity and the change in price will always have opposite signs if the demand slopes down from left to right.) Some economists, however, omit the (-1) from the definition of price elasticity of demand and work with it as a negative number.

The formula above can be used to calculate price elasticity of demand for the two demand curves in Figure 1.14.

In case (a)

proportional change in quantity is $-200/300$

proportional change in price is $1/2$

$$e = (-1)\frac{\left(\dfrac{-200}{300}\right)}{\dfrac{1}{2}} = \frac{2}{3} \times 2 = 1.33.$$

In case (b)

$$e = (-1)\frac{\left(\dfrac{-50}{300}\right)}{\dfrac{1}{2}} = \frac{1}{6} \times 2 = 0.33.$$

Arc elasticity

The method used above to calculate price elasticity of demand can be rather inaccurate when significant proportional changes in price or quantity take place. It can be seen that the answer obtained will vary depending on whether the changes in price and quantity are taken as proportions of their initial or final values. For example, suppose that in case (a), above, instead of rising from £2 to £3, price fell from £3 to £2.

Elasticity would then be calculated as

$$e = (-1)\dfrac{\dfrac{200}{100}}{\left(-\dfrac{1}{3}\right)} = 2 \times 3 = 6.$$

Thus for the same stretch of the same demand curve elasticity is calculated as 1.33 when price rises and 6 when price falls. This problem arises because price elasticity of demand can vary along the length of a demand curve (see below) and the above methods are attempting to obtain one measure for elasticity over a section of its length. One method of trying to overcome this problem is to use the concept of *arc elasticity*. This measure takes the changes in price and quantity as proportions of the *averages* of their initial and final values and is defined by the formula

$$\text{arc } e = (-1)\dfrac{\left[\dfrac{\Delta Q}{0.5(Q_1 + Q_2)}\right]}{\left[\dfrac{\Delta P}{0.5(P_1 + P_2)}\right]}$$

Although the formula is perhaps easiest remembered in terms of the averages of price and quantity, in any calculations the two 0.5s can be ommitted because they will always cancel out top and bottom. For case (a) then arc elasticity is

$$\dfrac{\dfrac{200}{400}}{\dfrac{1}{5}} = 0.5 \times 5 = 2.5$$

which is somewhere between the two values of elasticity obtained by using the simple measure above. It is not just the average of these two figures though and is, in fact, a measure of elasticity at a point half way along a chord joining the two positions on the demand curve between which elasticity is being measured. It can, however, usefully serve as an approximation of the value of elasticity along the intervening section, and it always results in the same figure whether price rises or falls.

For practical purposes the arc elasticity measure is usually employed when there are relatively large changes in price and quantity, as in the above examples. When the relative changes are small the simple measure can be used without any great loss of accuracy; for example, if price increased from £99 to £100 it would not make much difference if the £1 increase was taken as a proportion of £99, £100 or £99.50.

Changes in total revenue

One of the most important uses of the concept of price elasticity of demand is that it can be used to predict the changes in total revenue that will result from changes in price.

When price elasticity of demand is greater than one then demand is said to be *elastic*. A rise in price will cause a fall in total revenue because quantity demanded decreases by a greater proportion than price rises. Demand is elastic in case (a) above. Arc elasticity is 2.5 and total revenue falls from £600 to £300 when price rises from £2 to £3.

When the value of price elasticity of demand is less than one then demand is said to be *inelastic*. A rise in price brings about a less than proportional fall in quantity demanded and hence total revenue will rise. Similarly, a fall in price will cause total revenue to rise. Case (b) above illustrates an elastic demand curve. Arc elasticity is 5/11 and total revenue increases from £600 to £750 when price increases from £2 to £3. In practice demand schedules are usually either elastic or inelastic but there are three other limiting cases which it is useful to look at, and these are illustrated in Figure 1.15.

(a)   A *perfectly elastic* demand curve is a horizontal line and

$$e \rightarrow \infty.$$

An infinite amount is demanded at, or below, the price at which the demand curve is horizontal. Any increase in price above this level will cause quantity

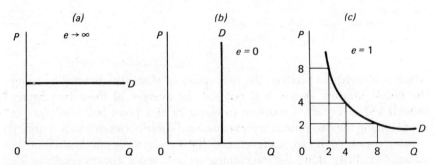

FIGURE 1.15   Infinite, zero and unit price elasticity of demand

demanded, and hence sales revenue, to drop to zero; that is, there will be an infinitely large change in revenue.

(b)   A *perfectly inelastic* demand curve is a vertical line and

$$e = 0.$$

The same quantity is always demanded whatever the price charged.

(c)   A *unit elasticity* demand curve will take a shape similar to that shown in Figure 1.15 (c) and along its length

$$e = 1.$$

The mathematical term for this type of curve is a 'rectangular hyperbola' and it has the property that price multiplied by quantity always equals the same number, i.e. total revenue does not change when price alters.

Factors affecting price elasticity of demand

The value of price elasticity of demand will vary for different products and can only be determined by empirical observation. However, a number of factors which will influence its value can be identified:

1.   The availability of close substitutes. If close substitutes exist then the demand for a good will tend to be elastic because if its price rises consumers will switch to these substitutes. The availability of substitutes will depend on how one defines a product, however, and the narrower the definition the more elastic will demand be. For example, the demand for pears will be more elastic than the demand for fruit in general because consumers can substitute other types of fruit if the price of pears rises, but if the price of all fruit goes up it is more difficult to find a suitable substitute.

2.   The proportion of income spent on a good. The smaller the proportion of one's income that one spends on a good the less will be the impact of a rise in its price and consequently the more inelastic its demand schedule is likely to be. For example, if the price of matches doubles smokers are not likely to change their demand for matches very much, but if the price of cigarettes were to double there would be a significant drop in the quantity demanded.

3.   Degree of necessity. This is a 'taste' factor and it is not possible to precisely define what is meant by a necessity. For example, some people might argue that tobacco is not a necessity in the sense that one does not need it to survive (and it may indeed decrease one's changes of survival). However, the fact that some people on low incomes still spend a significant proportion of their income on tobacco is an indication that

for these people it is an essential item of expenditure. The greater the degree of necessity the more inelastic demand will be. One should only really apply this criterion to broad product groups, however. For example, even though food is a necessity the demand for particular types of food may still be elastic because substitutes exist.

4. Time. The longer the time period that the flow of demand is being measured over the more elastic a demand schedule is likely to be. This is because when the price of a good changes consumers may sometimes take a while to make allowances for this in their expenditure patterns, particularly where a cost is involved in switching from one good to another. For example, in the 1960s many people installed oil-fired central heating systems in their homes. When the price of oil rose steeply in 1974 people were not able without expense to switch to other fuels and so the fall in the quantity of domestic heating oil demanded was not particularly substantial in the first few months after the initial price rise. However, throughout the following decade increasing numbers of people converted their existing central heating systems to other fuels, in particular gas, which was also more popular among consumers installing new central heating systems. Thus over a ten-year period the demand for domestic heating oil was more responsive than in the first few months after the initial oil price rise. There were of course changes in other variables that affected demand over this period, as well as further oil price rises.

Applications of price elasticity of demand

Agricultural Markets

One of the problems facing farmers is that climatic and other uncontrollable factors can cause unplanned fluctuations in supply. The demand for many agricultural products is price inelastic; for example, if the price of potatoes falls by 50 per cent the quantity demanded is likely to increase by a much smaller percentage. This means that when there is a good yield of a particular product the resulting increase in supply will cause farmers' earnings to fall, and vice versa when there is a poor yield. Thus farmers' incomes in total are subject to substantial fluctuations but they vary inversely with the change in supply. (NB This example assumes that there is a free market for agricultural produce whereas in the United Kingdom the prices of many agricultural products are controlled through the EEC Common Agricultural Policy.)

This situation is illustrated in the example in Figure 1.16. If Q represents, say, thousands of tons of potatoes per week then a poor crop will shift the supply schedule from S_1 to S_2, causing price to rise from £2.30 to £4.00 and quantity demanded to fall from 47 to 29 thousand tons. This means that total

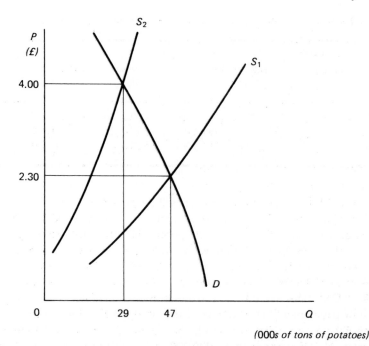

FIGURE 1.16   Fluctuating agricultural incomes and price inelastic demand

revenue increases from £108 100 to £116 000 because over this price range the demand schedule D is inelastic. (The arc elasticity is 0.877.)

Note, however, that this analysis only explains what happens to total revenue. Unless all farmers experience equal proportional unplanned fluctuations in production then individual farmers' incomes can vary in different directions. For example, a contraction in supply that causes total revenue to rise may be the result of poor crop in certain parts of the country and so some farmers may lose a great deal of income while others, whose production has been unaffected, enjoy a large gain.

Devaluation and Exports

It is sometimes argued that a fall in the value of the pound against other currencies will help increase United Kingdom exports because their price in foreign currency will fall, and will also cut imports because their price in sterling will rise. Consider the example in Table 1.1, however. Only considering exports to West Germany, assume that a United Kingdom car manufacturer exports a car which is priced at £10 000, and that transport and transactions costs can be ignored. If the Deutschmark/£ exchange rate is initially 4 DM

TABLE 1.1   Devaluation and export earnings from car sales

UK price	DM/£ exchange rate	Price in DM	Export sales	Export earnings in DM	Manufacturer's sales revenue
£10 000	4	40 000	100	4 000 000	£1 000 000
£10 000	3	30 000	(a) 110	3 300 000	£1 100 000
£10 000	3	30 000	(b) 150	4 500 000	£1 500 000

to the pound then in Germany this car will be priced at 40 000 DM, and if sales are initially 100 cars then export earnings will be 4 000 000 DM. A devaluation to a rate of 3 DM to the pound will cause the export price of the car to fall to 30 000 DM. If, however, this 33.3 per cent fall in price only causes the number of cars sold to increase by 10 per cent to 110 (that is to say, demand is inelastic), as in case (a), then export earnings will fall to 3 300 000 DM. This would cause a deterioration in the United Kingdom balance of payments. (Note however that, although the British government might not be happy with this result, the car manufacturer would enjoy an increase in sales revenue from £1 000 000 to £1 100 000.) For a devaluation of the pound to improve export earnings in foreign currency demand must be elastic, as in case (b), where sales are increased to 150 cars as a result of the same price change and this causes export earnings to rise to 4 500 000 DM.

Point elasticity

It has already been mentioned that elasticity can change along the length of a demand curve. To find out what elasticity is at the point X on demand curve D in Figure 1.17, consider a small movement along the curve to Y, corresponding to a small fall in price, ΔP, and a small increase in quantity, ΔQ. Over this section of the demand curve

$$e = (-1) \frac{\dfrac{\Delta Q}{Q_1}}{\dfrac{\Delta P}{P_1}}$$

(The simple method for calculating elasticity can be used because the changes in price and quantity are assumed to be small.)

    If the straight line TT′ is drawn at a tangent to the demand curve at point

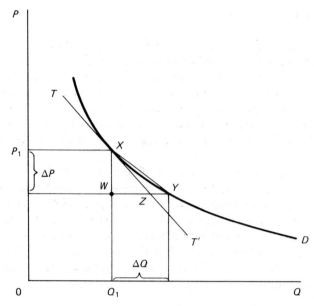

FIGURE 1.17   Point elasticity of demand

X, its slope is equal to $(-)XW/WZ$. If the distance from X to Y is decreased then the distance between points Y and Z becomes very small and the slope of the line XY gets closer to the slope of XZ. For an infinitely small movement along the demand curve then

$$XW/WZ = XW/WY$$

and so $(-)\Delta P/\Delta Q$ is equal to the slope of the tangent drawn at point X.
Therefore at point X

$$e = (-1)\left(\frac{\dfrac{\Delta Q}{Q_1}}{\dfrac{\Delta P}{P_1}}\right) = (-1)\frac{P_1}{Q_1} \times \frac{1}{\left(\dfrac{\Delta P}{\Delta Q}\right)}$$

Since $\Delta P/\Delta Q$ is equal to $(-)$ the slope of the demand curve at X this means that point elasticity $= -(P_1/Q_1) \times 1/(\text{slope of demand curve})$.

The slope of a straight line demand curve is constant along its length but the ratio of P to Q falls as one moves along it from left to right. Therefore elasticity must also continuously decline along the length of a straight line demand schedule.

Elasticity and total revenue

To explain what happens to elasticity and total revenue as one moves along the length of a demand curve it is necessary to introduce a new term, *marginal revenue*. Marginal revenue can be defined as the increase in total revenue that results from the sale of one more unit of a good. For a horizontal demand curve marginal revenue is simply the same as the price per unit because each unit can be sold at the same price. When a demand curve is downward sloping, however, the marginal revenue schedule will lie below it, as shown in Figure 1.18.

This is because when price is reduced all units, not just the extra units, are sold at this lower price and hence less revenue is received from the sale of those units that were previously sold at a higher price. In this example, when quantity is increased from 5 to 6 units price falls from £30 to £28. Total revenue increases from £150 to £168 and so the marginal revenue of the sixth unit is £18. (In Figure 1.18 *MR* is shown as £16 when *Q* is exactly 6 because the calculated figure of £18 is only an approximate measure of *MR* *between* 5 and 6 units.) When quantity is increased from 12 to 13 units price

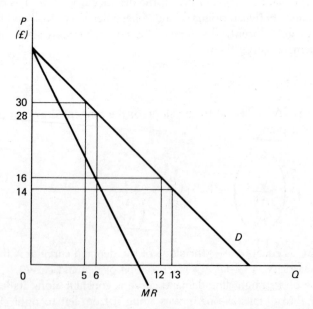

FIGURE 1.18   Marginal revenue for a downward sloping demand schedule

falls from £16 to £14. Total revenue falls from £192 to £182 and so the marginal revenue of the thirteenth unit is − £10.

Whole unit increases in quantity were used in the above example which

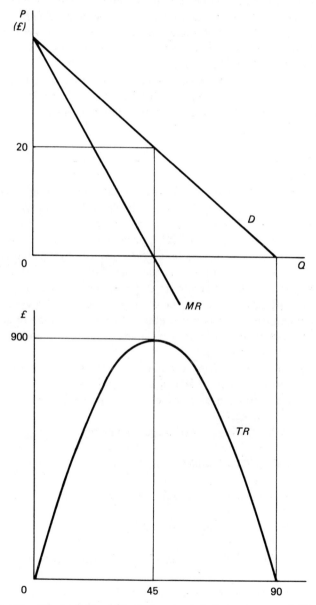

FIGURE 1.19 **The relationship between total revenue and the demand schedule**

introduced the concept of marginal revenue. However, like elasticity, marginal revenue can change along the length of a demand curve and a more precise way of determining marginal revenue for any given quantity can be found by considering the total revenue curve. In Figure 1.19 the total revenue curve TR is drawn corresponding to the straight line demand schedule D. Total revenue is bound to be zero when nothing is sold and it will also be zero at a quantity of 90 units because price is zero. Between these two quantities it will rise to a maximum of £900 and then fall.

In Figure 1.20, consider a small increase in quantity, ΔQ, from Q_1 to Q_2. This will cause a total revenue to rise by ΔTR from TR_1 to TR_2. The increase in quantity may not be exactly one unit, but marginal revenue can be calculated as

$$MR = \Delta TR / \Delta Q.$$

This is also the value of the slope of a straight line joining X and Y. If Y was closer to X then the slope of a straight line joining XY would be closer to the slope of the TR schedule at X. Thus when the change in quantity is infinitesimally small the slope of XY approximates to the slope of the TR schedule at X. In other words, for any given quantity marginal revenue is the same as the slope of the total revenue curve at that quantity. As the TR schedule approaches its maximum its slope becomes flatter and so MR gets smaller. The MR curve takes a value of zero at the output level at which TR is at a maximum; that is, it is horizontal and thus has a slope of zero. Above this output total revenue declines as quantity increases and consequently marginal revenue is negative.

It can be proved that a MR schedule will always have the same intercept on the price axis as a demand schedule, and twice its slope.
*Assume that demand can be represented by the relationship

$$Q = a - bP \qquad \text{where } a \text{ and } b \text{ are parameters.}$$

Thus $TR = P.Q = aP - bP^2$

MR is the rate of change of TR and so by differentiating

$$MR = dTR / dQ = a - 2bP,$$

that is, the MR schedule has the same intercept as the demand schedule and twice its slope.

The change in elasticity along a straight line demand curve can now be linked to the changes in marginal revenue and total revenue. Starting at point A in the middle of demand curve D in Figure 1.20, it can be seen that this

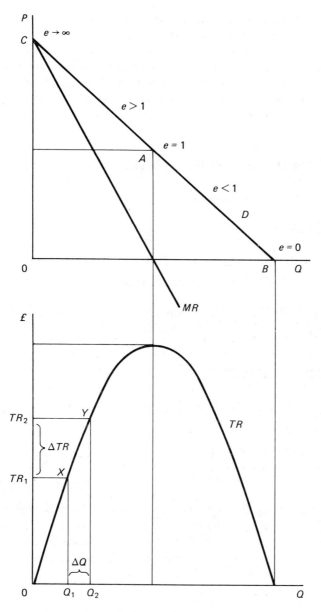

FIGURE 1.20   Elasticity of demand along a straight line demand schedule

corresponds to the maximum total revenue and so marginal revenue is zero. Elasticity must be equal to one because for (very small) changes in quantity total revenue does not change.

Moving down the demand curve away from A, total revenue falls as quantity increases. If total revenue falls when quantity increases then demand must be inelastic. The value of elasticity decreases from unity at A to zero at B. (The fact that it is zero at B can be checked using the formula for point elasticity.) Moving in the other direction from A, as quantity decreases total revenue falls and so demand must be elastic. The value of elasticity increases from one at A to infinity at C.

OTHER MEASURES OF ELASTICITY

Income elasticity of demand (e_m)

This is defined as

$$e_m = \frac{\text{proportional change in quantity demanded}}{\text{proportional change in income}}$$

Thus for normal goods e_m is a positive number, but for inferior goods it will be negative because a positive change in price will cause a negative change in quantity demanded.

Cross elasticity of demand (e_{AB})

The cross elasticity between the price of good B and the quantity demanded of good A is defined as

$$e_{AB} = \frac{\text{proportional change in quantity demanded of good } A}{\text{proportional change in price of good } B}$$

Thus for two goods that are substitutes cross elasticity of demand will be positive because a rise in the price of one will cause an increase in demand for the other. The reverse will be true for goods that are complements and so cross elasticity of demand will be negative. If there is no relationship then cross elasticity of demand will be zero.

Elasticity of supply (e_S)

This is defined as

$$e_S = \frac{\text{proportional change in quantity supplied}}{\text{proportional change in price}}$$

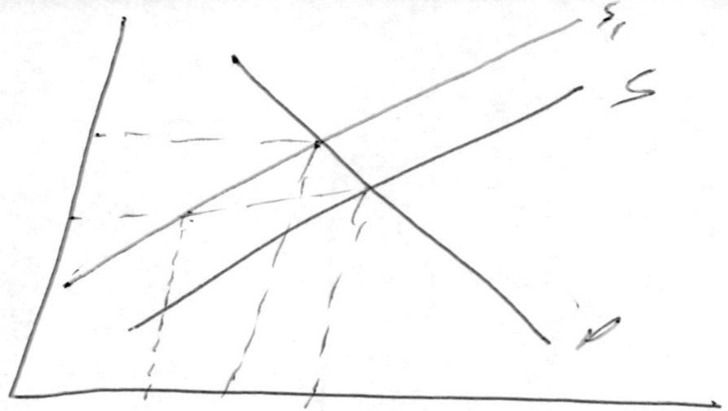

143

(6)

(a)

(b)

$s > 0$ stabil

$0 < s$ instabil

(c)

(d)

(e) ...

144

It will usually be positive and, as is explained in Chapter 5, the longer the time period that is being considered, the more elastic supply is likely to be.

QUESTIONS

1. Do you agree with the assertion that in a market economy the allocation of resources to the production of goods and services is determined by the tastes and preferences of consumers?

2. Identify the following as normative or positive statements, where possible:

    (a) The USA has a larger population than the United Kingdom.
    (b) The United Kingdom has a larger population than the USA.
    (c) Men and women should be able to retire at the same age.
    (d) The earth travels round the sun.
    (e) Euthanasia is immoral.
    (f) Students' grants are too low.
    (g) Most students prefer to live away from home.
    (h) The Government ought to increase public expenditure in order to reduce employment.
    (i) The air belongs to everyone.
    (j) There is life after death.

3. Why might the government wish to intervene in the operation of a free market economy?

4. What are the main differences between the physical sciences and the social science of economics?

5. In which ways do you think microeconomics may be of use to business men and women?

6. What effect on the demand curve for apples do you think the following would have?

    (a) A fall in the price of pears.
    (b) The government enforcing a fixed price for apples of 40p a pound.
    (c) A health warning that dangerous chemical fertilisers have been used on apple trees.
    (d) A blight that destroys a large proportion of the apple crop.
    (e) An increase in the rate of income tax on salaries over £30 000 a year, together with a rise in social security payments, such that the total net income of the population remains constant.

7. Explain, where possible, what would happen to the price and quantity

of chips sold by fish and chips shops in the following circumstances:

(a)   A failure of the potato crop is caused by bad weather.
(b)   Publication of evidence that excessive consumption of fats and carbohydrates leads to ill health is taken seriously by many people.
(c)   Both (a) and (b) occur.

8.   Using demand and supply analysis explain what would happen in the market for bread if there was a large increase in the price of flour, but the price of a loaf of bread was fixed by the Government at the original equilibrium price. How might the Government try to alleviate any disruption caused? Can you say which would be the best policy to adopt? How would each policy affect the total revenue received by bakeries compared with the original amount received?

9.   If the demand for oranges is linear and stable, and quantity demanded falls by 25 per cent when price rises from 6p to 9p each, does this imply that price returning to 6p will cause quantity demanded to rise by 25 per cent?

10.   Explain why the existence of ticket touts implies that the Football Association is not maximising the revenue it could get from the sale of Cup Final tickets.

11.   In what range would you expect the following elasticity measures to lie for the United Kingdom?

(a)   Price elasticity of demand for matches.
(b)   Price elasticity of demand for toothpaste in general.
(c)   Price elasticity of demand for toothpaste with stripes.
(d)   Income elasticity of demand for holidays abroad.
(e)   Price elasticity of supply for vintage cars.
(f)   Cross elasticity between the price of cigarettes and demand for matches.
(g)   Cross elasticity between the price of matches and demand for cigarettes.
(h)   Cross elasticity between the price of peanuts and the demand for soap.
(i)   Income elasticity of demand for bread.
(j)   Price elasticity of supply for carrots over (i) one month (ii) three years.

12.   The table below gives some information about the demand schedule for commodity X.

Price (£)	50	30	20	10	0	p
Quantity of X demanded	0	10	15	20	25	25 − 0.5 p

(a) What is the arc elasticity of demand for a price rise from £10 to £20?

(b) What is the arc elasticity of demand for a price rise from £20 to £30?

(c) If price rises from £30 will total revenue decrease?

CHAPTER 2

Production

This chapter analyses the production relationship between inputs and output. Given that the cost of producing any given output depends on:

1. the quantities of the different inputs used, and
2. the prices of the inputs,

then the production relationship will directly determine the cost of producing any given level of output if it is assumed that input prices do not change. The economic theory of production also assumes that the state of technology does not change and that all firms use the most efficient technology available. Changes in input prices, the state of technology and technical efficiency do, of course, occur but these changes are not usually related to the output level of a given firm. In some circumstances, though, input prices may change as a direct result of changes in a firm's output level (see under Pecuniary Economies of Scale in Chapter 3).

THE PRODUCTION FUNCTION

The production function is just a means of expressing the relationship between the inputs a firm uses and the output produced. It may be represented in a general form, for example,

$$Q = f(X_1, X_2 \ldots X_n)$$

where Q is units of output per time period and $X_1, X_2 \ldots X_n$ are quantities of the inputs $1, 2 \ldots n$, respectively, used in the same time period.

The general form production function above only tells us that the different inputs $X_1, X_2 \ldots X_n$ are used to produce output Q. The specific form of a production function tells us the relationship between the actual quantities of inputs used and the quantity of the good that is produced. An example of a specific form production function is

$$Q = 25X_1^{0.5} X_2^{0.5}$$

The output per time period that can be produced by using any given combination of the inputs 1 and 2 can be calculated by simply entering the respective values of X_1 and X_2 into this equation. Some possible combinations of inputs and output are given in Table 2.1.

TABLE 2.1   Input and output values for the production function $Q = 25X_1^{0.5} X_2^{0.5}$

X_1	X_2	Q
1	1	25
4	1	50
1	4	50
4	4	100
9	4	150
4	9	150
100	25	1250

Substitutability

In the above example it can be seen that the inputs can be substituted for each other and so the same output level may be achieved by different combinations of inputs. Indeed, if there is complete divisibility of the inputs then this mathematical formula suggests that, in theory, there will be an infinite number of possible combinations of the two inputs that can be used to produce any given output level. In practice perfect substitutability of inputs is not usual, but many production processes allow a certain degree of substitutability, although this may not always be immediately obvious. In house construction, for example, bricks and glass are substitutes to a certain extent. If bricks become more expensive houses with bigger windows can be built. There are some production processes that require fixed proportions of inputs, which are considered at the end of this chapter, but the theory of production assumes that in general inputs can be substituted for each other.

Production functions must be defined by specific mathematical formulae for statistical estimation and when there are more than two inputs. However, if it is assumed that there are only two inputs then certain properties of production functions can be explained diagrammatically, which is the approach adopted here in order to make the analysis easier to follow. The same results can be derived from algebraic analysis of the more realistic multi-input case.

The short-run and the long-run

A firm's ability to change its output level depends on how easily it can change the usage of its inputs. It may be fairly easy to get employees to put in more overtime work, or to buy more raw materials, but it will usually take a relatively longer time to install new plant and machinery. Economists define the short run as that time period during which at least one input is fixed whilst the other inputs can be varied. In reality there may be several short runs corresponding to the different lengths of time required to change different inputs. However, if there are only the inputs capital K and labour L then there is only one short run and it is usually assumed that L can be varied and K is fixed. Although most real firms use more than two inputs, these two time periods roughly correspond to what are sometimes known as the operating and the planning decision periods. Most firms have to make day-to-day operating decisions constrained by the availability of fixed amounts of plant and machinery and only take possible changes in plant and machinery into account when making planning decisions over a longer time horizon.

PRODUCTION IN THE LONG-RUN

Isoquants

An isoquant is a line joining all combinations of inputs that will produce the same output level. In Figure 2.1 an isoquant map is drawn to illustrate the production function $Q = (K, L)$, where Q is output, in tons per day, and K and L are the inputs of capital and labour, measured in machine days and worker days, respectively. Isoquants I, II and III represent output levels of 100, 200 and 300 tons, respectively. Thus it can be seen that an output of 100 units can be produced, for example, by using 2 units of L and 16 units of K, or by a combination of 3 units of L and 11 units of K. The smooth continuous lines representing the isoquants are drawn on the assumption that there is complete divisibility and continuous substitutability between inputs. This assumption is unlikely to hold true for most actual production processes, but the points where any discontinuities or indivisibilities occur will be different in every case, and so it is assumed for the general case that isoquants are continuous lines.

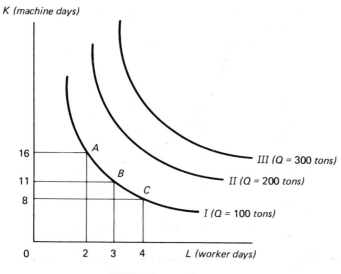

FIGURE 2.1   **Isoquants**

The marginal rate of technical substitution

The slope of an isoquant at any point represents the degree of substitutability between inputs. The marginal rate of technical substitution of K for L ($MRTS_{KL}$), is defined as the ratio in which K must be increased in proportion to any reduction in L in order to keep output at the same level. Between points A and B on isoquant I in Figure 2.1 the $MRTS_{KL}$ is 5 because an increase of 5 units of K will compensate for a reduction in L of 1 unit. On the same isoquant between points B and C the $MRTS_{KL}$ is 3.

The examples above only give an approximate value for the $MRTS_{KL}$ between two points on an isoquant and the $MRTS_{KL}$ in fact changes continually along the length of an isoquant. It can be shown that the $MRTS_{KL}$ is equal to the negative of an isoquant's slope at any given point. In Figure 2.2 overleaf the $MRTS_{KL}$ between A and B is the ratio of AC to CB. This is the negative of the slope of line AB. (The slope of a line is the negative of height over base if it slopes to the left.) The smaller the distance between A and B the closer the slope of line AB approximates to the slope of the isoquant at point A, which is shown by the tangent TT'. Therefore, for an infinitesimally small movement from any point on an isoquant the $MRTS_{KL}$ is equal to the negative of the slope of the isoquant at that point.

The slope and shape of an isoquant will vary according to the production process that it illustrates. However, it is normally expected that the $MRTS_{KL}$ will decline as one moves along an isoquant from left to right (if L is measured

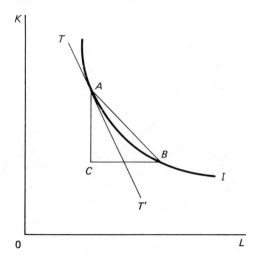

FIGURE 2.2   The *MRTS*$_{KL}$ and the slope of an isoquant

on the horizontal axis) giving a curve that is convex to the origin. Perhaps the easiest way to explain why this is so is to consider the two extreme cases of perfect substitutes and perfect complements.

In Figure 2.3 an isoquant map is shown for two inputs that are perfect substitutes. An example of perfect substitutability might occur where red bricks and grey bricks are being used to build a wall which is to be painted when finished. If the bricks are identical in every respect other than their colour then one grey brick can always be substituted for one red brick, or vice versa, without effectively changing the finished product. The marginal rate of technical substitution is, therefore, always equal to 1 and so the slope of any isoquant will be − 1 along its whole length, that is, isoquants will be straight lines sloping down from left to right. In this case (where it is assumed that any other materials and the labour input can be ignored) there is one to one substitutability, but any other constant value for the marginal rate of substitution would still yield straight line isoquants.

An example of perfect complementarity of inputs is illustrated in Figure 2.4. This case assumes that one machine operator is needed to operate each machine and that the addition of one extra machine without an operator, or one more operator without a machine to work with, will not add any more to output. The isoquants corresponding to this type of fixed proportions production relationship are consequently a series of right angles. Only when both inputs are increased is there a movement to a higher isoquant.

As most production funtions will lie somewhere between these two extreme cases isoquants are usually expected to take a shape somewhere between a

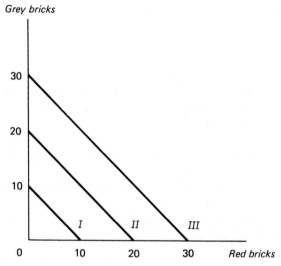

FIGURE 2.3   Perfect substitutability of inputs

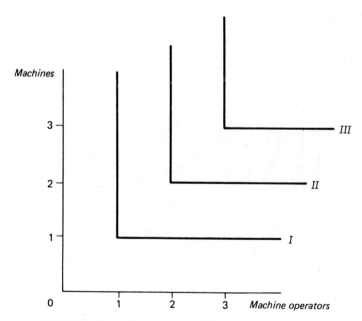

FIGURE 2.4   Perfect complementarity of inputs

right angle and a downward sloping straight line, that is, a curve convex to the origin.

Returns to scale

The degree of returns to scale of a production function describes what happens to output if all inputs are increased in the same proportion. There are three possibilities:

1. If output increases by a larger proportion than the increase in the inputs there are *increasing returns to scale*.
2. If output increases by a smaller proportion than the increase in the inputs there are *decreasing returns to scale*.
3. If output increases by the same proportion as the increase in the inputs there are *constant returns to scale*.

In Figure 2.5 equiproportional increases in inputs K and L can be illustrated by movements out along a ray from the origin, such as OA. The spacing of the isoquants is related to the degree of returns to scale that are present if successive isoquants represent equal increments in output. When isoquants come closer together it means that a smaller increase in the inputs is required

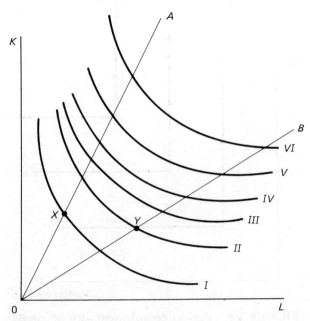

FIGURE 2.5   Returns to scale and the isoquant map

to achieve the same increase in output. When isoquants become spaced further apart it means that the same increase in output requires larger proportional increases in the inputs. The following points should be noted, however.

1. Inputs need not necessarily be proportionately increased in order to increase output. In Figure 2.5 one possible method of moving from isoquant I to isoquant II is represented by the movement from X to Y, where L is more than doubled and K is slightly reduced.
2. Even if all inputs are increased in the same proportion the degree of returns to scale can be different for different input ratios. In Figure 2.5 the spacing of the isoquants, and hence the degree of returns to scale, is different along rays OA and OB.
3. Although the spacing of the isoquants gives some indication of the changes in the input requirements for given increments in output one cannot always specifically identify the presence of increasing, decreasing or constant returns to scale just from this spacing. For example, in Figure 2.6 the isoquants are equally spaced along ray OA but, in moving from one isoquant to the next, output increases more than in proportion to the increase in the inputs used and so increasing returns to scale must be present.

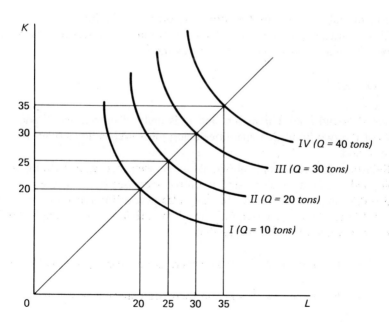

FIGURE 2.6   Evenly spaced isoquants and increasing returns to scale

A production function that can be represented by an isoquant map where the degree of returns to scale is the same along all rays from the origin is described as *homogeneous*. The degree of homogeneity indicates whether returns to scale are increasing, decreasing or constant. The specific production function

$$Q = 25K^{0.5}L^{0.5}$$

is *linear homogeneous*, which means that there are always constant returns to scale. To prove this, assume that the values of both inputs are multiplied by some constant m. If the initial values of K and L are K_1 and L_1, then the new values will be mK_1 and mL_1, respectively.

The new output level Q_2 will then be

$$= 25(mK_1)^{0.5}(mL_1)^{0.5}$$

$$= 25m^{0.5}K_1^{0.5}m^{0.5}L_1^{0.5}$$

$$= m^{0.5+0.5}25K_1^{0.5}L_1^{0.5}$$

$$= mQ_1$$

that is, output increases by the same proportion as the inputs.

This is an example of a Cobb–Douglas production function. A two-input Cobb–Douglas production function takes the form

$$Q = AL^aK^b$$

where A, a and b are parameters and Q is units of output and K and L are units of the two inputs, all quantities being measured as flows over the same time period.

Returning to the example above, it can be seen that when both inputs are multiplied by the same constant, m, output increases by m to the power of $(0.5 + 0.5)$. In general, for a Cobb–Douglas production function output will be m^{a+b} times the original output level when both inputs are multiplied by m.

For any value of m this means that:

If $a + b > 1$ then $m^{a+b} > m$ and there are increasing returns to scale.

If $a + b = 1$ then $m^{a+b} = m$ and there are constant returns to scale.

If $a + b < 1$ then $m^{a+b} < m$ and there are decreasing returns to scale.

Thus for any Cobb–Douglas production function the degree of returns to scale can be determined simply by adding up the indices of the inputs in the function and seeing whether the total is greater or less than, or equal to, unity. The same method can be used to find the degree of returns to scale of Cobb–Douglas production functions where there are more than two inputs. For example, the production function

$$Q = 20X_1^{0.4}X_2^{0.2}X_3^{0.3}X_4^{0.3}$$

exhibits increasing returns to scale as the indices of the variables representing the quantities of inputs sum to more than unity.

PRODUCTION IN THE SHORT RUN

Assume that a firm produces output Q measured in tons per day, using the two inputs K and L and that K is fixed and L, measured in worker days, can be varied. The data in Table 2.2 illustrate one possible such case.

In order to explain what happens to production it is necessary to define some terms:

Total product of labour (TP_L) is the total output of Q produced with a given amount of L.

TABLE 2.2 Production in the short run

L (*worker days*)	$Q = TP_L$ (tons)	AP_L	MP_L
0	0	–	–
1	5	5.0	5
2	12	6.0	7
3	26	8.67	14
4	43	10.75	17
5	59	11.8	16
6	72	12.0	13
7	82	11.71	10
8	89	11.12	7
9	93	10.33	4
10	95	9.5	2
11	95	8.64	0
12	95	7.92	0
13	90	6.92	– 5
14	80	5.71	– 10

Average product of labour (AP_L) is average output per unit of L used, more commonly called 'labour productivity'. Thus $AP_L = TP_L / L$.

Marginal product of labour (MP_L) is the rate of increase of TP_L with respect to L. When L is increased by equal increments of one unit, as in the example in Table 2.2, an approximate value of MP_L can be calculated by measuring the addition to TP_L that would result from using one more unit of the variable input L, that is, by using the formula.

$$MP_L^i = TP_L^i - TP_L^{i-1}$$

It can be seen that MP_L rises over the first few units of L. If only one or two workers are employed in a factory it may taken them so long to start up all the machinery that hardly anything is produced before it is time to start turning everything off again, but when more labour is employed production starts to rise more quickly. After 4 units of L, however, MP_L starts to decline as extra labour increases output by successively smaller increments. Above 12 units of of L MP_L actually becomes negative. This may be due to problems of organisation and overcrowding which cause additional workers actually to reduce output.

The law of diminishing marginal productivity

The example above illustrates the *law of diminishing marginal productivity*, which states that if more of one input is used when all other inputs are fixed then the increase in output resulting from equal increments of the variable input will eventually decline. In other words, the marginal product of the variable input will start to get smaller once the variable input has reached a certain value. This law cannot be proved from an initial set of assumptions. It is based on observation of what happens in actual production processes. If any example is considered where increasing units of a variable factor, such as labour, are used in conjunction with a given amount of a fixed factor, such as a factory, there must come a point where extra workers will add less to output than did previous workers. If a factory normally operates with a hundred workers and the labour force is increased to a thousand there would almost certainly be some fall in the marginal product of labour, and if there was not then there would be if the labour force rose to a million.

Although the law of diminishing marginal productivity is taken to apply to all production processes, it should be noted that:

1. The marginal product need not necessarily become negative, as it does in the example above. In certain cases, including Cobb–Douglas

production functions, its value will decline and approach zero but will always be positive.

2. The law of diminishing marginal productivity does not say that the marginal product will rise for the first few units of the variable input, although in practice this usually happens. Some mathematical formulations for production functions, however, such as the Cobb–Douglas production function, suggest that marginal product continually declines from infinity, which is its value when the variable input is zero.

3. In practice marginal product will often be constant over a range of values of the variable input. Economics textbooks, though, often present examples, such as the one above, where marginal product rises to a peak and then falls. This explains the comment sometimes made that the economist's theory of production is inconsistent with what happens in practice. Many businesses only experience short-run fluctuations in output which can be achieved by altering the variable input without moving outside the range where marginal product is constant. If, however, they attempted to produce output levels that were far greater than the range of output that their factory was designed to cope with then marginal product would eventually decline (see break-even chart analysis in Chapter 3).

4. The extra output produced by additional units of a variable input depends on how much of the other input(s) it is used in conjunction with. Although in the short-run the other input(s) is/are assumed to be fixed, there are many different levels at which they may be fixed. This means that the level of the variable input at which diminishing marginal productivity starts to occur will not always be the same and will depend on how much of the fixed input is used.

The law of diminishing marginal productivity is sometimes referred to as the 'law of diminishing returns'. This can be confused with the term 'decreasing returns to scale', explained in Chapter 3, which refers to long-run changes when all inputs are altered, and which is a completely different concept. For this reason this book sticks to the term 'law of diminishing marginal productivity'.

In the above example whole unit increments in the variable input L were considered. If L and Q are assumed to be completely divisible then TP_L can be represented by a continuous line such as that shown in Figure 2.7.

It can be shown that the MP_L is the slope of the TP_L schedule at any given level of L. Consider the move from A to B along the TP_L curve in Figure 2.7 overleaf. Over this range the MP_L is the increase in output divided by the increase in the amount of L used, which is BC/AC. This is equal to the slope of the line AB. The smaller the distance between A and B becomes the closer the slope of AB gets to the slope of the tangent TT', which represents the slope of the

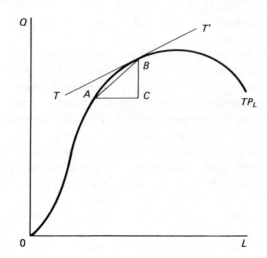

FIGURE 2.7   The total product of labour schedule

TP_L curve at B. Thus for an infinitesimally small change in L from its value at B the slope of AB will equal the slope of TT' and so, for any given value of L, MP_L is equal to the slope of the TP_L schedule.

This relationship between TP_L and MP_L is shown in Figure 2.8. The maximum value of MP_L corresponds to M, where the slope of the TP_L is greatest, and the point at which it cuts the L axis corresponds to the value of L at which the TP_L is horizontal, that is, its slope is zero.

The shape of the AP_L schedule can also be determined from the graph of the TP_L schedule. At L_1 in Figure 2.9 on page 60 AP_L is equal to AL_1/OL_1, which is the slope of OA. Thus the AP_L has the same value as the slope of a line from the origin to the point on the TP_L curve corresponding to the value of L for which AP_L is being determined. The value of AP_L for L_3 will be the same as that for L_1 because OC is just a continuation of the line OA. The maximum value of AP_L will be where a line from the origin is a tangent to the TP_L curve, at B. As MP_L is equal to the slope of the TP_L curve then AP_L at its maximum must be equal to MP_L. The relationship between TP_L, AP_L and MP_L schedules is summed up in Figure 2.10 (page 61).

THE RELATIONSHIP BETWEEN THE SHORT-RUN AND THE LONG-RUN

The slope of an isoquant

The short-run and long-run analyses of production can now be linked and the relationship between the $MRTS_{KL}$ and marginal product explained. Suppose

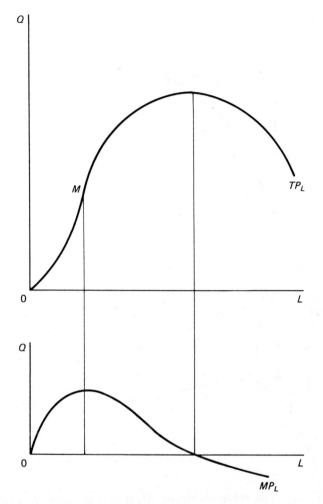

FIGURE 2.8   The relationship between marginal and total product

that the movement from *A* to *B* along isoquant II in Figure 2.11 (p. 62) is accomplished in two stages, from *A* to *C* and then from *C* to *B*. In going from *A* to *C* there is a reduction of ΔK in input *K*. This will cause a reduction in output *Q* of ΔQ where

$$\Delta Q = \Delta K . MP_K$$

If *L* is then increased by ΔL there will be an increase in *Q* of

$$\Delta Q = \Delta L . MP_L$$

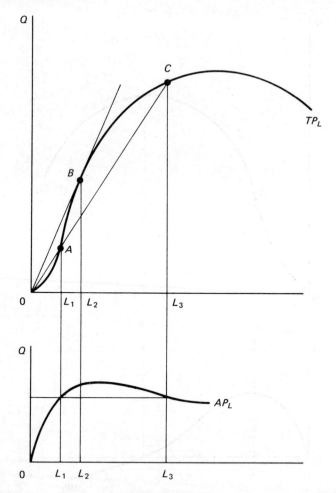

FIGURE 2.9   The relationship between average and total product

As A and B are on the same isoquant this means that the fall in output caused by the reduction in K is exactly balanced by the increase in output caused by the increase in L. Thus

$$\Delta K.MP_K = \Delta L.MP_L$$

and so

$$\Delta K/\Delta L = MP_L/MP_K$$

As the distance from A to B becomes smaller $\Delta K/\Delta L$ becomes closer to the

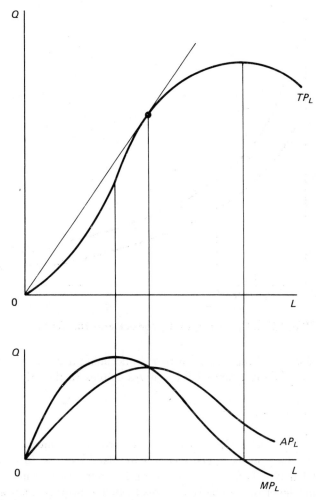

FIGURE 2.10   Total, marginal and average product of labour

negative of the slope of the isoquant II at A. Thus MP_L/MP_K equals the negative of the slope of the isoquant at A.

It has already been established that the $MRTS_{KL}$ at any point on an isoquant is equal to the negative of its slope. Thus at any point on an isoquant

$$MRTS_{KL} = MP_L/MP_K$$

If there is a movement along an isoquant from left to right it is expected that MP_L will decline, as more of L is used, and MP_K will rise, as less of K is used. Thus the $MRTS_{KL}$ will decline and the isoquant will become flatter (but with

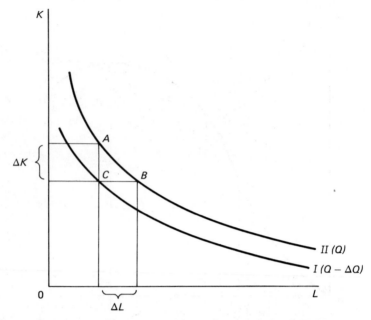

FIGURE 2.11   Marginal product and the $MRTS_{KL}$

a negative slope). In other words, if there is declining marginal productivity for both inputs then isoquants will be curves convex to the origin.

The economic region

The TP_L and MP_L schedules can be derived from an isoquant map, their position depending on the given value of the fixed input K. In Figure 2.12 it is assumed that K is fixed at a value of 20 units. As L is increased the corresponding level of output can be read off the isoquant map and then plotted as the TP_L curve, the two graphs in Figure 2.12 having the same horizontal axis. This exercise is rather like plotting a cross section of a hill in geography using a contour map, only this time the 'contours' represent output levels. When L is 5 units the highest isoquant, representing 39 units of output, is reached and TP_L is at its 'peak'.

If MP_L is measured over whole unit increases in L, rather than by equating it to the slope of the TP_L curve, its approximate position can also be plotted. For example, when L is increased from 1 to 2 units output increases from 16 to 29 units, as shown by the respective isoquants, and so MP_L is 13. (Note that, because this method only gives an approximate value for MP_L over a section of the TP_L schedule, the graph of MP_L is not the smooth line that it should be.)

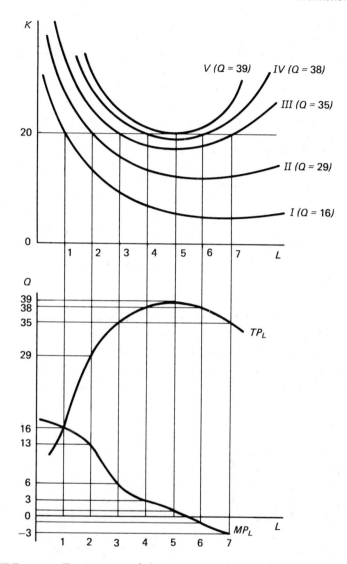

FIGURE 2.12   **Derivation of short-run product curves from an isoquant map**

Unlike the previous isoquant maps that have so far been encountered, the set of isoquants in Figure 2.12 start to 'bend back', that is, their slope becomes positive instead of the usual negative. This means that when K is fixed and L is increased output will initially rise but then after some point it will start to fall. In this example, as L is increased with K fixed at 20, output increases to a maximum of 39 units, when L is 5, and then falls. If total output falls then the MP_L must be negative, as is shown in the bottom section of Figure 2.12. Similarly, if K was increased with L held constant then MP_K would become negative if there was a backward bending section at the other end of the isoquants.

In Figure 2.13 the lines RR' and UU' are known as 'ridge lines'. They are drawn through the points on each isoquant where it starts to bend back, that is, when its slope is either vertical or horizontal. The area between these ridge lines is known as the 'economic region' of the isoquant map and the area outside is called the 'uneconomic region'. Whatever the prices of inputs, or the time period within which a decision is made, if a firm is acting rationally it will always use a combination of inputs that is within the economic region. No firm would choose to operate in the uneconomic region because any given output could always be produced by using less of at least one input. In the example in Figure 2.12 the same output of 35 units can be produced using either 3 or 7 units of L in conjunction with the fixed input of K. Obviously a firm will choose the input mix that uses the lesser amount of L and therefore costs less.

ESTIMATING PRODUCTION FUNCTIONS

Production functions can be statistically estimated from a series of different

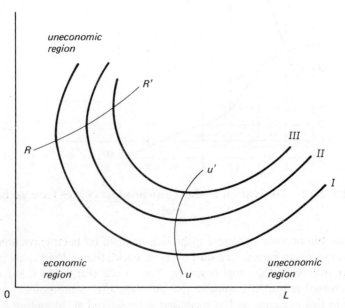

FIGURE 2.13   The economic and uneconomic regions

observations or they can be estimated from technical production information provided by production managers.

Statistical studies

A production function may be statistically estimated from time series or from cross-section data. There are several problems faced whichever method is used:

1. It may be difficult to obtain a sufficient number of observations. Statistical analysis requires that the number of observations used must be sufficiently greater than the number of variables in the function being estimated for any meaningful conclusions to be drawn.
2. Firms vary in efficiency and so data which includes observations of inefficient firms may cause the production function to be incorrectly estimated. (Remember that the production function assumes that the most efficient method of production is being used.) This means that the usual statistical approach of estimating which line best fits a sample of data, which will be distributed on either side of this line, will not give the true technically efficient production function. This problem is illustrated in Figure 2.14, where observations of the amounts of K and L used by different firms all producing the same output level correspond to the

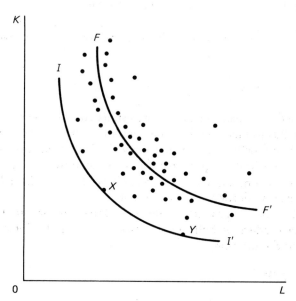

FIGURE 2.14   Estimation of production functions

points marked and the line of best fit is shown (approximately) by FF'. However, points such as X and Y lie below this line, which would not be possible if FF' was an isoquant. Given this set of observations the isoquant should be line II', which is the lower boundary of the observations, rather than FF'. (This method of deriving the true isoquant cannot be used for the more usual multi-input case and when the production function has to be estimated by statistical analysis, and is only used here to illustrate the problem.)

3. Technology changes over time and so the position of an isoquant will move, usually shifting inwards, causing time series estimations of production functions to be distorted.

4. It is difficult to measure the quantity of capital used. The many different types of plant and machinery that constitute a firm's capital cannot simply be added together in the same way as fairly homogeneous inputs such as coal or oil that can be measured in physical units such as tonnes or litres. The amount of capital a firm uses is therefore usually measured in terms of the total cost of this capital. The problem is that this method of measuring makes it difficult to distinguish between changes in the amount of capital used and changes in its price.

5. Even if all the problems mentioned above were overcome there would still remain the problem of finding the best functional form to describe the production function. To estimate the parameters of a production function using statistical analysis it is necessary to specify the algebraic formula that best describes its expected form.

The simplest form a two-input production function might take would be the additive function

$$Q = a + bK + cL$$

where a, b and c are parameters that are estimated from the data.

However, this formulation does not conform with the expected properties of a production function. It does not obey the law of diminishing marginal productivity because it suggests that if L is increased by one unit then Q will always rise by a constant amount, c, regardless of the levels of L or K, that is, the marginal production of L is constant.

The Cobb–Douglas production function overcomes this problem because the marginal product of both inputs always declines. In Table 2.3 this is illustrated for the function

$$Q = 36K^{0.25}L^{0.5}$$

where input K is held fixed at 16 and as L is increased MP_L declines.

TABLE 2.3   Values of the production function $Q = 36K^{0.25}L^{0.5}$

| | | | MP_L | |
K	L	Q	(a)	(b)
16	0	0	–	–
16	1	72.0	36.0	72.0
16	2	101.8	25.5	29.8
16	3	124.7	20.8	22.9
16	4	144.0	18.0	19.3
16	5	161.0	16.1	17.0

(a) is precise measure of MP_L at a point.
(b) is approximate measure of MP_L for unit increases in L.

(Two measures of MP_L are calculated in Table 2.3. One is the approximate measure used for unit increases in L and the other is the more precise measure which is the slope of the TP_L schedule.)

*Mathematically MP_L is the partial derivative of TP_L with respect to L. For any Cobb–Douglas production function

$$Q = AK^aL^b.$$

MP_L is equal to the slope of the TP_L schedule and so

$$MP_L = \partial TP/\partial L = bAK^aL^{b-1} = AK^aL^b.(b/L) = bAK^a/L^{1-b}.$$

If K is fixed, as L increases then L^{1-b} also increases and therefore the whole term declines. Thus MP_L continuously declines.

Similarly it can be shown that if K is increased with L held constant then the MP_K also declines continuously. *Using logarithms a Cobb–Douglas production function can be transformed into a linear form. The function

$$Q = AK^aL^b$$

can be written as

$$\log Q = \log A + a \log K + b \log L$$

and estimates of log A, a and b can then be made using linear regression

TABLE 2.4   **Estimates of Cobb–Douglas form production functions**

			Labour a_1	*Capital* a_2	*Raw materials* a_3	*Researcher*
1945	Gas	France	0.83	0.1		Verhulst
1936	Railroads	USA	0.89	0.12	0.28	Klein
1950	Coal	UK	0.79	0.29		Lomax
1955	Coal	UK	0.51	0.49		Leser

Source: A. A. Walters, 'Production and Cost Functions: An Econometric Society', *Econometrica*, vol. 31, nos. 1–2, January–April, pp. 1–66, 1963.

analysis. The estimated value of the constant term A is the antilog of the estimate of log A.

Some examples of actual estimates of Cobb–Douglas production functions are given in Table 2.4. These figures are rather dated, but more recent empirical research on production functions tends to use more sophisticated formulations, designed to try to overcome some of the problems mentioned above, which are rather too complex to explain here.

Given the problems that may be encountered in trying to estimate production functions any published estimates may not necessarily be accepted as completely accurate. As well as the problem of measuring capital, mentioned earlier, it has been argued that empirical studies often omit a measure of management and administration, which again is difficult to quantify. The Cobb–Douglas production function assumes that the same degree of returns to scale is present throughout the whole range of inputs and output. Studies of cost curves (see Chapter 3) have suggested that in many cases the degree of returns to scale will alter as output increases and so even the Cobb–Douglas production function may not be the best formula for describing a production function.

Technical studies

It is sometimes possible to obtain information from production managers about the input requirements for different levels of production. However, although this approach may give details of the usage of inputs such as raw materials, labour, energy and capital equipment, it does not usually give a complete picture of all the inputs that would be used. A firm also has to pay for inputs such as management and administration, personnel management, marketing and distribution, which would not be included in technical studies.

Technical studies will still be useful from the managerial economics viewpoint but from an economist's viewpoint they are incomplete and so may reduce the accuracy of predictions about the pricing and output behaviour of a group of firms.

LINEAR PRODUCTION THEORY

Instead of making the usual assumption of substitutability of inputs, linear production theory assumes that different inputs can only be used together in fixed proportions. It is possible though that there may be several fixed proportions production processes that a firm can use.

Consider the example of a firm that uses the two inputs K and L, measured in machine and worker days, respectively, to manufacture output Q, measured in tons per day. Assume that there are three possible fixed proportions production processes A, B and C.

To produce 1 ton of output the requirements of three processes are:

Method A: 5 units of K and 20 units of L.
Method B: 10 units of K and 10 units of L.
Method C: 15 units of K and 8 units of L.

To produce any other output level, the input requirements for each process are simply multiplied by output; that is to say, there are always constant returns to scale. For example, to produce 3 tons by method A the input requirements are 15 units of K and 60 of L. The rays OA, OB and OC in Figure 2.15 (p. 70) show the different input combinations that correspond to the fixed proportions production processes A, B and C, respectively, and are known as 'activity rays'. Thus one ton can be produced using combinations A_1, B_1 or C_1, 2 tons by A_2, B_2 or C_2, and so on.

It is also possible to use a mix of different fixed proportions production processes. For example, 0.2 tons made by method B requires 2 of K plus 2 of L and 0.8 tons made by method A requires 4 of K plus 16 of L. Thus one ton made by this combination of production processes requires 6 of K plus 18 of L. This particular input mix is shown by point X in Figure 2.15, which is one fifth of the way along the line joining A_1 and B_1. Any other mix of production processes used to manufacture a given output will similarly be represented by a point on the line joining the points representing this output level on the relevant activity rays. Its position on this line will reflect the relative proportions of the different methods used. If x per cent of output is produced using method A, and $(100 - x)$ per cent using method B, then the input mix will be represented by a point by a point $(100 - x)$ per cent of the distance along the line joining the relevant points on rays A and B.

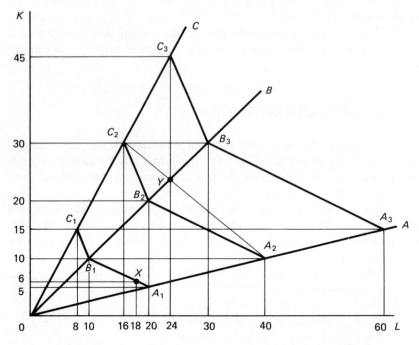

FIGURE 2.15   Fixed proportions production methods

It is not efficient to use all such combinations of methods, however. For example, point Y on the line A_2C_2 represents a production mix of 2/3 of method C and 1/3 of method A which therefore requires 23.33 units of K and 24 of L. However, combination B_2 requires less of both inputs (20 of K and 20 of L) and is clearly more efficient. Thus in this example the combination of method A with B, or method B with C, would be efficient, but not the combination of A and C.

The cheapest way of producing any given output can be found either by direct calculation or by drawing a budget line on the activity ray diagram. (Budget lines are explained in the next chapter and so when you have read it return to Figure 2.15 and as an exercise see if you can obtain the same solution as the direct calculation method below by using a budget line.) If the prices of K and L per unit are £16 and £4, respectively, then to produce one ton the total cost would be:

Method A $5 \times £16 + 20 \times £4 = £160$
Method B $10 \times £16 + 10 \times £4 = £200$
Method C $15 \times £16 + 8 \times £4 = £272$

Thus method A is cheapest. If the input price ratio was the same as the

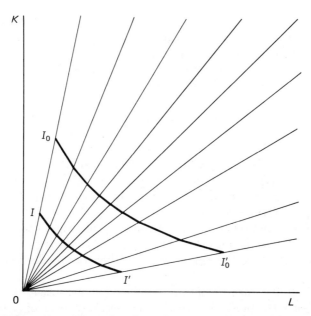

FIGURE 2.16   Many fixed proportions production processes

negative of the slope of any of the lines representing efficient mixes of methods, such as A_1B_1, then it would not matter which of the two methods, or which proportional mix, was used. For example, if the price of K was £8 per unit and L still cost £4 a unit then methods A and B would cost the same.

The more fixed proportions production processes that a firm can use the closer the lines linking efficient mixes of methods for producing any given output level will resemble the usual curved isoquants, as is shown by II' and I_0I_0' in Figure 2.16.

QUESTIONS

1. A firm uses inputs of labour L, capital K, raw material R and energy E to manufacture its product Q. If it faces the production function

   $$Q = 0.4 \ L^{0.3}K^{0.2}R^{0.1}E^{0.25}$$

   What kind of returns to scale are present?
2. What is the $MRTS_{KL}$ of the production function

   $$Q = 10L + 3K$$

   at any output level?

3.   No rational manager would use an input mix that corresponded to a position in the uneconomic region of the isoquant map describing her firm's production function. Why?

4.   The two production functions (a) and (b) below show the relationship between inputs L and K and output Q.

    (a) $Q = 0.5K + 0.5L$
    (b) $Q = K^{0.5}L^{0.5}$

Answer the following questions for both (a) and (b):
(i)   What types of returns to scale are present?
(ii)   Is there an uneconomic region on the isoquant map illustrating the production function?
(iii)   If K is held constant at some level what shapes will the AP_L and MP_L schedules take?
Which do you think is the more realistic of these two production functions? Why?

5.   What are the main problems involved in statistically estimating a production function? Why may a technical estimate of a production function be useful to a firm's manager but not be of use to an economist trying to explain the behaviour of a large group of firms?

6.   A firm uses inputs K and L to make output Q but it is constrained to using the three processes A, B and C, or any combination of these processes. Assume inputs and outputs are divisible into small units.
Process A requires 6 units of K and 1 unit of L to make 100 units of Q.
Process B requires 3 units of K and 3 units of L to make 100 units of Q.
Process C requires 2 units of K and 8 units of L to make 100 units of Q.
Draw an isoquant map to illustrate this firm's production choices.
If the price of K is £40 a unit and the price of L is £90 a unit what is the minimum cost of producing 300 Q? With the same input prices what is the maximum output that can be produced for a budget of £165? Are there any combinations of processes A, B and C that it will never be efficient to use? Can a marginal product curve for L be derived?

CHAPTER 3

Costs

An efficient firm will produce any given output level by the cheapest feasible method. Taking this principle as its starting point, this chapter explains how production costs are related to a firm's output level. This relationship is based on the theory of production set out in Chapter 2 and is analysed in the long-run and in the short-run.

OPPORTUNITY COST

The inputs that an economist takes into consideration when calculating a firm's costs are not necessarily the same as those that an accountant would. Instead of just taking into account those inputs where there is an actual monetary payment, economists also include the opportunity cost (or benefit forgone) of inputs used where there is no actual payment. For example, if a firm uses its own premises then it forgoes the rent it could have earned from leasing them out. This concept of opportunity cost is explained more fully in Chapter 4, where its relevance to the economist's definition of profit is also considered.

LONG-RUN COSTS

In the long-run a firm can adjust all inputs in order to achieve the lowest cost method of producing a given output. In some cases output will be specified and a firm will seek the lowest cost combination of inputs that can achieve this output level. Alternatively, it may try to maximise the output that can be produced within a given cost constraint. Isoquant analysis can be used to show that the solutions to both of these problems require the same set of conditions.

The budget constraint

The budget constraint is the maximum expenditure on inputs that a firm is allowed. For the two-input case the budget constraint can be illustrated by a straight line such as AB in Figure 3.1. In this example it is assumed that a firm has a total budget of £200 and that the prices of the two inputs K and L are £5 and £2 per unit, respectively. The intercepts A and B show the respective amounts of K and L that could be purchased if the whole of the budget was only spent on one input; for example, if £200 was spent on K then 40 units could be purchased. Other possible patterns of a total expenditure of £200 on K and L will lie on the straight line joining A and B (assuming divisibility) because each combination of K and L must satisfy the budget equation

$$5K + 2L = 200.$$

The firm may spend less than its budget, but not more, and so the combinations of K and L that it is feasible to purchase lie within the triangle OAB.

The slope of the budget line is determined by the relative prices of the

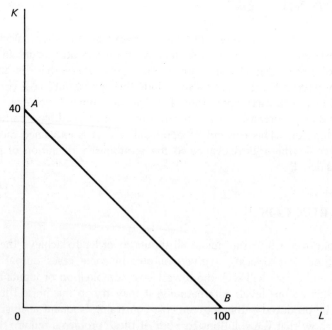

FIGURE 3.1   The budget constraint

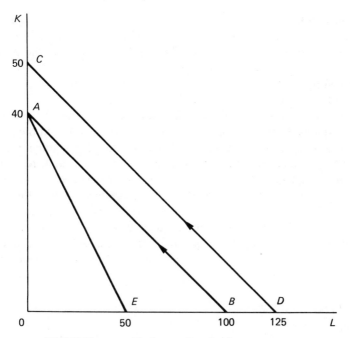

FIGURE 3.2   Shifts in the budget constraint

two inputs and does not depend on the size of the budget. Assume that a firm has a budget of £M to spend on inputs K and L with prices P_K and P_L per unit, respectively. The intercepts of the budget constraint will be M/P_K on the K axis and M/P_L on the L axis. Its slope is therefore

$$- (M/P_K)/(M/P_L) = - P_L/P_K$$

Although the magnitude of the budget does not affect the slope of a budget line, it does determine its position. If the total budget available increases from £200 to £250 then the budget line will then shift to CD, which is parallel to the original budget line AB but further out from the origin, as shown in Figure 3.2.

Continuing with the same example, assume that with the original budget of £200 P_L increases from £2 to £4. The new budget line will then be AE, which has a slope equal to

$$- P_L/P_K = - £4/£5 = - 0.8$$

compared with a slope of -0.4 for budget line AB. Thus a change in the relative prices of the inputs causes the slope of the budget line to alter. Note that if both input prices change by the same proportion then the slope of the budget line will not change and there will just be a parallel shift of the budget line, that is, the effect will be the same as a change in the budget.

Optimal input combination

To determine the optimal input combination, first consider the problem of achieving the maximum feasible output for a given budget. On the isoquant map in Figure 3.3 the budget line *AB* is drawn representing a budget constraint of £100 and input prices for *K* and *L* of £10 and £4 per unit, respectively. The highest isoquant that passes through the feasible expenditure range *OAB* will represent the greatest output that can be produced within this budget constraint. This maximum feasible output is 200 tons and the optimal input combination will be at *X* where the isoquant *II* just touches the budget line *AB*. Although lower output levels can be produced with this budget (for example, 100 tons at *Y*) there is no higher isoquant that can be reached. The

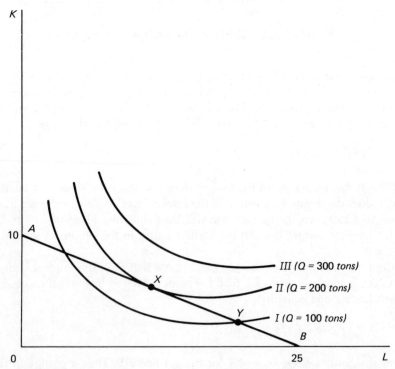

FIGURE 3.3   Optimal input combination–output maximisation

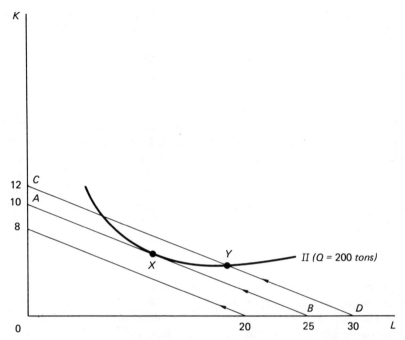

FIGURE 3.4   Optimal input combination–cost minimisation

optimal input combination is therefore found at the point of tangency between the budget line and the isoquant representing the greatest feasible output.

To explain the method of finding the cheapest input combination that will produce a given level of output, assume that the required output is 200 tons and that the prices of the two inputs are the same as in the example above. The slope of the budget line is therefore

$$- P_L / P_K = - £4/£10 = - 0.4.$$

Its position is determined in Figure 3.4 by finding the line with a slope of $- 0.4$ that is closest to the origin but still touches isoquant *II*. This is budget line *AB* with the optimal input combination at *X*, which is the same solution as that found for the output maximisation problem illustrated in Figure 3.3. There are other ways of achieving the same output but they will cost more; for example, the budget line *CD* through input combination *Y* on the isoquant *II* represents a larger budget than does *AB*.

The optimal input combination will therefore be either:

(a)   where the highest feasible isoquant is tangent to the given budget constraint (for the output maximisation problem), or

(b)   where the isoquant representing the given output is tangent to the lowest possible budget constraint (for the cost minimisation problem).

There are, however, two possible exceptions to this rule.

1.   Corner Solutions

It is possible that isowuants may touch one or more of the axes, as in Figure 3.5. Mathematically the lines representing the isoquants would continue as shown by the dotted sections but, of course, it is impossible to have a negative quantity of an input. If the budget constraint is AB then in this example the greatest feasible output is determined at point A. Although isoquant I represents this maximum feasible output it is not tangent to the budget line at A. This is an example of a 'corner solution'.

2.   Tangency in the Uneconomic Region

If the marginal products of both inputs become negative then isoquants may take the shape shown in Figure 3.6. Assume that a firm wishes to produce the output represented by isoquant I and the prices of the two inputs yield a budget constraint with a slope of -0.5. There will be two points, X and

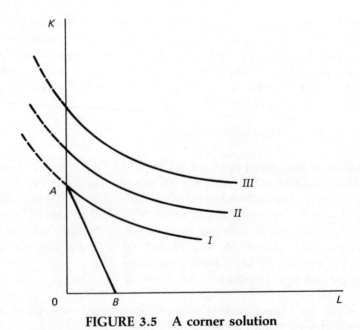

FIGURE 3.5   A corner solution

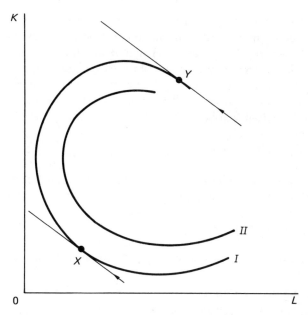

FIGURE 3.6   Tangency in the uneconomic region

Y, where lines with this slope are tangent to isoquant *I*. Only *X* represents an optimal input combination, however. Point *Y* is outside the economic region and is, in fact, the most expensive combination of inputs that will produce this output level. Thus, in addition to the tangency condition, the optimal input combination must also be in the economic region of a firm's isoquant map, that is, the point of tangency must be on a section of an isoquant that is convex to the origin.

Optimal input combination and the marginal product

The result that the optimal input combination normally occurs at the point of tangency between an isoquant and a budget line in the two-input case follows from a more general rule which applies for any number of inputs. This states that a firm is only operating efficiently when the marginal product of the last £1 spent on all inputs is equal, that is, when an extra £1 is spent on any input it will produce the same additional output as an extra £1 spent on any other input. This means that

$$MP_1/P_1 = MP_2/P_2 = \ldots = MP_n/P_n \qquad \text{for any number, } n, \text{ of inputs.}$$

The rationale for this rule is explained in the following example.

Suppose that a firm uses two inputs, A and B, to manufacture good X and that both inputs are utilised past the point where diminishing marginal productivity sets in. The prices of A and B are £25 and £40 per unit, respectively. If the firm is initially allocating its budget so that MP_A is 150 and MP_B is 180 then it is not making the best use of its resources.

If £1 more is spent on A it will purchase 1/25th of a unit of A and so the addition to output will be

$$MP_A/P_A = 150/25 = 6.$$

If £1 less is spent on B the firm will use 1/40th of a unit less of B and the consequent drop in output will be

$$MP_B/P_B = 180/40 = 4.5.$$

Thus the net effect on output of switching £1 of expenditure from B to A is

$$+6 - 4.5 = +1.5 \text{ units.}$$

That is to say, there is a net increase in production without any increase in total expenditure on inputs. These calculations have assumed that the marginal product of both inputs is the same for fractional increases and decreases in input usage. However, as more of input A is used, its marginal product is expected to decline and as less of B is used its marginal product is expected to rise. Thus if expenditure is gradually transferred from A to B eventually the situation will be reached where

$$MP_A/P_A = MP_B/P_B$$

and it will then not be possible to achieve any further increases in output simply by transferring expenditure from one input to the other. It should be noted that the marginal products of the two inputs will change not only because there is a movement along the MP_A and MP_B schedules but also because the whole marginal product curve of each input will shift when the amount of the other input used alters.

Given the optimal combination rule that

$$MP_A/P_A = MP_B/P_B$$

then

$$P_A/P_B = MP_A/MP_B.$$

Given that

$$MP_A/MP_B = -(\text{slope of an isoquant})$$

and

$$P_A/P_B = -(\text{slope of the budget line})$$

then, in the two-input case, the optimal input combination occurs where the slope of the budget line equals the slope of an isoquant. It is important to remember that the general optimal input combination rule is the cause of this result in the diagrammatic illustration of the two-input case and not the other way around.

The expansion path and long-run average cost

If for some reason a firm wishes to change its output level then, because all inputs are variable in the long-run, it will be able to move to another position where the conditions for optimal input combination are satisfied. This is illustrated in Figure 3.7, where the prices of K and L are £20 and £10 per unit, respectively. If output is initially 10 tons then, given these input prices,

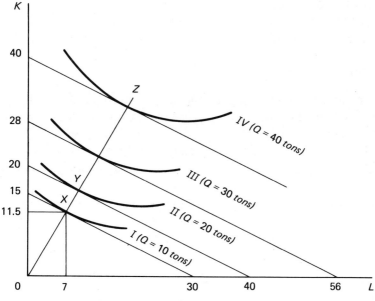

FIGURE 3.7   The expansion path

the optimal input combination is at X where the budget line with a slope of -0.5 is tangent to the 10 tons isoquant, and input usage is 11.5 units of K and 7 units of L. If output is increased to 20 tons then the new optimal input combination is at Y. This is found by drawing a line which is parallel to the original budget line and tangent to the 20 tons isoquant. In a similar fashion the cheapest method of producing other output levels can be found. The line XZ which joins these optimal input combinations is known as the *expansion path*. In this particular example the expansion path is a straight line because there is a symmetrical isoquant map corresponding to a homogeneous production function. In other cases the expansion path may take different shapes. Note also that the expansion path will alter if relative input prices change.

The total cost TC of producing an output of 10 tons can be read off the diagram in three ways as all combinations of inputs on the budget line through X involve the same total cost. The optimal input combination is 11.5 units of K and 7 units of L and so TC can be calculated as

$$(11.5 \times £20) + (7 \times £10) = £300.$$

It would be even simpler, though, to read off the axes the maximum amount of either input that could be bought. The budget line cuts the K axis at 15 and so the total budget can be calculated as

$$15 \times £20 = £300.$$

Average cost AC is total cost divided by output. For an output of 10 tons

$$AC = TC/Q = £300/10 = £30.$$

The TC and AC for other output levels are given in Table 3.1 and the values of AC are plotted in Figure 3.8. The line joining these points is the *long-run*

TABLE 3.1   **Output and cost**

Output	TC	AC
10 tons	£300	£30
20 tons	£400	£20
30 tons	£560	£18.67
40 tons	£800	£20

(Data refers to Figure 3.8)

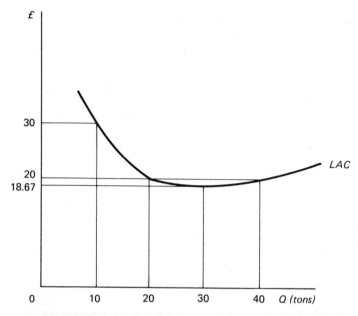

FIGURE 3.8 · **The long-run average cost curve**

average cost LAC curve. This shows the cheapest average cost of producing any given output level in the long-run when a firm can vary all inputs in order to achieve the optimal input combination.

In the example in Figure 3.8 the *LAC* is U-shaped. Over the first section of the *LAC* when average cost is falling there are *economies of scale* and when the *LAC* rises there are *diseconomies of scale*. In this particular case economies of scale occur when there are increasing returns to scale and diseconomies of scale occur when there are decreasing returns to scale. The 'returns to scale' property of a production function only refers to what happens when all inputs are increased in the same proportion, however, and in practice and other methods of increasing output may be used.

Economies of scale

There are several different possible reasons why economies of scale may be present but basically they all entail either one, or both, of the following occurring as a result of an increase in output:

1. A decrease in the amount of inputs required per unit of output.
2. A fall in input prices.

There are, of course, other reasons why (1) or (2) might occur, for example, the discovery of a new source of a raw material may lower input prices. However, the concern here is to identify reasons why there may be a change in average cost solely due to increases in a firm's output. Economies of scale due to reasons that fall into category (1) are known as *real* economies of scale and those that are due to category (2) reasons are called *pecuniary* economies of scale. It is not possible to list here all the different sources of economies of scale but some of the main ones can be considered:

Real Economies of Scale

1.   Increasing returns to scale   It has already been explained that one possible source of real economies of scale is a production function that exhibits increasing returns to scale, but why should any actual production process exhibit this property? One possibility occurs when output is in the form of an area or a volume. For example, the material needed to construct a storage tank will not increase in proportion to the volume of the tank. Similarly, the total floor-space of a house can be doubled without doubling the number of bricks needed. In reality things are, of course, not always quite this simple. Stronger and thicker material may be needed if a bigger tank is built. However, what can be said is that where there is an area or volume involved in output then this may increase the likelihood of economies of scale being present. Other possible reasons for pure increasing returns to scale (that is, output increasing more than in proportion to an equal proportional increase in all inputs, without the nature of the inputs changing) will be specific to particular production processes.

2.   Indivisibilities   Much of the preceding analysis assumes divisibility of inputs and output but in practice indivisibilities do exist and can be a source of economies of scale. If a particular indivisible piece of equipment is necessary for production then a firm that does not produce enough to utilise fully the equipment's capacity will face higher unit costs than a firm that produces enough to use it to its full capacity. In motor vehicle production, for example, the outer shell of a vehicle is stamped out by a body press and it has been estimated that one press can cope with up to 2 million vehicle shells. This is greater than the total annual production of all United Kingdom car producers combined. (See Table 3.4 on page 95).

To illustrate how indivisibilities affect a firm's average costs consider the hypothetical example of a firm that uses a piece of equipment which is capable of producing up to 20 000 units of output a year and costs £50 000 a year to operate, regardless of the output level Q that is actually produced. Assume also that labour and raw materials together are a constant £12 per unit of output.

Thus when $Q = 1000$ then $AC = (£50\,000 + £12\,000)/1000 = £62$, and

when $Q = 20\,000$ then $AC = (£50\,000 + £240\,000)/20\,000 = £14.50$. When output exceeds 20 000 a second machine must be paid for and so if $Q = 20\,001$ then $AC = (£100\,000 + £240\,012)/20\,001 = £17.00$

The resulting AC curve is plotted in Figure 3.9.

This example seems similar to the short-run situation, considered later in this chapter, where a firm faces a fixed cost of £50 000. However, there is a difference because this analysis refers to the long-run and, although the machine may be indivisible, the firm is still free to get rid of it or to install new machines if it wishes. Sometimes a small firm may be able to overcome this indivisibility problem by leasing a machine only when it is required (for instance, it can buy computer time) but this is not always feasible.

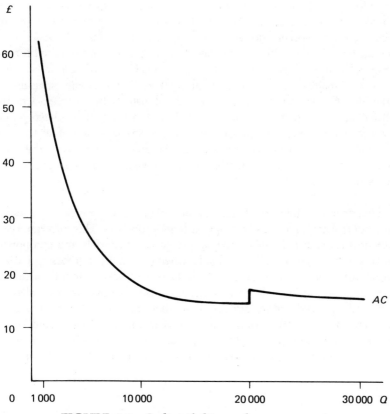

FIGURE 3.9   Indivisibility and average cost

Indivisibilities do not apply to machinery alone. Another possible example of an indivisible item of expenditure might be a security guard employed to patrol a firm's premises at night.

3.   *Set-up costs*   Before production even commences most firms incur set-up costs. They may just involve the labour cost of setting the specifications on a pressing machine before a batch of metal components is pressed out. In other cases, though, set-up costs can run into many millions of pounds. If a car manufacturer launches a new model it usually has to pay for research and development, retooling the production line and retraining workers before a single car can be manufactured. The higher a firm's output the greater the number of units that these set-up costs can be spread over and consequently the lower average cost per unit will be.

4.   *Specialisation of labour*   A small firm may only be able to afford one worker to perform several different tasks whereas a large firm may be able to employ specialised workers who only perform one task each and are able to become more efficient at this one job. Costs may also be reduced through specialisation if workers do not have to move from place to place to do different tasks and if individual special clothing or tools are required for each worker who does a particular task. The specialisation of labour can occur among non-manual as well as manual workers. For example, specialists in marketing, finance and production control will usually be more efficient than one manager who is responsible for all these functions. It has been argued, however, that the increased productivity due to specialisation of labour is not an example of increasing returns to scale because the nature of the inputs changes and so it is not just a matter of the same inputs being proportionately increased.

5.   *Uncertainty*   The unpredictability of certain events which are outside a firm's control can give an advantage to large producers. This uncertainty can occur on the input side, when the supply of raw materials and components may be erratic, and on the demand side, when customers' purchasing patterns fluctuate over time. It is expensive to hold large stocks of inputs or finished goods because the firm has to pay storage costs and because capital is tied up. It can be proved mathematically[1] that when there are random fluctuations in demand or supply the optimal amount of inventories that should be held increases less than proportionately to average output. Therefore average cost per unit of output of keeping inventories will be lower the higher output is.

---

1.   See Chapter 3 of David Johnson, *Quantitative Business Analysis* (London: Butterworths, 1986).

A simple example can illustrate another instance of uncertainty causing economies of scale. Assume that a firm uses a particular machine which has a probability of 0.05 of breaking down during any given week and that any breakdown causes a machine to be out of action until the following week. Given that the industry is such that any unplanned loss of production would be catastrophic, every firm keeps enough spare machines to cover possible breakdowns. This means that one spare machine should be kept for every twenty machines that a firm uses if the remote (1 in 400) chance of two machines breaking down, and the even remoter possibility of more than two breakdowns, are ignored. A firm which uses less than twenty machines will still have to keep one spare however. The average cost per unit of output of keeping a spare machine will therefore fall as output increases up to the level that can be produced by twenty machines; in other words, there will be economies of scale. Past this output another spare will have to be paid for and so *LAC* will take a shape similar to that shown in Figure 3.9 above.

6. *Marketing and distribution*   To reach a given number of people advertising requires the same outlay whether sales are high or low and so average advertising costs will fall the greater the output that is sold. This particular economy of scale can consciously be created by large firms in order to keep smaller rivals out of an industry (see Chapter 7). It also costs a firm money every time a sales representative or a delivery vehicle visits a retail outlet. The greater the output sold or delivered at each visit the lower will be average cost.

7. *By-products*   Certain production processes create waste materials that may be profitably collected and reused for by-products if they are generated in sufficient quantities, thus bringing down the average cost of the main product. For example, a single carpenter may just sweep up any sawdust and small off-cuts of wood and throw them away, but a large manufacturer of timber products may generate enough to make it worthwhile to use them to make chipboard or hardboard.

Pecuniary Economies of Scale

1. *Bulk purchasing*   Materials and components are often sold at a discount if they are bought in bulk. This may be an established practice by sellers or it may be a matter of negotiation on each sales contract. Large producers who are major buyers of particular inputs are in a strong bargaining position and may be able to dictate their price, within limits, particularly if they are supplied by a number of small firms.

2.   *Finance*   The cost of raising finance can be less for large firms. The higher risk involved in lending large sums to small firms is reflected in the higher interest rates they have to pay on loans (or the refusal of finance). Large companies whose shares are quoted on the stock exchange may also find it cheaper to raise finance by launching a new issue of shares than by straightforward borrowing. A new issue involves a substantial expenditure on publicity and administration and is only worthwhile when large amounts of finance are required.

Diseconomies of scale

When a firm expands output past a certain point unit costs may start to rise for several reasons, both 'real' and 'pecuniary', some of which are explained below.

1.   *Organisational problems*   As a firm grows bigger unit costs may rise because of delays and difficulties in communications, internal power struggles that lead to the pursuit of objectives other than overall profit, and other inefficiencies due to the scale and complexity of running a large organisation. This need not necessarily occur in every industry, however, and it has been suggested that when a production unit reaches the size at which diseconomies of scale start to set in then a firm can keep down average cost by opening a second production unit.

2.   *Over-specialisation of labour*   The specialisation of labour can only be taken so far. Workers who do the same mundane repetitive task all the time can lose incentive and concentration. Mistakes will occur and work may be disrupted more frequently, with a consequent increase in average cost. Over-specialisation of labour, however, is not always an inevitable consequence of increasing output and may be avoided if working practices are reorganised.

3.   *Saturated markets*   If a firm has saturated a market with its product then further increases in sales may only be possible if new markets are entered. This may involve higher distribution costs if they are further away and extra transactions costs if the firm has to start selling in foreign markets. Alternatively, a firm may launch a very heavy marketing campaign to try to squeeze a few more sales out of its existing market. In these situations the expansion of production will cause average cost to rise.

Time periods

Output is a flow per period of time and the choice of the time period is important when analysing economies of scale. If, say, a year is used as the relevant time period then the cost situation of a firm that operates for this period only will be different from that of a firm that will carry on producing for a number of years. The latter will be able to spread the cost of machinery, setting up production and so on, over a large output, and inputs may be bought more cheaply because more are purchased from suppliers. This will cause its *LAC* schedule to be below the *LAC* schedule of a firm that only operates for a shorter period, as illustrated in Figure 3.10. The quantity axis measures output per annum and LAC_1 and LAC_2 are the *LAC* curves for two firms who are in production for one year and ten years, respectively.

To illustrate this concept, consider the case of the launch of a new car. At the time of the launch of the Austin–Rover Maestro it was reported that approximately £200 million had been spent on its development and planned production was about 100 000 vehicles a year. Working with these estimated figures (which are not necessarily accurate) it can be calculated that if this production run was only to take place for one year then average development costs per vehicle would be £2000. This would clearly be uneconomic given all the other production costs involved. If, however, production were to continue at the same rate for ten years then average development costs would only be £200 per vehicle.

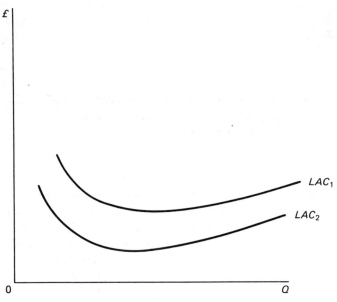

FIGURE 3.10   Shifts in long-run average cost

Economies of Size

Some of the factors which have been mentioned above as possible causes of economies of scale (for example, the relative cheapness of finance for large firms) may be related to a firm's total size rather than to the rate of output of the particular product in question. A large multi-product company may be able to take advantage of cheaper finance, specialised managers, established brand images and retail outlets and the rest, even though its output of individual products may be relatively low. Economies of size will shift the position of the *LAC* curve in the same way that an increased operating period is likely to do. If LAC_1 in Figure 3.10 refers to a firm that produces good Q only then LAC_2 refers to a firm that also produces a range of other goods and so exploits certain economies of size.

External Economies and Diseconomies of Scale

An *LAC* curve shows what happens to average costs if one firm expands output. If, however, all the firms in an industry simultaneously increase output then each individual firm may find its average costs falling by more than if it alone increased output. This is most likely to occur in new industries, or in industries setting up in new locations, where for example, components or supplementary service industries find it worthwhile to set up as the total industry output expands and so bring down the costs of these inputs. Individual firms would find their *LAC* curve shifting downwards (once again shown by the movement from LAC_1 to LAC_2 in Figure 3.10) if external economies of scale were present and a large number of firms in the industry all expanded output at the same time.

The reverse would happen, and individual firms' *LAC* curves would shift upward, if external diseconomies of scale were present, for example, if increased production by all firms brought about a significant increase in the demand for an input and so caused its price to rise. This would be an example of a pecuniary external diseconomy of scale.

Empirical Evidence

Although the *LAC* curves usually presented by economists are U-shaped, most of the evidence available from empirical studies of long-run costs suggests that firms' *LAC* curves are usually L-shaped, that is, that firms experience economies of scale but not diseconomies of scale. Some estimates of the relationship between average cost and output results are presented in Table 3.2.

Empirical studies which suggest that *LAC* curves are L-shaped are not necessarily conclusive. In addition to the problems discussed in Chapter 2 with respect to the estimation of production functions, such as variations in

TABLE 3.2   Economies of scale in UK manufacturing industry

Industry	MES* in absolute terms	MES as % of UK output 1969	% Increase in value added at 50% of MES
Oil	10 million tons p.a.	10	27
Sulphuric Acid	1 million tons p.a.	30	19
Synthetic Fibre (polymer plant)	80 000 tons p.a.	33	23
Bread	Throughput of 30 sacks of flour per hour	1	30
Detergent	70 000 tons tons p.a.	20	20
Bricks	25 million bricks p.a.	0.5	30
Steel	9 million tons p.a.	33	12–17
Cars (a) one model	500 000 cars p.a.	25	10
(b) range of models	1 million cars p.a.	50	13
Aircraft (one type)	> 50 aircract	> 100	> 25
Bicycles (range of models)	10 000 bicycles p.a.	4	(small)
Turbo Generators (one design)	4 p.a.	100	10
Books (one title, hardback)	10 000 copies	100	50

* MES = Minimum Efficient Scale
Source: C. F. Pratten, *Economies of Scale in Manufacturing Industry*, University of Cambridge Department of Applied, Economics, Occasional Papers 28 (Cambridge University Press, 1971).

the state of technology, there are a number of other possible reasons why accurate estimates of *LAC* schedules can be difficult to obtain:

1.   Technical estimates that use information about specific production

processes may not give a complete picture of the overall costs facing a firm, although they may be useful for managerial decision making. They are not likely to include any additional expenditure that might be needed for, say, extra secretaries in the accounts department or higher distribution costs, which may be just as necessary to maintain a higher output as more raw materials and machinery. For example, although there are production-related economies of scale in the brewing industry, as shown by AC_P in Figure 3.11, if more beer is produced it has to be distributed over a wider area, given the geographical dispersion of customers. Increasing distribution costs will thus eventually offset the production economies of scale and total average costs will increase, that is, there will be diseconomies of scale. In this case when output starts to exceed the level at which average costs are a minimum it may be best to build another brewery in another location in order to reduce distribution costs.

2.   Another cost that might be hidden, even in statistical studies that try to include all relevant costs, is the opportunity cost of assets that have been paid for in the past and hence do not involve current expenditure. If firms took into account the true cost of using land, buildings, machinery and other assets that they already owned, and perhaps management expertise also, then estimates of *LAC* curves might be different. One cannot say

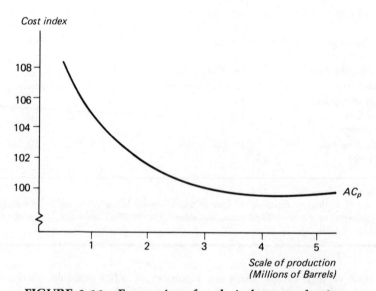

FIGURE 3.11   Economies of scale in beer production

Source: A. Cockerill, 'The Merger Movement in the Brewing Industry', *Journal of Industrial Affairs*, vol. 4, no. 1, Autumn 1976, p. 13.

that the inclusion of these costs would necessarily result in a U-shape, however.

3. It may be the case that firms stop expanding when long-run average cost starts to rise. Thus one reason why a rising section of the *LAC* schedule is not usually observed may be that no firms actually operate on it. In some cases diseconomies of scale may not set in until an output level is reached which is far above that normally encountered and there may be a long flat section of the *LAC* curve after all economies of scale have been exploited. It could be argued that, because within a given time period there will be a finite supply of resources that can be used for production, increases in the demand for inputs must eventually cause their prices to rise and so create a diseconomy of scale. For practical purposes, though, many firms need not take this distant possibility into account.

Implications for Market Structure

The shape of the *LAC* curve in relation to market demand will influence the structure of an industry. The output level at which the *LAC* curve flattens out gives an indication of the size that firms will usually tend to grow to, although this will depend on whether or not increasing output will increase profits (see Chapter 4). In markets where demand *D* is such that there is only room for one firm operating at minimum efficient scale (see Figure 3.12) the market will tend towards a monopoly. Some indications of which United Kingdom industries this tendency towards monopolisation is likely to apply to are given in Table 3.2 above.

The relationship between *LAC* and market demand can help explain some of the problems faced by United Kingdom car manufacturers. The output at which the minimum efficient scale *MES* is reached in private car production differs for different stages in the production process. Estimates vary, but it has been suggested that the *MES* has in the past been close to 2 million for body pressing, 1 million for engine and transmission manufacture, and 200 000 for final assembly. However, recent advances in technology have tended to bring down these figures. Some estimates of the relationship between overall production costs and output of private cars are presented in Table 3.3. If these are compared with the data in Table 3.4 it is obvious that the major United Kingdom car manufacturers have not been producing enough vehicles to reduce unit costs to the minimum. Some foreign producers have much higher output levels and consequently a cost advantage. In 1985 annual private car production figures for other countries' major car producers were: General Motors (USA)–4.9 million (8.2); Toyota (Japan)–2.6 million (7.6); Renault (France)–1.3 million (2.6); Volkswagen (W. Germany)–1.4 million (4.2);

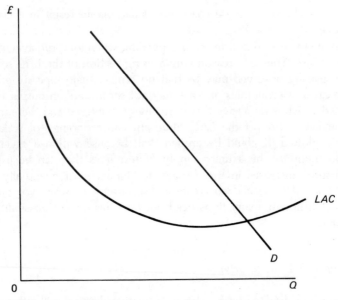

FIGURE 3.12   LAC and market demand

TABLE 3.3   Average production costs in car manufacturing

Output per year	Index of unit average cost (cars)
100 000	100
250 000	83
500 000	74
1 000 000	70
2 000 000	66

Source: G. Rhys, 'Economics of the Motor Industry', *The Economic Review*, vol. 3, no. 3, January 1986, pp. 32–38.

Fiat (Italy)–1.2 million (1.4). (Figures in brackets are total annual production, in millions, for each country.)

It is, of course, not a simple matter to expand output to reap economies of scale. There is a vicious circle in that the smaller producers, like Rover, have to sell in the same market as the other larger producers and if prices are similar their profit margins will be smaller due to the cost disadvantage. If one looks with hindsight at the United Kingdom motor industry of the

TABLE 3.4 Private car production and sales

Production by major UK manufacturers	1975	1979	1982	1985
Austin Morris/ Rover Triumph	*	*	369 839	450 982
Jaguar/Daimler	*	*	22 042	(38 378)**
Range Rover	*	*	13 235	14 212
Total BL	605 141	503 767	405 116	465 104**
Ford	329 648	398 694	306 635	317 689
Vauxhall	98 621	58 765	112 669	162 587
Talbot Dodge	226 612	102 977	56 235	67 066
Total UK Production	1 267 695	1 070 452	887 679	1 047 973
UK New Registrations	1 194 115	1 716 275	1 555 027	1 832 408
Imports into UK	448 749	1 060 645	934 141	1 071 892
Exports from UK	516 219	410 118	313 025	240 247

*   Included in Total BL (now Rover).
** Jaguar/Daimler privatised and not included in BL 1985 total.
Source: Society of Motor Manufacturers and Traders, *Motor Industry of Great Britain: World Automotive Statistics*, SMMT Ltd, 1986.

1950s and 1960s one might take the view that United Kingdom manufacturers should have followed a strategy of greater volume and less variety of models. Other European manufacturers and the Japanese, whose output after the war was negligible, have successfully managed to do this and overtake the United Kingdom.

SHORT-RUN COSTS

According to the law of diminishing marginal productivity, if increasing units of a variable input, L, are used in conjunction with a fixed input, K, then after some point additional units of L will add less to ouput than previous ones. If additional units of L add diminishing amounts of output then it must be the case that equal increments of output will require increasing amounts of L. Thus in the short-run the average cost of additional units of output will increase when diminishing marginal productivity sets in. To explain how this will affect the short-run cost structure of a firm a few terms must be defined:

Total Cost (TC) = the total cost of producing any given output level, Q.
Total Variable Cost (TVC) = the total cost of the variable input, L.

Total Fixed Cost (TFC) = the total cost of the fixed input, K.

Average Total Cost (ATC) = average total cost per unit of output. (This is sometimes just referred to as Average Cost, AC, when the distinction between variable and fixed costs is not relevant.)

Average Variable Cost (AVC) = average cost of the variable input per unit of output.

Average Fixed Cost (AFC) = average cost of the fixed input per unit of output.

By definition

$$ATC = TC/Q \qquad AVC = TVC/Q \qquad AFC = TFC/Q \text{ and}$$

$$TC = TVC + TFC, \text{ therefore}$$

$$AC = AVC + AFC.$$

Marginal Cost (MC) = the change in TC brought about by a unit change in Q.

Strictly speaking MC is the rate of change of TC and will continually change as the slope of the TC curve alters. However, an approximate value for MC between two output levels can be found by calculating the average increase in TC caused by each unit increment in output.

The example shown in Table 3.5 assumes that input L is increased while K is held fixed at one unit, which costs £20, with each unit of L costing £15. After 3 units of L have been added the law of diminishing marginal productivity starts to operate. Thus above an output of 48 units any additional increments of output will require increasing amounts of L. This means that MC will rise

TABLE 3.5   Short-run costs

K	L	Q	MP_L	AP_L	TFC	TVC	TC	AFC	AVC	AC	MC
1	0	0	–	–	£20	£0	£20	–	–	–	–
1	1	12	12	12	£20	£15	£35	£1.67	£1.25	£2.95	£1.25
1	2	30	18	15	£20	£30	£50	£0.67	£1.00	£1.67	£0.83
1	3	48	18	16	£20	£45	£65	£0.42	£0.94	£1.36	£0.83
1	4	64	16	16	£20	£60	£80	£0.31	£0.94	£1.25	£0.94
1	5	77	13	15.4	£20	£75	£95	£0.26	£0.97	£1.23	£1.15
1	6	86	9	14.3	£20	£90	£110	£0.23	£1.05	£1.28	£1.67
1	7	90	4	12.8	£20	£105	£125	£0.22	£1.17	£1.39	£3.75
1	8	90	0	11.3	£20	£120	£140	£0.22	£1.33	£1.55	–

when output exceeds 48 units. Once diminishing marginal productivity sets in the decline in MP_L soon causes AP_L to start to fall. When AP_L falls AVC rises.

The general shape that a firm's short-run cost curves take is illustrated in Figure 3.13. As Q increases AFC will always get progressively smaller because a fixed sum is being divided by an increasing quantity. Diminishing marginal productivity causes MC to rise and when this rising MC curve cuts the AVC curve this too will start to rise. This is because the increase in MC is due purely to the increased cost of L, that is, increasing TVC. If additional units of output add more to TVC than the average cost of the previous ones then AVC must increase.

For similar reasons MC always cuts the ATC curve at its minimum point. If the cost of an additional unit of output is less than the average cost of previous units then this must cause a fall in ATC, and if an extra unit of output adds more to costs than the previous ATC then it must cause ATC to rise. Thus when ATC is falling MC is below it and when ATC is rising MC is above it, and so MC must go through the minimum point of the ATC schedule. As ATC is the vertical sum of AFC, which continually declines, and AVC, which must eventually rise, then the ATC schedule is also expected to fall and then rise; in other words, it will be U-shaped.

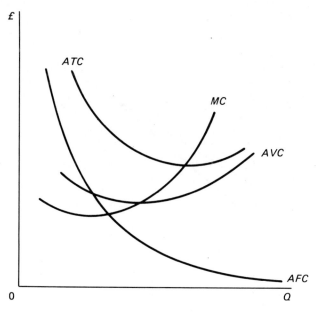

FIGURE 3.13   Short-run cost curves

Accounting costs and break-even charts

It is sometimes argued that the preceding analysis of short-run costs bears little resemblance to the way that actual firms treat costs when making output and pricing decisions. In practice it is often assumed that each extra unit of output will have the same variable input requirement, that is, that the marginal cost of extra units of output will be constant. This assumption also underlies the use of break-even chart analysis, a method sometimes used to estimate profit. In the example in Figure 3.14 the straight line *TC* schedule corresponds to a constant *MC* of £0.65 and *TFC* of £10. The straight line *TR* schedule is drawn on the assumption that each unit of output can be sold at the same price, in this case £0.90. If the firm does not operate in a perfectly competitive market (see Chapter 5) this assumption of a constant price may not hold, but here the main concern is to examine how the nature of the cost schedule affects the analysis.

The expected profit (or loss) for any given output level is the vertical distance between *TR* and *TC*. Profit is greater than zero above an output of 40 units, which corresponds to the break-even point, *X*. Although this

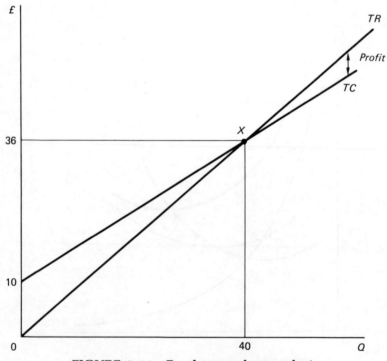

FIGURE 3.14　Break-even chart analysis

break-even chart analysis may be of some use for management decision making, such as estimating profit from any given output level, from the viewpoint of an economist it has no predictive value. It is usually assumed that firms try to maximise profits (see Chapter 4), but in a break-even chart profit increases continually as output expands. Therefore, to maximise profit a firm should in theory perpetually expand output towards infinity. This is obviously impossible and means that output cannot be predicted.

Break-even chart analysis does appear to conflict with the usual assumptions made about short-run costs by economists, but this apparent contradiction may be resolved. Although economists usually illustrate a firm's MC and AVC curves as smooth U-shapes, the law of diminishing marginal productivity does not rule out the possibility of the marginal product being constant for a range of values of the variable input before it starts to decline, as explained in Chapter 2. If this is the case then MC will be constant over the range of output when MP_L is constant and a firm's short-run cost curves will take shapes similar to those shown in Figure 3.15.

Although Figure 3.15 may describe a firm that faces constant marginal productivity for normal day to day fluctuations in its output, the law of

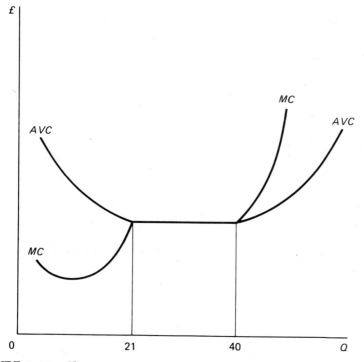

FIGURE 3.15   Short-run cost curves with constant marginal product

diminishing marginal productivity ensures that if output is expanded far enough then the marginal product will eventually start to decline, in this case when output exceeds 40 units. Thus, although break-even chart analysis may be used for normal changes in production levels, once output goes outside this range then the assumptions on which this method is based do not hold and *MC* will rise, as the economic model predicts. In Figure 3.15 this means that break-even chart analysis can be used as long as output remains between 21 and 40 units (if the assumption of a straight line *TR* schedule also holds).

THE RELATIONSHIP BETWEEN SHORT-RUN AND LONG-RUN COST CURVES

Suppose that in the long-run a firm has the choice of using three possible sizes of plant, *A*, *B* and *C*, whose corresponding *SAC* curves, SAC_A, SAC_B and SAC_C, are shown in Figure 3.16. Plant *A* does not involve much capital expenditure and so average cost of production is not high at low output

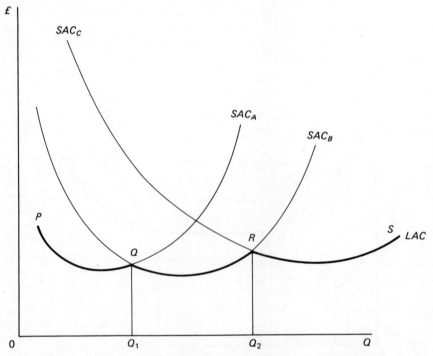

FIGURE 3.16   Different short-run average cost curves and the long-run average cost curve

levels, but it rises quickly when the plant's limited capacity is reached and the marginal product of the variable input starts to decline rapidly. Plants B and C involve greater capital expenditure so that average cost does not start to rise until relatively higher output levels are reached. To minimise the cost of any given output the firm will use plant A if planned output is below Q_1, plant B if output is between Q_1 and Q_2, and plant C if output exceeds Q_2. The long-run average cost (LAC) curve is therefore the 'scalloped' shaped line $PQRS$.

The greater the range of possible sizes of plant then the nearer the LAC curve will approximate to the smooth U-shape in Figure 3.17. Kinks and discontinuities may occur in some firms' LAC schedules, depending on individual circumstances, but this smooth shape is used to illustrate the general case. As already explained, however, empirical studies have suggested that there may not be an upward sloping section. Note also that although the LAC curve is an outer envelope of different SAC curves it only goes through the minimum point of one SAC curve in Figure 3.17. This is at X, which is also the minimum point of the LAC schedule.

The relationship between a firm's short- and long-run cost curves can also be derived from an isoquant map. This is an extension of the analysis explained earlier that related a firm's LAC to its isoquant map. Assume that a firm's

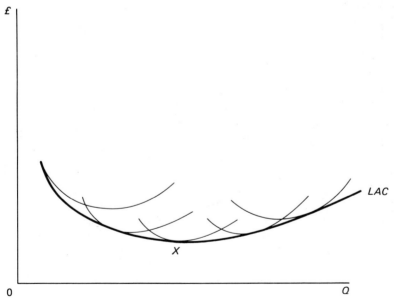

FIGURE 3.17   The relationship between short-run and long-run average cost curves

production function corresponds to the isoquant map in Figure 3.18 and that the prices of the two inputs K and L are £40 and £20 a unit, respectively. Thus any budget line will have a slope of -0.5. If output is initially 100 units then the cheapest way of producing this output level is found at X, where a line with slope of -0.5 is tangent to the 100 unit isoquant. This budget line corresponds to a total expenditure on inputs of £800 and so average cost will be £8, as shown in Table 3.6. If output is increased to 200 units then if both K and L can be adjusted the optimal input combination will be at Y, corresponding to a total expenditure of £1200 and an average cost of £6. The two points X' and Y' can now be plotted on the *LAC* curve in Figure 3.19, corresponding to the long-run optimal input combinations X and Y, respectively, in Figure 3.18.

Now consider what would happen if, starting from the optimal input combination for producing 100 units at X, the firm wished to expand output to 200 units in the short run, that is, with K fixed at 10 units. As the only way that output can be increased is by employing more of L then the firm

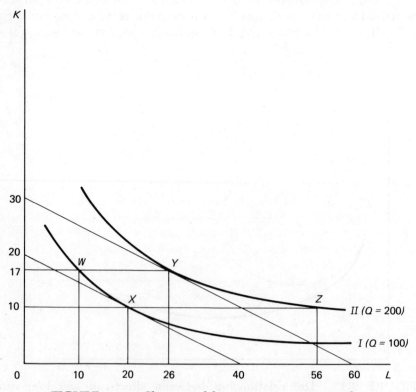

FIGURE 3.18   Short- and long-run expansion paths

TABLE 3.6 **Long-run and short-run costs**

	Output	Units of K	Units of L	TC	AC
(Optimum input mix)	100	10	20	£800	£8.00
(Optimum input mix)	200	17	26	£1200	£6.00
(K fixed at 17 units)	100	17	10	£880	£8.80
(K fixed at 10 units)	200	10	56	£1520	£7.60

(Data refer to Figure 3.18)

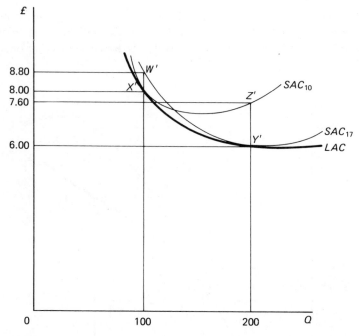

FIGURE 3.19 **Long-run and short-run average cost curves**

would have to find the least amount of L that would need to be added. This can be determined by moving horizontally across from point X until the 200 units isoquant is reached, at point Z. Input combination Z is clearly outside the budget constraint through Y, and total expenditure rises to £1520 and average cost is £7.60. Thus because in the short-run both inputs cannot be adjusted to achieve the optimal input combination, total costs rise more than when expanding output in the long-run. Point Z' can now be plotted on the curve SAC_{10}, which corresponds to K being fixed at 10 units, in Figure 3.19.

Consider next a reduction in output from 200 to 100 units in the short-run, assuming that the firm is initially at the optimal input combination for producing 200 units, at Y. Given that 17 units of the fixed input K have to be paid for, the cheapest way of doing this is to move to W. Total cost falls to £880 and so average cost is £8.80. Point W' can then be plotted on the curve SAC_{17}. Thus it can be seen that the optimal input combinations in Figure 3.18 correspond to points on the LAC curve in Figure 3.19, and other combinations of inputs will correspond to points that lie above the LAC curve on different SAC curves.

Long-run and short-run total cost curves

Using the data in Table 3.3, the points W'', X'', Y'' and Z'' can be plotted on the long-run total cost (LTC) and the two relevant short-run total cost (STC) curves in Figure 3.20. Each STC will only touch the LTC at one point

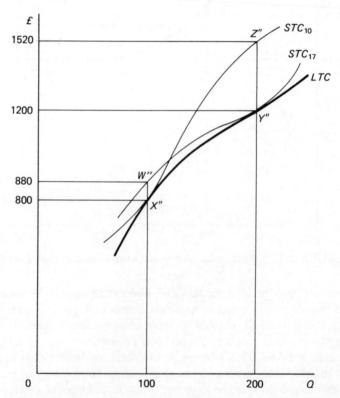

FIGURE 3.20   Long-run and short-run total cost curves

because there is only one output level for which any given amount of the fixed input is optimal.

The long-run marginal cost curve

The Long-Run Marginal Cost (*LMC*) curve shows the marginal cost of a unit change in output when the firm is free to alter all inputs. It is the rate of change of *LTC* with respect to Q and so it will take a U-shape because the slope of the *LTC* is expected first to decline and then to increase.

Each *STC* schedule, such as those shown in Figure 3.20, will have the same slope as the *LTC* at the output for which the fixed amount of capital is optimal, for example, at X'' and Y''. Thus the corresponding short-run marginal cost (*SMC*) must be equal to *LMC* at this output as marginal cost reflects the slope of a total cost schedule. Below this output the *STC* schedule is flatter than the *LTC* schedule and so *SMC* must be below *LMC*. Above this output the *STC* schedule is steeper than the *LTC* schedule and so *SMC* must be greater than *LMC*. Thus each of the *SMC* curves shown in Figure 3.21 cuts the *LMC* at the output level for which the fixed input is optimal, that is, the output at which the corresponding *SAC* touches the *LAC*. For example, SMC_1 cuts *LMC* at output Q_1, which is also the output at which SAC_1 touches *LAC*.

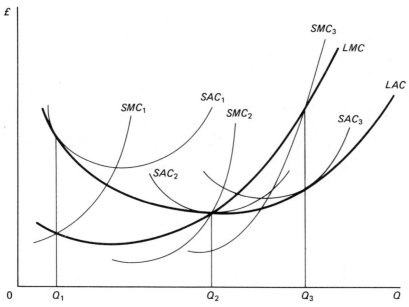

FIGURE 3.21   The long-run marginal cost curve

Just as each *SMC* schedule cuts the corresponding *SAC* curve at its lowest point so the *LMC* schedule must cut the *LAC* curve at its lowest point. In the long run if additional units of output cost less than the previous average cost then *LAC* must fall and if they cost more then it must rise.

QUESTIONS

1. Assume that a firm has the production function that is illustrated by the isoquant map in Figure 3.Q1, below, and that it can buy input *L* at £20 a unit and input *K* at £15 a unit.

    (i)   What is the cheapest method of producing 100 units of output?
    (ii) If the firm increased output from 100 to 200 units by adjusting

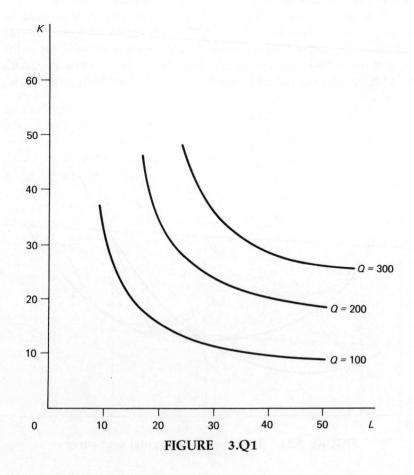

FIGURE   3.Q1

both K and L to their optimal values would the *LAC* schedule rise or fall?

(iii) If the firm expanded output from 100 to 200 units in the short-run, with K fixed at the optimal level of K for producing 100 units, what would happen to average production costs?

(iv) If the firm decreased output from 200 to 100 units in the short-run, with K fixed at the optimal level of K for producing 200 units, what would happen to average production costs?

(v) Using your answers to (i) to (iv) plot the approximate shape of this firm's *LAC* and relevant *SAC* schedules.

2. Would a 10 per cent increase in the prices of both inputs have the same effect on a firm's budget constraint as would a 10 per cent reduction in its budget?

3. Explain the difference between the terms 'diminishing marginal productivity' and 'decreasing returns to scale' and their relevance to the shape of a firm's cost curves.

4. Are there any circumstances under which a firm's *LAC* curve will correspond to the minimum point of more than one *SAC* curve?

5. The results of many empirical studies suggest that firms' *LAC* curves are L-shaped. Does this mean that the assumption of U-shaped *LAC* curves, often made in economics, must be incorrect?

6. A firm operates on the assumption that it can sell every unit of output that it products at a price of £20, no matter what its output level is, and that each unit produced adds £15 to costs. If fixed costs are £50, even if nothing is produced, is it possible for this firm to determine (a) the output at which it will break even? (b) the output at which profits will be maximised?

7. What part do you think economies of scale in passenger car production have played in the relative decline of the United Kingdom motor industry?

CHAPTER 4

Theories of the firm

This chapter explains the rationale for the profit maximising theory of the firm, which is used as a basis for most of the analysis in Chapters 5, 6, 7, 8 and 10, and also assesses the usefulness of some alternative theories of the firm.

FIRMS' OBJECTIVES

The internal operations of a firm are a complex process and all firms are different. Therefore, as explained in Chapter 1, simplifying assumptions have to be made to construct a theory that will explain the behaviour of firms in general, and a theory's usefulness is judged by its ability to predict behaviour successfully and not by the realism of the assumptions on which it is based. To construct a theory of the firm it is necessary to establish the objectives that a firm is assumed to pursue and then analyse how it will attempt to achieve these objectives subject to the constraints that it faces. The most important constraints are the costs of production and the demand for the firm's product, taking into account any competition from rival producers. Other constraints include the legal, political and social framework within which a firm operates, although these are not usually explicitly taken into account in theories of the firm.

It is the differences in the objectives that firms are assumed to pursue that constitute the main distinguishing feature of most of the different theories of the firm that have been put forward. The theories of the firm considered in this chapter attempt to explain the behaviour of those firms operating in a free market economy and whose profit accrues to the owners of the firm's capital. This means that they cannot be directly applied to all sections of industry in the United Kingdom. Nationalised industries, for example, may be directed by the government to pursue different objectives from those pursued by private industry. Some of the former state monopolies which have been privatised still have their prices regulated by the government. Also excluded are worker co-operatives, which are not very widespread in the United Kingdom at present. Although a theory designed to predict the behaviour of private firms cannot be used to predict the behaviour of other types of firm, the decision-making rules yielded by such a theory may nevertheless still be useful to other types of firms seeking to improve efficiency.

How can one find out what the objectives of firms in private industry are? One cannot simply use a questionnaire survey that asks a sample of managers what objectives their firms pursue. Not all will reply to the questionnaire and some will not give completely honest answers. Even if some answers are truthful, in that they correctly state what managers might wish to do, circumstances may prevent them ever actually pursuing these objectives. Different replies may be conflicting and it will be difficult to discover a commonly held objective that can be incorporated into a theory that is meant to apply to firms in general. For example, how could the stated objective of 'maintaining customer goodwill' be used to explain price and output decisions?

To make progress, it is first necessary to distinguish between targets and objectives. In day to day operations no section of a firm can easily relate every decision to some underlying objective such as the maximisation of annual profits for the whole company. Instead, targets are usually set for intermediate objectives that are consistent with a firm's main objectives, and operational decisions are then based on these targets. For example, a production manager may be set the target of bringing down the cost of manufacturing a given output. Lower production costs are not an end in themselves, however, and are usually just a means to securing greater profit.

The sort of replies that one might get from a management questionnaire survey are likely to confuse targets and objectives. It cannot be denied that in some cases personal pride, job satisfaction and genuine altruism may be the objectives satisfied by 'maintaining customer goodwill'. However, for most firms the main purpose of trying to achieve this intermediate objective is to maintain customers' demand for the product and hence increase profits, profit maximisation being the underlying main objective.

Although there is a considerable volume of literature on the theory and practice of management, which stresses that a firm should clearly set out its objectives and then use intermediate targets and objectives to achieve these principal objectives, there is no general agreement on what these main objectives should be. One view is that the interests of the owners should always be put first and that only the minimum legal obligations to other parties be met. Others would argue that the interests of customers, workers and society in general should receive more than this minimum attention. In order to determine which set of objectives best explains the behaviour of firms it is necessary to examine how successfully the different theories of the firm that have been put forward, incorporating different sets of objectives, fulfill the purpose of an economic theory, that is, to be able to explain and predict the behaviour of firms in general and to yield a useful set of management decision-making tools.

PROFIT MAXIMISATION

The most commonly made assumption is that firms aim to maximise profits. However, to incorporate this objective into an economic model the term 'profit maximisation' must be more precisely defined. Profit is the difference between a firm's sales revenue and its expenditure on inputs. When any necessary taxes have been paid it is then the property of the firm's owners, and may be paid out as income to them or ploughed back into the firm.

Opportunity cost and economic profit

An economist's definition of profit is not necessarily the same as an accountant's because they define costs differently, as mentioned in Chapter 3. An economist considers the opportunity costs of an input, defined as the benefit forgone by not using it in its next best alternative use. In some cases this is the same as the monetary payment made; for example, if a firm spends £1000 on electricity then it forgoes the benefits from spending £1000 on something else. However, the opportunity cost of some inputs is not the same as the monetary expenditure on them. Assume, for example, that a self-employed worker has a surplus of £12 000 of revenue over expenditure in her annual accounts and could earn £15 000 by working as an employee for another company. Assume also that taxes and any non-monetary benefits from being self-employed can be ignored, and that these figures will be the same for future years. An economist would argue that this worker should take into account the opportunity cost of the contribution of her own labour to her self-employed business, that is, the £15 000 she could have earned by selling her labour to another employer. Her net economic profit would then be — £3000, in other words she would be £3000 worse off than if she worked for this other company. Although in practice legislation usually obliges firms to calculate their profits on the normal accounting basis for taxation assessment purposes, which in this case would show a profit of £12 000, the economist's definition of costs is more useful for managerial decision making. The individual in this example would obviously be financially better off by £3000 if she worked for the other company.

Depreciation charges and opportunity cost

The concept of opportunity cost is particularly relevant when calculating depreciation charges for capital equipment. Firms' profit and loss accounts are usually calculated on an annual basis. Some inputs, however, such as capital equipment, will contribute to production over a number of years and so their cost is not just charged against revenue for the year in which they are purchased, but is spread out over a period of time. Arbitrary methods of calculating annual depreciation charges, such as dividing the initial cost of a machine by the number of years that is expected to be in use, will not necessarily reflect its true opportunity cost, however.

Consider the example of a firm that spends £50 000 on a specialised piece of machinery that has no resale value or leasing value once it has been installed. Assume that the expected working life of this machine is 10 years and that the annual cost of the other inputs that are used with it to manufacture a particular product is £20 000. If, after one year of production, the firm discovers that annual sales revenue is £23 000 what should it do if the same set of sales figures can be expected for the next nine years? One might suggest that the initial £50 000 capital expenditure on the machine should be charged at the rate of £5000 a year over the expected 10 years of the machine's operation. This would mean that the firm's annual accounts would show a profit of

$$£23\,000 - £20\,000 - £5000 = -£2000,$$

that is, a loss of £2000, and would imply that the firm should cease production. This would be the wrong course of action, however. An economist would argue that if the machinery has no other use once it has been purchased then the opportunity cost of using it is zero. This implies that the firm should stay in production because annual economic profits will be

$$£23\,000 - £20\,000 = £3000$$

Given that the decision to buy the machine has already been made then the firm can earn an operating profit of £3000 a year to set against the initial purchasing cost. It will still make an overall loss, but this will be substantially lower than the loss that would be incurred if the firm ceased production after the first year, illustrating the economist's rule that 'historical costs are irrelevant'. Although the firm should take into account the machine's initial price, and the consequent overall loss, when faced with the decision of whether or not to purchase another similar machine, operating decisions should be based on current opportunity costs, not historical costs.

In the above example the opportunity cost of using the machine is zero because it has no alternative use once purchased. If, however, the firm could lease the machine out for an annual rental of £2000 then this would be the opportunity cost to the firm of using it in its own production process.

Economic profit and resource allocation

When a firm is making zero economic profit it is exactly covering all its opportunity costs. This means that it is making a return no greater and no less than it could earn from employing its factors of production in their next best alternative use. If in an industry all firms were making zero economic profit, and there was no opportunity to increase profits through price or production changes, then there would be no incentive for resources to be transferred into or out of the industry, either through existing firms expanding production or through new firms setting up. The existence of economic profits would, however, be a signal that would attract new resources, unless entry into the industry was barred in some way.

Short- and long-run profit maximisation

Profit is a flow, just like supply and demand, and so the time period within which firms try to maximise profits must be defined. The profit maximising theory of the firm assumes that firms try to maximise profits in the short-run. In the long-run firms will take into account the profit flows that can be expected from investments before planning their capital expenditure programme.[1] In other words, it is assumed that a firm splits the problem of how to maximise profits into a short-run output and pricing decision and a long-run investment decision.

If the time dimension was not precisely defined and it was just assumed that firms tried to pursue something called 'long-term profit maximisation' then no predictions could be made about firms' behaviour. One could argue, for example, that firms might not automatically pass on cost increases in price rises, even though this would increase short-run profits, because they would wish to ensure customer loyalty and hence future profits. However, it is impossible to measure exactly how much this motive may affect a firm's price and output decision making. Any deviation from short-run profit maximisation could be conceivably explained away by the argument that this is due to the firm maximising 'long-run profits', but this would just be guessing. The weakness of the long-run profit maximisation hypothesis is made clear when this question is turned on its head and one asks, 'If firms maximise long-run profits, by what amounts will price and output differ from the values predicted by the short-run profit maximisation theory?' This question cannot be answered without specific information about the rate at which individual firms would be willing to trade off future profits against current profits. Thus a

---

1.   For an explanation of investment analysis see, for example, J. L. Pappas, E. F. Brigham and B. Shipley, *Managerial Economics*, UK edn (London: Holt, Rinehart and Winston, 1983).

theory based on the assumption that firms maximise long-run profits cannot make any general predictions and so fails the test by which the usefulness of an economic theory is judged. This assertion does not deny the fact that in reality some firms actually do try to maintain some sort of balance between long-run and short-run profits; it just means that the extent of this behaviour, as applied to firms in general, cannot be measured and incorporated into a theory of the firm.

Profit maximising price and output

The basic profit maximising theory of the firm considers a firm with one plant that produces one product. This analysis can be extended, for instance, to cover the multi-product and multi-plant cases, but only the basic model is considered here. It is first necessary to understand the fundamental ideas involved before applying the theory to these more complex cases.

If it is assumed that technology does not change, the quality of the production is not varied, and there is no advertising, then profit will depend on the difference between revenue and costs which, in turn, will depend on a firm's output level. The relationship between costs and output has already been explained in Chapter 3. The relationship between a firm's sales revenue and output will depend on the market demand for the good being produced and the state of competition in the industry. The ways in which different market structures can affect the demand for an individual firm's output are examined in more depth in Chapters 5, 6, 7 and 8, but here, in order to explain the basic principles of the profit maximising theory of the firm, it is simply assumed that a firm faces a downward sloping demand curve.

The determination of the profit maximising price and output is explained using the example illustrated in Figure 4.1. It is assumed that the relationship between price and quantity demanded is as shown by the demand curve DD', in the top section, and the relationship between the total cost of production and output is as shown by TC, in the middle section. The rest of the graphs shown in Figure 4.1 can be derived from these two relationships. The TR curve is found by multiplying price by quantity demanded, and MR has the same intercept on the vertical axis and twice the slope of DD'. It is also equal to the slope of TR (as explained in Chapter 1). As DD' is straight, line MR is also a straight line, cutting the quantity axis at a distance half way between the origin and the point at which the demand curve cuts the axis. Marginal Cost (MC) is equal to the slope of the TC schedule.

The total profit function PP', in the bottom section of Figure 4.1, is at a maximum when the vertical distance between TR and TC is at its greatest. Thus the profit maximising output is 23 units. Instead of having to actually plot the TR and TC schedules and then measure the distance between them, the profit maximising output can instead be directly determined from the

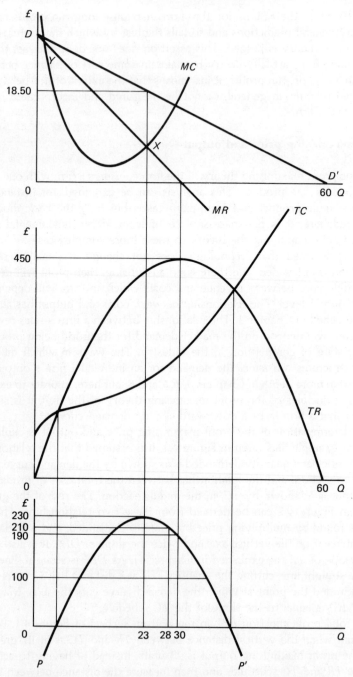

FIGURE 4.1   Profit maximising output determination

information given in the top section of Figure 4.1. The fundamental profit maximisation rule is that output should be expanded up to the point where:

1. marginal revenue equals marginal cost, and
2. the marginal cost schedule cuts the marginal revenue schedule from below.

The logic of this rule, or at least the first part, should be obvious. If the extra revenue from the sale of one more unit exceeds the extra cost of producing it, profits will increase if output is expanded. If, on the other hand, the *MC* of an extra unit exceeds its *MR* then profits will fall and so a firm should not expand production.

To explain the second part of the profit maximising rule, consider the two points of intersection of the *MR* and *MC* schedules in Figure 4.1, at *X* and *Y*. Even though *MC* equals *MR*, a firm does not maximise profits if it operates at *Y* because profits can be increased by expanding output, since *MR* is greater than *MC* to the right of *Y*, or by reducing output, since *MC* is greater than *MR* to the left of *Y*. At *X*, however, a firm cannot increase profit any further by either reducing or increasing output. Once the profit maximising output of 23 units has been determined the corresponding price of £18.50 can be read off the demand schedule.

The above example shows how the profit maximising theory of the firm can predict price and profit for a given set of cost and revenue schedules. It can also therefore predict the changes in price and output that would result from any changes in these schedules. In addition, the profit maximising '*MC* equals *MR*' rule can be useful for management decision making. Some other approaches to the theory of the firm are now considered to see how well they stand up against the profit maximising theory with respect to these criteria.

MANAGERIAL THEORIES OF THE FIRM

In the nineteenth century the typical firm was both owned and managed by the same entrepreneur. Maximising profit was naturally considered the main objective. Today, however, the major part of industrial output in the United Kingdom is controlled by large public companies which are owned by shareholders and run by salaried managers. Only very broad policy guidelines are laid down at shareholder meetings and widely dispersed shareholding means that individual shareholders can have little say in company decisions. The growth of large institutional shareholders, such as insurance companies and pension funds, has to some extent countered this, but there is still a significant degree of separation of ownership from control.

There are several different managerial theories of the firm that are based on this observation of the separation of ownership from control. A common assumption that the managerial theories make is that the managers who run these shareholder-owned companies will try to pursue their own personal objectives, such as a high salary, security, or prestige, subject to certain constraints. Most of these objectives cannot actually be quantified, but it is assumed that they are correlated with variables such as the firm's total sales revenue or its rate of growth.

The main constraint imposed on managers is that they must ensure that their firm makes at least a given minimum level of profit. There are two reasons for this constraint. Firstly, shareholders may vote to replace the management team if they are not satisfied with the profit that the firm earns for them. Secondly, low profits will tend to depress the price at which a firm's shares are traded. If the firm is actually capable of making a higher profit this will mean that its shares are undervalued. Another firm that recognises this undervaluation may seize the opportunity of buying the shares up at a bargain price and if there is a complete take-over then the original management team may be removed.

The main managerial theories of the firm are Baumol's sales revenue maximisation theory,[2] Williamson's managerial utility maximisation theory,[3] and Marris's growth maximisation theory.[4] As it would require a complete chapter each to explain these theories properly, only the main ideas behind Baumol's model are outlined here. This, however, is sufficient to illustrate certain shortcomings that are common to all the managerial theories, in particular the fact that insufficient information on the minimum profit constraint can make prediction impossible.

Sales revenue maximisation

Baumol assumed that managers tried to maximise sales revenue subject to a minimum profit constraint. This assumption was based on observations of the way that a number of firms conducted their operations. To see what predictions this theory can make, return to the example illustrated in Figure 4.1. Sales revenue is at its maximum of £450 when output is 30 units. If there was no minimum profit constraint then this is the output at which a sales revenue maximising firm would operate. It is always greater than the profit maximising output because the point where MC cuts MR will always be to the left of the point where MR is zero (that is, where sales revenue is at a maximum)

---

2.   W. J. Baumol, *Business Behavior, Value and Growth* (New York: Macmillan, 1959).
3.   O. E. Williamson, *The Economics of Discretionary Behavior* (Chicago: Markham, 1967).
4.   R. L. Marris, *The Economic Theory of Managerial Capitalism* (London: Macmillan 1964).

because MC is always positive. If, however, there was a minimum profit constraint of £210 then a sales revenue maximising firm would have to reduce output to 28 units. Should the minimum profit constraint be £230, which is the maximum possible profit, then output will be the same as that predicted by the profit maximising theory of the firm. If the minimum profit constraint is below this maximum profit then the firm will operate at a higher output level than the profit maximising output. Reductions in the constraint will cause output to rise until the sales revenue maximising output is reached. A minimum profit constraint lower than the profit earned at this sales revenue maximising output will not 'bite', that is, it will be irrelevant because the firm will be already making more than this minimum. For example, if the firm faced a minimum profit constraint of £100 then it would operate at the sales revenue maximising output of 30 units. This yields a profit of £190 and so easily satisfies the constraint.

The difficulty with testing this theory is that the minimum profit constraint is not usually known. Any observations of firms that are operating above the profit maximising output level could conceivably be interpreted as support for the sales revenue maximising theory of the firm, but this cannot be proved. Unless the minimum profit constraint is known, and it will vary from firm to firm, one cannot predict by how much output and price will deviate from their profit maximising values. Thus, in a similar way to the idea of long-run profit maximisation discussed earlier, the weakness of this approach is demonstrated when one tries to use it to make predictions. The same basic problem is also confronted in the other managerial theories of the firm. Without knowledge of the minimum profit constraint it is difficult to make any predictions that can be tested.

Another feature of the managerial theories is that they can only be applied to firms that are making economic profits over and above the opportunity cost of all inputs, and where the threat of new entry into the industry that may erode these profits may be ignored. In a perfectly competitive industry (see Chapter 5) new competitors will be attracted into the industry by any economic profit and thus ensure that, in the long run, even profit maximising firms cannot earn more than a zero economic profit. Any firm that tries to do anything other than maximise profits will thus find itself making a loss and be driven out of business. This 'survivor theory', which is sometimes put forward as an argument in support of the profit maximising theory of the firm, does not necessarily apply to imperfectly competitive markets, however. Barriers to entry may allow firms to persistently earn positive economic profits and thus allow some deviation from the profit maximising price and output. The problem with the managerial theories is that they cannot predict in general what the extent of this deviation will be if firms pursue objectives other than profit maximisation.

THE BEHAVIOURAL THEORY OF THE FIRM

The behavioural theory of the firm developed by Cyert and March[5] differs substantially from the managerial theories discussed above. It is maintained that, because of insufficient information, uncertainty, and the complexity of decision making, it is impossible for a firm to maximise anything, be it profit, sales revenue, or any other variable. It is recognised that a firm is not a uniform decision-making mechanism but a coalition of different groups with different interests, such as managers, shareholders and workers. All decisions are the result of a form of bargaining process between these various groups. It is assumed that, instead of finding the optimal value of some variable, a firm proceeds by a process that Cyert and March called 'satisficing'. This means that a firm sets itself target levels for different variables such as sales, productivity and so on, based on past experience and any other information that is available, and then tries to achieve these targets. If they are met then they are revised upward. If they are not met then the firm will instigate an investigation to try to find out the reasons for this failure, and ways of improving efficiency in order to achieve the targets. Only after exhaustive attempts to remedy the problem have failed will targets be revised downwards.

This theory appears to describe more realistically how firms actually operate than does the profit maximizing theory. However, it cannot make any general predictions about price or output levels, or even the direction in which these variables might move in response to exogenous changes in cost or demand. Cyert and March made a detailed study of a department in a retail store and observed rules that were used for adjusting prices that tallied with their theoretical model, and behavioural models have since been constructed to explain behaviour in other organisations. The problem is, however, that procedures for the setting and adjusting of targets are completely different for different firms and even within one firm they may change with time. Another limitation on the general usefulness of the behavioural theory is that those companies who have spent a great deal of time and money constructing detailed computer simulation models of their own operational systems will, for commercial reasons, be reluctant to release the information they contain to economists and others wishing to study firms' behaviour.

Thus, although the assumptions on which the behavioural theory of the firm is based may be realistic, it cannot predict the behaviour of firms in general. It also yields very little in the way of management decision-making rules that may help improve a firm's efficiency. The behavioural theory does have some uses, though. For certain aspects of government industrial policy

---

5.   R. M. Cyert and J. G. March, *A Behavioral Theory of the Firm* (Engelwood Cliffs, N. J.: Prentice Hall, 1963).

it makes sense to recognise that firms actually operate by a process of target setting and looking for ways of improving efficiency when targets are not met. For example, in the United Kingdom the government has over the years tried various measures to get firms to move to areas of high unemployment. Some opponents of this policy have argued that if left to themselves firms will choose the site that maximises their profits and so any measures that attempt to make them locate anywhere else will cause them to be less efficient. However, as Loasby observed,[6] most firms in fact do not continually scan the whole country to discover their optimal location. They only look for a new location when their existing site cannot meet their requirements, for example, when they wish to expand. When the decision to move has been made they will set out the necessary requirements for a new site and then search in the vicinity of their existing plants, or other known areas, until somewhere that meets these requirements is found. This is a form of 'satisficing' behaviour, and means that firms do not always choose the best possible site when relocating. Therefore making them move to areas of high unemployment need not necessarily reduce their efficiency. This explanation of the way firms make decisions also suggests that government industrial location policy should include a widespread publicity programme to make firms more aware of the benefits of locating in other areas.

FULL COST PRICING

It has been observed[7] that some firms determine their selling prices by adding a mark-up to the average cost of production. For example, if average cost per unit of output is £12.50 and the mark-up is 20 per cent then the selling price will be £15. As an explanation of firms' behaviour this is more realistic than the suggestion that they equate *MR* and *MC*. However, although it may be true that this is how some firms actually calculate their prices in the course of day to day business, it is not a general theory of the firm. One may be able to estimate prices in a particular industry in a particular time period if one knows what the percentage mark-up is and what average cost is. However, this theory does not explain how the mark-up itself is determined. All that one can say is that an individual firm will use a mark-up that it considers a reasonable figure in the light of current conditions in the industry.

This mark-up explanation of how prices are determined need not be inconsistent with the profit maximising theory of the firm, however. One view is that the mark-up method describes how some firms actually calculate prices

---

6. B. J. Loasby, 'Making Location Policy Work', *Lloyds Bank Review* (January, 1967).
7. See, for example, R. C. Skinner, 'The Determination of Selling Prices', *Journal of Industrial Economics* (July 1970), pp. 201–17.

but the profit maximising theory predicts what price and output will be, that is, it predicts the size of the mark-up. The mark-up may in practice only be altered periodically, so that price and output are kept close but not always exactly equal to their profit maximising values, as it would be costly and impractical to keep constantly changing it for every slight variation in a firm's circumstances.

In many industries, though, the mark-up approach is not even a realistic description of the way prices are calculated. When there are a large number of competitors an individual firm usually has to charge a similar price to its rivals'. Unless there is a significant difference in quality, customers will switch to rival producers if a firm charges more than the going market price, and if it can sell as much as it wishes at this market price then it would lose money by charging a lower price. In other less competitive industries, where mark-up pricing would be possible, firms may use a more sophisticated system of pricing in order to increase profit, perhaps borrowing some ideas from the economic theory of profit maximisation. The mark-up method is a rather crude rule of thumb that can usually be improved on from the managerial decision making viewpoint.

GALBRAITH'S TECHNOSTRUCTURE

Although he does not try to give precise predictions about prices and output, Galbraith[8] has put forward an alternative explanation of firms' behaviour. In highly industrialised nations he observes that many industries are now dominated by large corporations that wish to grow and prosper. To this end they will try to control consumer demand to ensure that they can sell their output profitably.

It has long been recognised that advertising and other forms of marketing campaigns can alter the demand for specific products, but the demand manipulation that Galbraith suggests goes on is at a different level. The relatively few large firms dominating industry, which he terms the 'technostructure', have certain common interests and this helps strengthen their control over markets. Widespread advertising, as well as influencing the demand for particular products, can have the effect of inducing a generally more materialistic attitude among consumers. Thus in the 'consumer society' the acquisition of more consumer goods is given greater importance than the satisfaction of other aspects of life such as the arts and environment. The large producers also limit consumer choice by only making those products that will bring them the most profitable return. In a more freely competitive

---

8. See, for example, J. K. Galbraith, *Economics and the Public Purpose* (London: Penguin, 1975).

environment smaller firms would normally step in to satisfy any unfilled consumer demand. However, larger firms are able to keep out new competitors and only sell what makes them the best profit regardless of the potential of other producers to be able to meet an unsatisfied consumer demand, albeit at a lower rate of profit.

Galbraith also suggests that large manufacturers can also ensure a continuing demand for their products by shortening the life of durable goods. This can be done in two ways. Firstly, products may be built to deteriorate physically or wear out within a relatively short timer period even though manufacturers have the technical ability to make them last longer if they wanted to do so. Secondly, producers may constantly change the style and design of products so that consumers will have to buy a new model to keep up with the latest developments even though older versions of the product can still fulfill the basic function for which it is intended. These changes can include both technological improvements as well as cosmetic design changes. Galbraith cites the car industry as an example of an industry where both of these practices occur. In addition to this direct influence on consumers, Galbraith also suggests that large corporations attempt to ensure a demand for their products by influencing government policy. He says that pressure is put on the government to favour the interests of these large corporations to the detriment of other interests, such as the quality of the environment. As examples he cites the vast expenditure on armaments and the space programme in the USA, which supports a large section of industry.

It is not possible statistically to test Galbraith's theory in the same way that the predictions of the profit maximising theory can be tested. There is evidence that many industries are now dominated by a few large firms who often spend a great deal on advertising and product changes, but it is difficult to find out if the motives behind their behaviour are as Galbraith suggests. Product changes can be genuine attempts to improve consumer satisfaction. Industry may receive government support, but this can benefit workers and the economic wealth of the country as a whole and does not necessarily mean that the government is under the influence of large corporations.

One's decision to accept or reject Galbraith's theory is likely to be clouded by value-judgements. Many people consider that there is some truth in these ideas even if the extent to which they are true cannot be measured. Some supporters of Galbraith's theory also consider that the dominance and power of the technostructure is not desirable, while some of those who disagree with Galbraith sometimes argue that there is nothing basically wrong with the way large companies operate. These views, however, are value-judgements about the way society ought to operate and not assessments of the ability of Galbraith's theory to explain how firms actually do operate. It would not be illogical to accept that Galbraith provides a truthful picture of the way firms operate and at the same time consider that there is nothing wrong with this form of behaviour. If one is concerned solely with finding a way of explaining the operation of firms in a free market economy then one should not pass over a particular proposition just because some people consider it describes an undesirable mode of operation.

CONCLUSIONS

In this chapter it has been shown that the profit maximising theory is more successful than other theories of the firm both in being able to predict behaviour and in yielding principles that may be useful for managerial decision making. The assumption of profit maximisation therefore underlies most of the explanations of firms' behaviour presented in the rest of this book, although there are exceptions; for example, Chapter 11 considers the Marxian theory of the firm. The other theories of the firm that have been considered in this chapter either do not allow any precise predictions to be made, or require specific information about individual firms, and are thus not able to predict the behaviour of a group of firms in general. However, these other theories can still have their uses, as has been explained. The unrealistic profit maximising model is only intended to predict the behaviour of a large group of firms, not individual companies. Today in the United Kingdom, and in other industrialised countries, output is becoming increasingly concentrated in the hands of a small group of large producers. Many are foreign-owned multinational companies. In these instances it could be argued that the unrealistic assumptions of the profit maximising theory cannot be justified because predictions are not being made about the behaviour of a large group of firms and that it may be more appropriate to use other explanations of behaviour even though specific information about individual firms may be required. Whatever future research is undertaken economists are never likely to discover the one 'correct' theory of the firm. The more information that is included in a theory the more complicated and difficult to work with it becomes and the more limited will be its applicability. Thus one's choice of an economic theory of the firm will depend on the degree of simplicity of explanation and generality of application that one is looking for.

QUESTIONS

1. 'The idea that firms maximise long-term profits can be used to explain any deviation from the short-run profit maximising price and output, but cannot predict what such deviations might be.' Comment.
2. Assume that a firm owns a machine and on 1 January each year has the choice of selling it, at its current market value, leasing it out to another

company for annual rent of £1250 (paid at the end of the year), or operating it for another 12 months. It cannot sell or lease out the machine at any other time during the year and it can invest any capital it might have at an interest rate of 10 per cent.

At the start of year 1 the value of the machine is £5000
At the start of year 2 the value of the machine is £4000
At the start of year 3 the value of the machine is £3000
At the start of year 4 the value of the machine is £1000
At the start of year 5 the value of the machine is £500
At the start of year 6 the value of the machine is £300

What is the opportunity cost to the firm of using the machine in (a) year 1, (b) year 2, (c), year 3, (d) year 4 and (e) year 5?

3. Explain, using simple numerical examples, how it may be possible for a firm to be making (a) zero accounting profit and a positive economic profit; (b) zero economic profit and a positive accounting profit.
   According to the profit maximising theory of the firm could situations (a) or (b) possibly be equilibrium situations?

4. If a firm faces a unit elasticity demand curve it can always increase profits by reducing output. True or false?

5. What do you think will enter a manager's utility function other than profit?

6. What is the difference between satisficing and optimising?

7. The sales revenue maximising theory predicts that a firm's output will always be lower than that predicted by the profit maximising theory. True or false?

8. 'The more realistic a theory of the firm is the less useful it becomes.' Comment.

CHAPTER 5

Perfect competition

The last chapter explained the basic principles of the profit maximising theory of the firm on the assumption that a firm faced a given demand curve. The demand for a firm's output will, however, depend on:
1. the market demand for the good that is produced, and
2. the state of competition in the market and the behaviour of rival producers.
This is the first of four chapters which consider how different possible states of competition can affect a firm's pricing and output behaviour. Markets can range from the case of perfect competition, analysed in this chapter, to pure monopoly, with a number of possible intermediate cases.

DEFINITION OF PERFECT COMPETITION

Perfect competition occurs when a market has the following properties:
1. A large number of buyers and sellers. Numbers must be large enough to ensure that no individual buyer or seller can exercise any significant control over the price of the product.
2. Perfect information. Everyone has full information about all opportunities to buy and sell. A firm cannot sell the good to a consumer at a higher price than a competitor would because the consumer would always be aware of the opportunity to buy at the lower price.
3. Free entry and exit. There are no restrictions on new firms setting up in the industry, if they think it will be profitable to do so, and existing firms are free to leave the industry if they wish.
4. A homogeneous product. All firms produce a homogeneous (that is, identical) product and consumers are indifferent as to which firm they buy it from.
5. Divisibility. The product can be divided into small units.
6. Profit maximisation. All firms try to maximise profits.

One is unlikely to find a real industry where all these conditions are satisfied completely. However, this set of assumptions allows a workable model to be constructed which can be applied to markets that come reasonably close to satisfying the conditions set out above. Most examples of almost perfectly competitive markets are to be found in agricultural and commodity markets.

THE DEMAND SCHEDULE FACING A SINGLE PRODUCER

In a perfectly competitive industry each firm supplies such a small proportion of the total output of the industry that it has to accept the going market price. The effect of this on a firm's demand schedule can be illustrated with an example.

Suppose that a market gardener supplies tomatoes to a large wholesale market. In the tomato growing season each day she sends an average of 100 kg (0.1 metric tonnes) to be sold at the wholesale market where the average daily trade in tomatoes total 200 tonnes. Assuming that there are no significant quality variations between the produce of different tomato growers, then if the going price of tomatoes is 20p a kilogramme no one is going to buy tomatoes from this market gardener if she tries to sell them at a higher price. On the other hand, she would not wish to sell any at a lower price if she can sell all her output at a market price of 20p. Thus this individual producer effectively faces a demand schedule which is a horizontal line at a price of 20p, as shown by D in Figure 5.1(a) overleaf. On the quantity axes, in Figure 5.1(a) q measures output per time period for a single producer and in Figure 5.1(b) Q measures quantity per time period for the whole industry. The same notation is used in other diagrams in this chapter.

Marginal revenue (MR) will also be a horizontal line at 20p because each extra kilogramme of tomatoes sold brings in an extra 20p revenue. This holds for reasonably sized fluctuations in the producer's output. Obviously if there was something like a thousand fold increase in its output then the condition (1) above that defines a perfectly competitive market would not hold and the market price would change.

A horizontal demand curve has an infinitely large price elasticity of demand. It can be shown that this is approximately true for the example above if it is assumed that the market demand for tomatoes is the downward sloping straight line D_m in Figure 5.1(b). This demand schedule can be expressed by the equation

$$Q_d = 400 - 10P$$

where Q_d is quantity demanded and P is price. This can be rewritten as

$$P = 40 - 0.1Q_d.$$

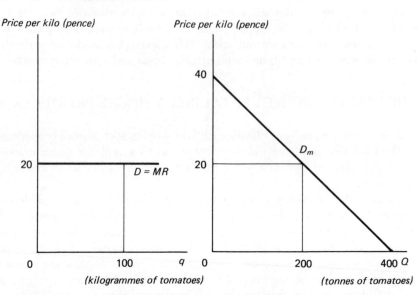

FIGURE 5.1   A firm's demand schedule in perfect competition

If this individual market gardener increased production by 10 per cent, from 0.1 to 0.11 tones per day, and all other producers did not change their output levels, the total amount sold on the market would increase to 200.01 tonnes. Assuming that price can be expressed in fractions of a penny, the market price would then be

$$40 - 0.1(200.01) = 40 - 20.001 = 19.999 \text{ pence.}$$

Using the arc elasticity measure, this individual producer therefore faces a demand schedule with a price elasticity of

$$\frac{0.01/(0.1 + 0.11)}{0.001/(20 + 19.999)} = \frac{0.01 \times 39.999}{0.001 \times 0.21} = 1904.7$$

This is an extremely large value for price elasticity of demand and effectively means a horizontal demand curve, although mathematically there will be a slight slope. Although the demand schedule facing a firm in a perfectly competitive market is for all intents and purposes a horizontal line at the ruling market price, the market demand for the good in question is not affected by the state of competition among suppliers and so takes the usual form of a line sloping down from left to right.

MARKET SUPPLY AND THE TIME PERIOD

In Chapter 1 the simple supply and demand analysis of a competitive market assumed that the supply curve sloped up from left to right without commenting on the time period except to say that supply is a flow and some time dimension has to be defined. The time period within which supply is analysed is, however, an important influence on the nature of the supply schedule. (It is also true that the demand curve may alter its elasticity over time, but it is assumed constant for the purposes of this analysis.)

There are four main time periods which can be considered in the analysis of supply in a perfectly competitive market: (1) the very short run, (2) the short run, (3) the long run with new entry, and (4) the long run with plant size adjustment.

THE VERY SHORT RUN (MARKET PERIOD)

The very short run is defined as the time period within which no inputs can be altered and hence only a fixed output can be supplied. For example, if consignments of freshly picked tomatoes from market gardeners are sold at a wholesale market two days after they are picked then the total quantity available for sale cannot be increased within any given day, even if there is an exogenous increase in demand. If the quantity available for sale cannot be changed when demand increases then price must increase, as shown in Figure 5.2 overleaf. The supply schedules for both the single producer and the industry, S_S and S_M respectively, will be vertical lines at the available quantity. In this example it is assumed that there are 100 similar producers all selling 300 kg of tomatoes a day. An exogenous increase in demand from D_1 to D_2 would cause price to increase from 15 to 25 pence per kilogramme and quantity supplied by the industry would remain unchanged at 30 tonnes.

THE SHORT RUN

The short-run equilibrium output of a firm whose short-run cost curves are as shown in Figure 5.3(a), and which sells its output in a market where the current market price is £30, can be determined using the 'MC equals MR' rule for profit maximisation which was explained in Chapter 4. The MR schedule is a horizontal line at £30 and is cut (from below) by MC at an output of 40 units.

At this output level AC is £21.50 and so profit can be calculated as

$$(P - AC) \times q = (£30 - £21.50) \times 40 = £340.$$

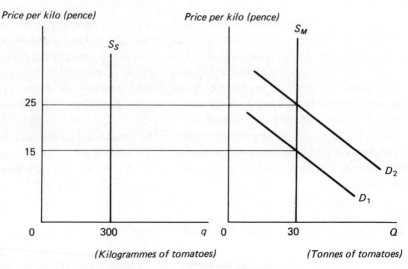

FIGURE 5.2   The very short run

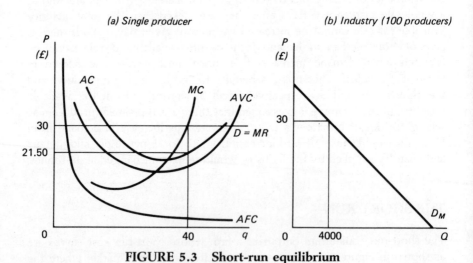

FIGURE 5.3   Short-run equilibrium

Note that the profit maximising output in this example, and in general, is not the output at which *AC* is a minimum. It is also possible that even when all the conditions for profit maximisation are satisfied a firm will not find it worthwhile to stay in production.

The decision to close down

The '*MC* equals *MR*' rule for profit maximisation is also the rule for loss minimisation. How this relates to the decision on when to stop production is explained using the example in Figure 5.4, where the cost curves are assumed to apply to a typical producer in a perfectly competitive industry. If price is £28 then the corresponding *MR* schedule cuts *MC* at an output of 44 units, at which *AC* is £31. The firm will therefore make a loss of

$$(£31 - £28) \times 44 = £132.$$

A firm cannot continue forever making a loss and in the long-run if these cost and demand conditions persist it will close down. In the short-run, however, even if a firm stops production completely it still has to pay its fixed costs, which in this example are £440. (This can be found from Figure 5.4 by multiplying *AFC* by output; for example, *AFC* is £10 when quantity is 44 and so *TFC* must be £10 multiplied by 44.) These fixed costs of £440 are greater than the £132 that would be lost if the firm kept producing.

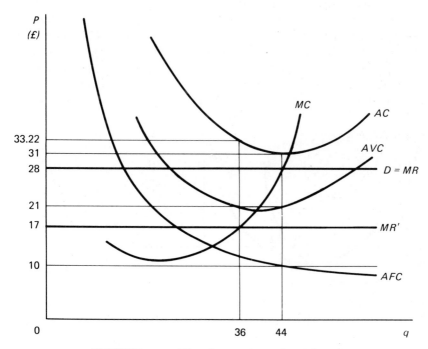

FIGURE 5.4   The decision to close down

Thus, in the short run, the firm would be financially better off by continuing production. Because the price of £28 is greater than the *AVC* of £21 at an output of 44 units, the firm is making an 'operating profit' of revenue over variable costs which it can set against its fixed costs in order to reduce its loss. In this situation total revenue is £1232 and total variable costs are £924. Thus there is an operating profit of £308 which can be set against the fixed costs of £440 and so reduce the loss to £132.

In the short run a firm should only cease production if price is less than *AVC* at the output at which *MC* cuts *MR* from below. If, for example, price is £17 in Figure 5.4 then *MC* cuts *MR'* at an output of 36 units, at which *AC* is £33.22 and *AVC* is £21. If the firm did produce this output it would bring in a *TR* of £612 and pay out *TC* of £1196. The consequent loss of £584 would be greater than the total fixed costs of £440 and so the firm would be better off if it closed down production.

The short-run supply curve

The industry's short-run supply curve can be derived from the short-run cost curves of the firms that make up the industry. Assume that an industry contains 100 identical producers whose short-run cost curves are shown in Figure 5.5(a). If the market price is £30 then the corresponding *MR* schedule will cut *MC* at *A* and so output will be 40 units. If each firm supplies 40 units then the total quantity supplied by the market will be 100 × 40 = 4000 units. Thus point *A'* can be plotted on the market supply curve, *S*, in Figure 5.5(b).

If the market price drops to £25 the new *MR* schedule cuts *MC* at *B*, the profit maximising output for each firm will be 38 units and the industry in total will supply 3800 units. The same exercise can be repeated for a number

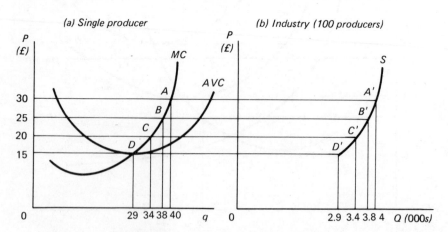

FIGURE 5.5   The short-run supply curve

of possible market prices, with the quantity supplied by an individual firm being read off its *MC* curve (as long as price is above *AVC* – otherwise production would cease). The industry supply curve is therefore found by horizontally summing the sections of individual producers' *MC* curves that lie above the *AVC* curve. This supply curve should really be labelled the short-run supply curve because it shows how much of the good existing producers are willing to supply at any given price when they can only vary one input.

THE LONG RUN

In the long run two types of adjustment may take place:
1. New firms may enter the industry or existing firms may leave.
2. Firms may alter the inputs that are fixed in the short-run and so change the size of plant that they operate.

Although both adjustments may take place simultaneously they are considered separately to make the analysis clearer.

1. Entry and exit

The short-run industry supply curve S_1 in Figure 5.6(b) is drawn on the assumption that the industry is made up of 100 firms all with the same cost structure as in Figure 5.6(a). If the market demand curve is initially D_1 then the equilibrium price is £14 and the total quantity supplied by the industry

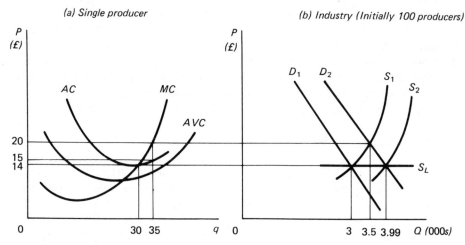

FIGURE 5.6   New entry and long-run equilibrium in a constant cost industry

is 3000 units. This price is equal to the minimum value of AC and so each firm will produce 30 units and make zero economic profit. Thus there is no incentive for new firms to enter the industry or for existing ones to leave and there is a long-run equilibrium.

Now assume that exogenous factors cause the demand curve to shift out to D_2. This intersects S_1 at a price of £20. At this short-run equilibrium price each of the original firms would supply an output of 35 units and face an AC of £15, thus making a profit of $(£20 - £15) \times 35 = £175$.

This is an economic profit over and above opportunity costs and so will attract other firms into the industry. New entry will have the effect of shifting the short-run supply curve to the right. At any given price existing firms will still supply the same amount as before, but there will now be extra supply from the new firms. As the supply curve moves to the right so the market price will fall. It will keep falling until there are no economic profits being earned and therefore no further incentive for any more firms to enter the industry. If it is assumed that new entrants have the same cost structure as the original firms then 33 more firms would cause the short run supply curve in Figure 5.6(b) to shift to S_2 and there will be a new long-run equilibrium at a price of £14. Once again each firm is making zero economic profit and producing 30 units, but as there are now 133 firms the total quantity supplied by the industry is 3990 units.

Constant Cost Industries

In the above example, whatever changes there may be in demand the profit incentive will cause new entry, or exit, to ensure that price always eventually returns to £14. Thus the long-run supply curve S_L is horizontal. It is implicitly assumed that the cost curves do not change, but this may not necessarily always be the case. As an industry's demand for inputs changes then input prices may alter and thus cause firms' cost curves to move up, or down. The effect on supply of these possibilities is explained below. An industry, such as the one described in the example above, where cost curves do not change when industry output alters, is known as a 'constant cost industry'.

Increasing Cost Industries

In an increasing cost industry, when new entrants are attracted and the whole industry output rises, the consequent increased demand for inputs causes their prices to rise. A rise in input prices will cause firms' cost curves to shift upwards, as illustrated in Figure 5.7(a), and is an example of pecuniary diseconomies of scale. The shape of the AC curve and the output at which it reaches its minimum point may both change, depending on the relative price increases of different inputs. (Although it is assumed here that existing firms do not change their fixed input, new entrants may increase the demand for this input and so cause its price to change.) The new average cost curve AC_2 in Figure 5.7(a), with its minimum point directly above the minimum point of the original average cost curve AC_1, is only one possibility.

To explain the effect of increasing costs on the long-run supply curve, assume that an industry has the short-run supply curve S_1 shown in Figure 5.7(b) and is initially in short- and long-run equilibrium at X with price equal to £13.50. If it is also assumed that there are initially 100 firms in the industry and that AC_1 and MC_1 in Figure 5.7(a) illustrate a typical firm's cost structure then at the equilibrium price £13.50 each firm will produce an output of 20 units and the market supply will be 2000 units. If there is an exogenous shift of the market demand curve to D_2 then in the short-run price will rise to £25 and existing firms will increase output to 30 units, each earning £285 profit. The entry of new firms attracted by this profit will shift the supply curve out to the right and so cause price to fall. However, as this is an increasing cost industry, the cost curves move upward, to AC_2 and MC_2, when the increase in output causes input prices to rise. Therefore the product's price will not fall all the way back to its original value. The new long-run equilibrium will be at Y, with price equal to £18. Each firm will again just cover its costs and there will be no incentive for further new entry. The long-run supply curve S_L therefore slopes upwards.

Decreasing Cost Industries

It is also possible for input prices to fall as the whole industry output increases,

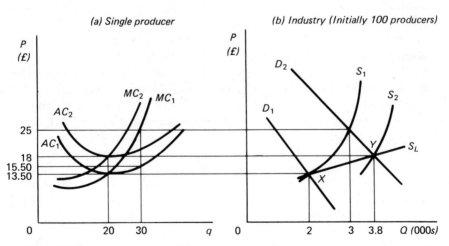

FIGURE 5.7   New entry and long-run equilibrium in an increasing cost industry

in other words, for pecuniary external economies of scale to exist. If this is the case then an increase in demand will bring about a downward shift in firms' cost curves and result in a downward sloping long-run supply curve.

It should be noted that industries may not be increasing, constant, or decreasing cost industries for every possible output level. It would be unusual for input prices to fall continually as industry output increased, and in some cases the long-run supply curve may initially fall and then turn upwards as increasing input prices are encountered.

2. Changes in size of plant

It is usual to analyse the long-run in a perfectly competitive market in terms of new entry and exit rather than the adjustment of plant size by existing firms. This may be a reasonable proposition given that in many industries it may be easier for a new firm to build a new plant than for an existing firm to alter the size of, or replace, existing production facilities. In some cases, though, the reverse may be true and existing firms may be able to alter their fixed inputs more quickly than new firms can enter the industry.

Assume that a typical firm in a constant cost industry has short- and long-run cost curves as shown in Figure 5.8 and is initially in equilibrium with price equal to £6 and output at 25 units. Assume also that there are 100 firms in the industry and that initially each operates on the short-run cost curves SAC_1 and SMC_1. If an exogenous change in market demand, from D_1 to D_2, causes the market price to increase to £21 then in the short run the firm will increase output to 28 units. If new entry is assumed to take a relatively long time and the firm thinks that price will remain at £21 for a significant time then in the long-run it will consider changing its size of plant. If price is £21 then MR cuts LMC at an output of 38 units and so the firm will increase profits if it changes the amount of its fixed input to that which is optimal for producing this output level. However, even without new entry price will not remain at £21 if all firms undertake such long-run adjustments to plant size, because the increased output brings price down. The industry supply curve will no longer be S_1, the horizontal sum of the SMC_1 curves, but S_L the horizontal sum of the LMC curves. Although this still slopes upward, it is flatter than S_1 and so price falls to £17. At this new long-run equilibrium price each firm produces an output of 35 units and has a plant size corresponding to SAC_2. There will also be a new short-run supply curve S_2 corresponding to SMC_2. Eventually, of course, price may fall even further as a result of new entry as economic profits are still made when price is £17.

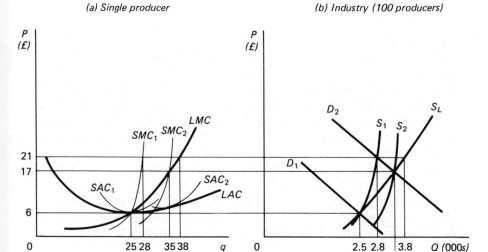

(a) Single producer   (b) Industry (100 producers)

FIGURE 5.8   Plant size adjustment and long-run equilibrium

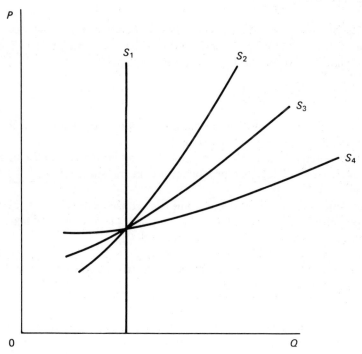

FIGURE 5.9   Elasticity of supply and the time period in a perfectly competitive market

CONCLUSIONS

The long-run adjustments of new entry and plant size changes have been considered separately above for ease of analysis. In reality both adjustments may take place simultaneously, although the order of events can differ from industry to industry. In general all that can be said is that in a perfectly competitive industry the longer the time period considered the more elastic the supply curve is usually expected to be. Returning to the example of tomato growing used earlier, Figure 5.9 illustrates a case where there are four possible supply curves. Schedule S_1 represents the supply curve for the market period. Schedule S_2 represents the short-run supply curve when the firm is free to vary inputs such as labour or fertilizer but not the acreage of land under glass available for growing tomatoes. Schedule S_3 represents supply when existing growers can increase their land, and S_4 is the supply schedule when the time period is long enough to allow new entrants to set up in the industry.

QUESTIONS

1. Assume that an industry comprises a hundred firms each currently producing an output of 20 units, and that the relationship between market demand Q and price P is given by the equation

    $$Q = 5000 - 500P.$$

    If a single firm is considering expanding output by 1 unit, calculate the elasticity of the demand schedule it faces.
2. What criteria should a firm in a perfectly competitive market use to decide whether or not to cease production (a) in the short-run, and (b) in the long run?
3. Distinguish the short- and long-run consequences for a perfectly competitive firm and industry of imposing (a) a lump-sum tax on the profit of each firm, and (b) a per unit sales tax.
4. Under what conditions would the long-run supply curve of a perfectly competitive industry slope (a) upwards (b) downwards? Could these conditions persist over time?

CHAPTER 6

Monopoly

A monopoly is usually defined as the sole seller of a product, but what is a product? Would it make sense to say that Ford are a monopoly producer of Ford Escort cars? A more precise definition of a monopoly is that it is the sole seller of a product with no close substitutes, although this still leaves open the question of what is meant by a 'close' substitute. It is fairly easy to define some markets where there are no close substitutes for the product, such as toothpaste, but in other cases it is more difficult to make this distinction. For example, if a firm was a monopoly producer of white sliced bread it could be argued that consumers could still purchase alternative close substitutes such as unsliced white bread or wholemeal bread. There is no precise definition of how close substitutes must be for there not to be a monopoly and in practice one just has to make a decision based on the information that is available.

In the United Kingdom and in many other countries legislation[1] has made private monopolies illegal, except under special circumstances, and the major monopolies in existence are nationalised industries. More recently, the privatisation of some former state-owned monopolies has been accompanied by measures to try to ensure that there is at least an element of competitition and to regulate the prices that a privatised monopoly can charge its consumers. What is the point, then, of analysing how a private unregulated monopoly behaves if private unregulated monopolies do not usually exist in the United Kingdom? One reason is to discover why it has been thought necessary to regulate them in the first place. An understanding of monopoly behaviour is also necessary to explain how international monopolies, and monopolies in

---

1. For an explanation of United Kingdom competition policy see J. R. Cable, 'Industry' (section IV: Competition Policy and Consumer Protection, pp. 227–44) in M. J. Artis (ed.), *The UK Economy: A Manual of Applied Economics*, 11th edn (London: Weidenfeld and Nicolson, 1986).

countries where they are not regulated, may operate. The theory of monopoly can also assist in explaining the operation of markets which, although not pure monopolies, are close approximations to it, perhaps because of collusion between producers. As explained in Chapters 7 and 8, it can be difficult to predict behaviour in the intermediate market structures between monopoly and perfect competition and so it is useful to know what is expected to happen in these two limiting cases.

SHORT-RUN EQUILIBRIUM

Because there is only one firm in the industry a monopolist's demand schedule is the same as the market demand. This will usually be downward sloping from left to right and so the corresponding *MR* schedule will lie below it, as shown in the example in Figure 6.1. Because it faces a downward sloping demand curve a monopoly can choose to set either price or output. This is a wider choice than that faced by a firm in perfect competition, which can only decide its output, but even a monopoly is constrained by the fact that consumers are only willing to buy a limited amount of a good at any given price.

Profit will be maximised at the output where *MC* intersects *MR* from below, which is 150 units in the example in Figure 6.1. To sell 150 units the

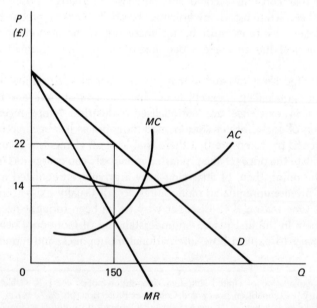

FIGURE 6.1   Short-run equilibrium for a monopoly

demand schedule shows that the firm must charge a price of £22. As *AC* is £14 at this output level, profit will therefore be

$$(£22 - £14) \times 150 = £1200.$$

LONG-RUN EQUILIBRIUM

Barriers to entry

The profits earned by the firm in the above example would attract new firms into the industry if it were not for barriers to entry. A pre-condition for a monopoly to exist, except for possible temporary short-run situations, is that new entry is barred. If new competitors were allowed to enter the industry then by definition it would no longer be a monopoly. Barriers to entry fall into three broad categories:

1. Legal. The state may make competition illegal for a variety of reasons; for example, patents are granted to allow firms to recoup in profits the money spent on the research and development of new products.
2. Sole ownership of inputs or retail outlets. If a particular raw material is essential for the manufacturing of a good and one firm owns all the sources of this raw material then obviously no other rival producer can manufacture the good. The same applies when one firm employs the only workers with the skills necessary to make the good or has exclusive access to capital equipment required for its manufacture.

   At the other end of the production chain, some products are sold through specialist retail outlets. If one firm owned all the retail outlets then rival producers would not be able to sell their product and would thus be excluded from the industry. For example, petrol can usually only be sold by petrol stations and so a petrol producer that owns every petrol station will be able to prevent potential competitors selling their petrol.[2]

   A similar situation has occurred in the market for beer, where large brewers have bought up public houses and made it difficult for smaller breweries to find sales outlets. In this case there is some competition from off-sales which can be made available through a wider range of different retail outlets. However, the sales potential from such alternative retail outlets is limited and the buying up of public houses by large brewing companies has led to the disappearance of many smaller breweries.

---

2. For a study of the market for retail petrol supply in the United Kingdom see R. W. Shaw and C. J. Sutton, *Industry and Competition: Industrial Case Studies* (London: Macmillan, 1976), ch. 2.

3. Economies of scale. When economies of scale are present in an industry then a large firm will be able to produce at a lower average cost than a small firm. If there is one large producer already established in the industry it may be able to keep out new entrants by keeping price below the level at which a new entrant could make a profit. For example, in Figure 6.2 a large established firm producing output Q_E at average cost C_E could set a price of P_1. This would make it impossible for a new entrant producing only Q_N, with average costs of C_N, to operate at a profit.

The above analysis assumes that a new entrant will, initially at least, produce less than an established firm. This will frequently be the case, but not always. A new entrant may be a large multi-product firm with enough resources to start up production at the same rate as the established firm. In this case the economies of scale are not an effective barrier to entry. Thus economies of scale *may* be a barrier to entry that maintains a monopoly, but this barrier to entry is relative to the possible initial scale of output of potential rivals. In some cases a monopoly may try to create barriers to entry by advertising, which itself can be a source of economies of scale (see Chapter 7).

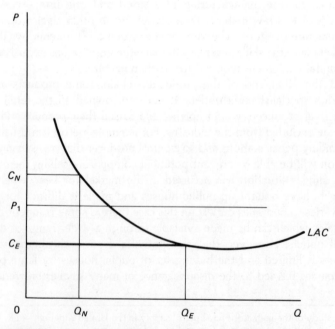

FIGURE 6.2   Economics of scale as a barrier to entry

Monopoly and competition

A monopoly can experience some indirect forms of competition. It has to compete for consumers' expenditure with the producers of other products even though these may not be substitutes in the usual sense. For example, if car production was a monopoly the demand for cars would still be affected by the price of housing, given that both goods take up a significant proportion of consumers' incomes. There is also the possibility that research and development by other firms will allow them to break into the market or perhaps produce a substitute for the monopolist's product. For example, CB radio can be a substitute for telephone calls.

Given the fact that international trade takes place then, strictly speaking, monopolies can only exist on a global scale. It is usual practice, however, to define monopolies in terms of a national market. In this case a national monopoly may still have competition from foreign producers, in export markets at least. A private profit maximising monopoly will usually be aware of this foreign competition and will act accordingly. However, this distinction is not always made when discussing monopoly price regulation. It has been argued that nationalised monopolies should charge a 'fair' price so as not to exploit the consumer (see Chapter 12). The results of such a common policy being applied to all nationalised monopolies regardless of foreign competition could be a potential economic disaster. It is one thing to ensure that domestic consumers' electricity prices are at a 'socially optimum' level because there is little foreign competition (although consumers could use imported oil for heating). However, other companies that have at one time been nationalised, such as British Steel, compete in the world market. If these were to face an enforced price above the going market price then sales would be lost, and if they charged a price below it then customers (including foreign ones) would gain at the expense of the government of the United Kingdom.

Optimum size of plant

Because barriers to entry prevent new firms setting up, the only long-run change in a monopolistic industry is the adjustment of inputs that are fixed in the short-run. In the long run a profit maximising firm will adjust its output until long-run marginal cost (LMC) equals MR.

Assume that a firm initially has a plant size corresponding to SAC_1 in Figure 6.3 overleaf. Its short-run equilibrium is where SMC_1 equals MR, at output Q_1 and price is P_1. However, in the long-run the firm can increase profits by expanding output to Q_2 where LMC equals MR, with price equal to P_2. This entails changing plant size so that the firm operates in the short run on SAC_2.

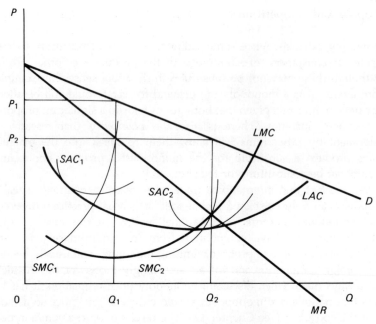

FIGURE 6.3   Long-run equilibrium for a monopoly

PRICE DISCRIMINATION

Price discrimination is the practice of selling the same good to different customers at different prices, or of selling different units of the good to the same customers at different prices. This is most likely to happen under monopoly because consumers do not have other sellers to turn to when faced with different prices. Even under monopoly, though, price discrimination will only occur under circumstances which make it (1) possible, and (2) profitable.

1.   For price discrimination to be *possible* two conditions are necessary:

(a)   Markets must be clearly separable.
(b)   Resale of the product between customers who pay different prices must be impossible or prohibitively expensive.

Markets which satisfy these conditions usually fall into the following categories:

(i)   Services. Examples of services where price discrimination is sometimes practised are medical treatment and transport. It is impossible to resell an operation or a train journey in the same way that a car or a book can be resold.

(ii)   Monitored sales through official installation. Utilities like gas, electricity and telephone calls come under this category. It is illegal to resell them and the same customers can pay different prices for different units.

(iii)   Geographically or politically separated markets. Transportation costs and/or trade controls and tariffs may prevent resale or make it uneconomic.

2.   For price discrimination to be *profitable* it is necessary for the different segments into which it is possible to separate the total market to have different elasticities of demand. If demand was identical in each segment of the market then a firm would maximise profits by always charging the same price.

As is explained below, price discrimination can take several different forms.

FIRST DEGREE PRICE DISCRIMINATION (PERFECT PRICE DISCRIMINATION)

First degree price discrimination occurs when each unit of a good can be sold at a different price. Assume that a firm faces the demand and cost schedules shown in Figure 6.4. To simplify the analysis it is assumed that MC is horizontal

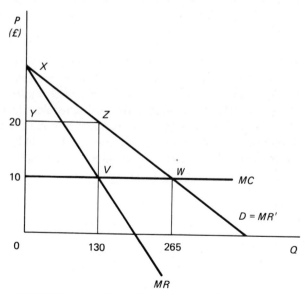

FIGURE 6.4   First degree price discrimination

and that fixed costs are zero, that is, each unit of output costs £10 to produce. If this firm is a monopoly selling at a single price then the profit maximising output is 130 units and price is £20. Now consider what would happen if this monopoly was able to sell each unit at a different price. To sell one more unit it would not have to lower the price(s) at which other units were sold. The marginal revenue from the sale of an extra unit of output would therefore be equal to the price at which it is sold and so the firm would face a new marginal revenue curve, MR', which is the same as the original demand curve, D. It will still maximise profits by expanding output up to the point where marginal revenue equals marginal cost, but this profit maximising output now becomes 265 units. There is no 'profit maximising price', though, because each unit is sold at a different price.

Profits will clearly be greater than the £1300 earned when a single price of £20 is charged. Firstly, the extra revenue shown by the area XYZ is earned on the same output that was sold at the single price of £10 and, secondly, the firm also earns profits equal to area ZVW on the extra output that it is now worth selling.

SECOND DEGREE PRICE DISCRIMINATION

Second degree price discrimination involves two or more different prices being charged for different amounts of the same good. Assume that a firm faces the demand schedule BD shown in Figure 6.5 and its marginal costs are a constant £10. A single pricing monopoly in this situation would produce 200 units which would be sold at a price of £26, earning profits of £3200 (assuming that there are no fixed costs).

Assume that the firm then starts a two-part pricing system and charges a price of £31 each for the first 130 units sold. This means that if the firm wishes to sell more than 130 units it must lower the price and so effectively operate on the section AD of the original demand schedule. Thus above an output of 130 units the firm faces the new marginal revenue curve MR' (it is as though the zero on the quantity axis was moved to the right by 130 units). To maximise profits it should therefore expand output to 265 units. Total profits will then be total revenue from the two batches of sales at the different prices minus total cost

$$= (130 \times £31) + (135 \times £21) - (£10 \times 265)$$
$$= £4030 + £2835 - £2650$$
$$= £4215$$

which is clearly greater than the single price maximum profits of £3200.

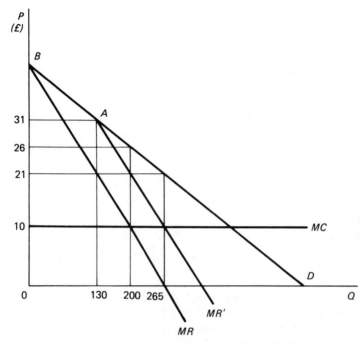

FIGURE 6.5 Second degree price discrimination

The example above shows a two-part system of price discrimination, but three or more different prices can be used to increase profits even further. In fact, the greater the number of different prices that can be charged the greater the profit that can be earned. The most profitable method, if it is possible, is to charge a different price for each unit sold, that is, first degree price discrimination.

Income effects

It is possible that the income effect of second degree price discrimination may mean that the result is not exactly as shown in the example above. A demand curve shows how much of a good consumers would be willing to buy at any given *single* price. If they have to pay more for the first few units then the quantity demanded of extra units may be less.

For example, in the case shown in Figure 6.6, at a single price of £10 the quantity demanded is 280 units and so total expenditure is £2800. If, however, the first 130 units were sold at a price of £20 then the expenditure on these units alone would be £2600. As this effectively reduces the income that consumers have left to spend on further units of output, below the price of

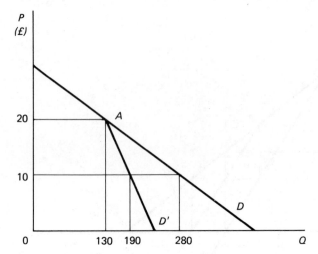

FIGURE 6.6   The income effect of second degree price discrimination

£20 the demand schedule may swing inwards to become AD'. The total amount sold if a price of £10 was charged for sales after the first 130 units would then be 190 and expenditure would be

$$(£20 \times 130) + (£10 \times 60) = £3200.$$

Below-cost pricing

When foreign manufacturers sell their output in another country at a price below the average cost of production this practice is sometimes criticised as being unfair 'dumping' that is intended to drive domestic firms out of business. This need not necessarily be the case, though, and it can be shown that below average cost pricing as a component of a second degree price discrimination policy may be the only way that a firm can produce the good at all.

Assume that a firm has long-run cost curves as shown in Figure 6.7 and is a monopoly in its domestic market, where demand is D_D, and can sell as much as it wishes in a competitive export market, where its effective demand schedule is D_E and the ruling price is £20. It can be seen that if the firm only sells in the domestic market there is no single price at which it can cover average cost in order to make a profit.

Consider what its options are, though, if it can sell in the home and export markets at different prices. It faces an effective marginal revenue curve of MR_D only up to an output of 120 units. Past this output it is not worth selling any more in the domestic market because the marginal revenue in the export market, MR_E, is higher, at a constant £20. Thus the firm's overall

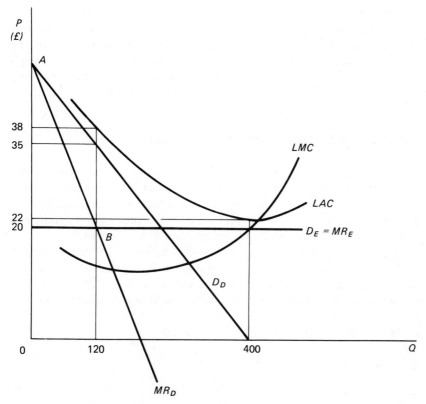

FIGURE 6.7 Below-cost pricing

marginal revenue schedule is the kinked line ABD_E. The profit maximising output where marginal revenue cuts marginal cost is therefore 400 units, of which 120 units are sold in the domestic market (at a price of £35) and the remaining 280 units in the export market (at the market price of £20). Average cost is £22 when production is 400 units. Thus:

Total revenue from domestic market = 120 × £35 = £4200
Total revenue from export market = 280 × £20 = £5600
Total cost   = 400 × £22 = £8800
Profit = TR(home + export) − TC = £9800 − £8800 = £1000.

Although the 280 units exported are sold below cost they help to increase profit because they bring down the average cost of production not only for exports but also for the 120 units sold in the home market. If only 120 units were produced for the home market average cost would be £38 and the firm would make a loss of £360. This example of two-part pricing allowing a profit to be made when average production cost falls as output increases illustrates how cars produced in the United Kingdom can be sold on the continent at a price below that charged in the domestic market. Although the situation is rather more complex and the details differ, it is still basically a question of increasing total sales in order to bring down average costs.

THIRD DEGREE PRICE DISCRIMINATION

Third degree price discrimination can take place when there are two or more separable markets for a good, each having its own downward sloping demand schedule. A firm has to decide how much to produce in total and how to split this output between the different markets, the prices being determined by the amount sold in each. This latter problem is tackled first.

Assume that a monopoly can split its sales between the two markets, 1 and 2, whose demand schedules are shown in Figure 6.8 as D_1 and D_2, respectively, and that it produces a total output of 180 units. If this total output is initially divided so that 90 units are sold in each market then:

$$P_1 = £24 \qquad MR_1 = £5 \qquad TR_1 = £2160$$

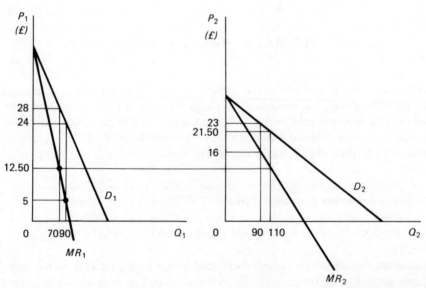

FIGURE 6.8   Third degree price discrimination and the distribution of sales

$P_2 = £23$ $MR_2 = £16$ $TR_2 = £2070.$

Total Revenue $= TR_1 + TR_2 = £4230.$

This is not the best way of dividing the sales, however. If it is assumed that marginal revenue is approximately the same for single unit increases and decreases in output it can be seen that:

If one more unit is sold in market 2 the gain in revenue is £16.
If one less unit is sold in market 1 the loss in revenue is £5.

Thus it will pay the firm to transfer sales from market 1 to market 2. As more is sold in market 2 the value of MR_2 will decline and as less is sold in market 1 then the value of MR_1 increases. Maximum revenue will be obtained when sales are split so that MR_1 equals MR_2. In this example this occurs when MR_1 and MR_2 both equal £12.50. Thus Q_1 is 70 units, Q_2 is 110 units and the prices in the two markets are £28 and £21.50, respectively. Total revenue will then be

$$(70 \times £28) + (110 \times £21.50) = £1960 + £2365 = £4325.$$

This is clearly greater than the original revenue earned and is the maximum obtainable revenue when output is 180 units. Switching sales from one market to another will not increase revenue any further because the revenue gained in one market will be the same as the revenue lost in the other market.

The second part of the problem is to decide on total output. The 'MR equals MC' profit maximising rule is still used, but exactly what is MR when there are two (or more) markets where different prices are charged? This problem is illustrated in Figure 6.9, where a firm is assumed to face two separable markets with demand curves D_1 and D_2. As the firm expands output from zero, consider where it should sell each unit in order to earn the maximum revenue. The first unit produced should be sold in market 1 because the marginal revenue from the first unit sold in market 1 is greater than the marginal revenue from the first unit sold in market 2. The same applies to the second unit, and the third. In fact each unit up to the 45th earns a marginal revenue in market 1 greater than the marginal revenue of the first unit in market 2. However, when more than 45 units are sold in market 1 marginal revenue becomes less than the marginal revenue from the first unit sold in market 2. Thus if the firm produces more than 45 units in total it should distribute its output between the two markets, basing this distribution on the rule that the marginal revenues in each market should be equal. This means that the firm's marginal revenue schedule for total output, MR_T, will be the horizontal summation of MR_1 and MR_2. If marginal revenue is above £30

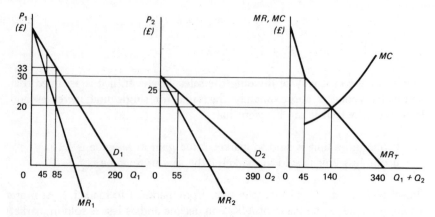

FIGURE 6.9   Price and output determination under third degree price discrimination

then only MR_1 is relevant and below this price MR_T is the sum of the sales in both markets.

When MR_T has been constructed then the profit maximising total output of 140 units can be determined, where MR_T equals MC. The split of this total output between the two markets can then be found by determining the output in each market where marginal revenue is the same as the value of MR_T. In Figure 6.9, as MR_T equals MC at a value of £20 then MR_1 and MR_2 will also equal £20. Thus, in market 1 output will be 85 units and price will be £33, and in market 2 output will be 55 units and price will be £25. As one would expect, price is higher in the market with the more inelastic demand curve.

QUESTIONS

1.   Assume that the relationship between a monopoly's output Q and price P is given by the equation

$$P = 25 - 1.5Q$$

and that marginal cost MC is defined as

$$MC = 2Q.$$

Fixed cost are £16.
What will be the profit maximising price and output, and the profit?

What will happen to these quantities if (a) a lump sum profits tax of £10 is imposed, and (b) a £2 per unit sales tax is imposed?

2. Is a monopolist subject to any kind of competition?
3. Is it possible that a profit maximising monopolist will produce (a) where it just breaks even, (b) at the minimum point of its average cost curve, (c) where (a) and (b) both occur?
4. Explain why some hoteliers in Mediterranean holiday resorts offer out-of-season rates that are below average cost.
5. A market trader in a bazaar sells souvenirs to foreign tourists who visit the place on day trips and, after bargaining with them, sells at the highest price that she thinks she can get from each visitor as long as the production costs of the souvenir are covered. Explain why this method can give a better profit than charging everyone a fixed price.
6. A firm can sell in two separate markets whose demand schedules are given by the formulae:

$$P_1 = 100 - 4Q_1$$

$$P_2 = 50 - Q_2$$

where P_1 and P_2 are the prices in the two markets and Q_1 and Q_2 are the respective quantities demanded. Marginal cost MC is given by the formula

$$MC = 2 + 0.5Q \qquad \text{where } Q \text{ is total output.}$$

What prices should the firm charge in each market in order to maximise profits? How much will then be sold in each market?

CHAPTER 7

Oligopoly

An oligopoly is an industry with only a few firms. 'Few' means a number small enough for the pricing and marketing policies of one firm to have a significant effect on the sales of other firms. Some theories of oligopoly assume that all firms produce a homogeneous product, which may be true in a number of cases, such as the market for petrol, but there are also many oligopolies where the product is differentiated, for instance, the car industry.

Because the output that a firm can sell at any given price will depend on the behaviour of rivals, as well as the market demand, the demand schedule facing any one firm cannot be known with certainty. Given this inter-dependence there are basically three broad strategies a firm in an oligopoly can take:

1. Ignoring interdependence. The firm does not take into account the fact that rivals may react to any decisions it takes; for example, it may set its selling price on the assumption that competitors keep their current prices unchanged.
2. Competition. The firm tries to 'out-guess' its rival; for example, in considering a price change it tries to take into account what retaliatory actions this might bring from competitors. If the other firms in the industry are also pursuing the same strategy then it can be impossible to predict accurately the final outcome. Each firm tries to stay a step ahead of its rivals and has to consider questions along the lines of 'Are they trying to guess what we're thinking about what their reaction would be to...etc..?'
3. Collusion. Firms collude to try to increase joint profits.

Because of the different possible strategies that can be adopted there are a number of different theories of oligopoly. Some assume one of the patterns of behaviour mentioned above while others assume some form of mix of strategies. In this chapter some of the main theories of oligopoly are explained, approximately in the chronological order that they were originally published.

CLASSICAL MODELS OF OLIGOPOLY

There are some 'classical' theories of oligopoly that were put forward in the nineteenth century which fall into category (1). In Cournot's model[1] firms decide on output assuming that rival producers keep their output levels unchanged. Edgeworth[2] suggested that firms operated on the assumption that other producers' output would not alter. Although these simplistic models readily lend themselves to mathematical analysis, and can be incorporated into more sophisticated models as limiting cases (such as Cowling[3]), their applicability is somewhat limited and they are not investigated further here.

THE KINKED DEMAND CURVE THEORY

In the 1930s Sweezy[4] put forward his 'kinked demand curve' explanation of the rigidity of prices that seemed common at that time. This theory makes the following assumptions:

1. A firm sets its price and then lets the market determine what is sold at this price.
2. An existing market price is already established.
3. Each firm believes that if it lowers its price all other competitors will follow this price reduction in order to maintain their share of the market.
4. Each firm believes that if it raises its price then other firms in the industry will *not* follow and suit and so it will lose sales to rivals.

The derivation of the name 'kinked demand curve theory' should be obvious from Figure 7.1, which shows the demand schedule facing a firm in an oligopoly where the above conditions hold. It is assumed that the already established price and output are P_1 and Q_1. The demand curve DD' is drawn on the assumption that rivals match any price change. It is relatively inelastic because

1. A. Cournot, *Researches into the Mathematical Principles of the Theory of Wealth*, translated by N. T. Bacon (New York: Macmillan, 1929). (Originally published in French in 1838.)
2. F. Y. Edgeworth, 'The Pure Theory of Monopoly', in F. Y. Edgeworth, *Papers Relating to Political Economy*, vol. 1 (London: Macmillan, 1925) pp. 111–42. (Originally published in Italian in 1897.)
3. K. Cowling, *Monopoly Capitalism* (London: Macmillan, 1982).
4. P. Sweezy, 'Demand Under Conditions of Oligopoly', *Journal of Political Economy*, vol. 47 (1939), pp. 568–73.

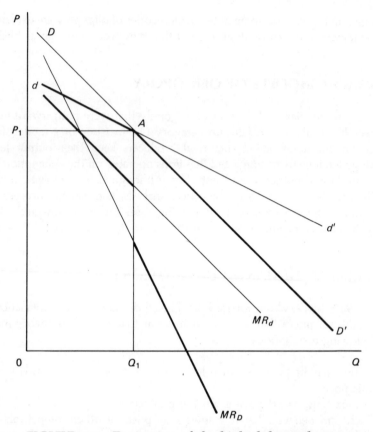

FIGURE 7.1   Derivation of the kinked demand curve

if rivals were to match any price rise, or price cut, that this firm might make then it would not lose, or gain, very much in sales. On the other hand, if rivals did not respond to any price changes then the quantity demanded would change more substantially and the firm would face the more elastic demand curve *dd'*.

From assumption (4) the firm believes that rivals will not follow price rises and so above price OP_1 it faces demand schedule *dd'*. Below this price it faces demand curve *DD'*, because from assumption (3) it believes that rivals will follow any price reduction. Thus the demand curve that the firm believes it faces is the kinked line *dAD'*.

Corresponding to demand curve *dd'* there is the marginal revenue curve MR_d and, similarly, MR_D corresponds to *DD'*. As the firm only faces *dd'* up to output Q_1 then MR_d also only applies for this output range. Above Q_1 the firm operates on *DD'*, and thus MR_D, and so there is a discontinuity in its marginal revenue curve at output Q_1.

In Figure 7.2 only the relevant parts of the demand and marginal revenue curves from Figure 7.1 are shown, together with the firm's MC curve. Below output Q_1 $MR > MC$ and above Q_1 $MC > MR$, thus Q_1 must be the profit maximising output. It can now be seen why this theory predicts price stability. If cost conditions alter and cause the MC curve to move, then as long as it only moves within the range MC_1 to MC_2 in Figure 7.3 the firm will keep price at P_1 (assuming that AC is low enough to allow sufficient profits for the firm to stay in business). A shift in the market demand would also leave price unchanged at P_1 if it still meant that MC passed through the discontinuous section of the MR schedule.

Although this theory can explain why price may remain stable when costs or market demand change within certain limits, what it cannot do is predict what will happen when the cost or demand changes exceed these limits and price does start to move. For example, if costs increased so that marginal cost

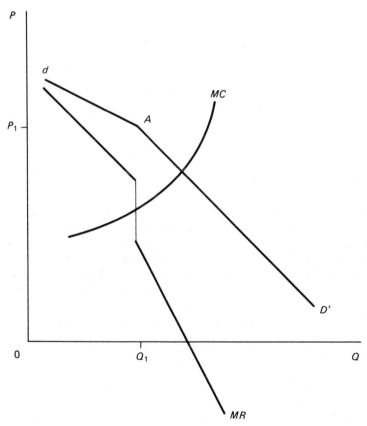

FIGURE 7.2   Price stability and the kinked demand curve

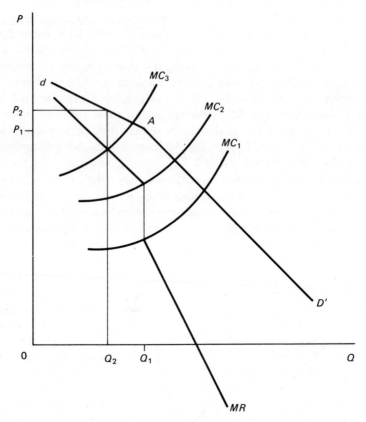

FIGURE 7.3   Price changes and the kinked demand curve

rose to MC_3 in Figure 7.3 then the profit maximising output would be Q_2 and the firm would charge price P_2. However, if this firm increased its price the amount that rival firms could sell at any given price would increase, that is, their demand curves would shift outward. This in turn might cause these rivals to alter their prices if these shifts in their demand meant that their MC schedules no longer went through the discontinuous sections of their MR schedules. This would then cause the demand curve facing the original firm to shift and so cause it to alter price again, with possible further repercussions for other firms. What cannot be predicted, however, is where, or if, a new equilibrium price will eventually be achieved.

One may ask, 'Doesn't the chain of events described above contradict the assumption that rivals do not follow price increases?' The answer to this question is 'No'. Although it is assumed that firms *believe* that rivals will not follow any price increases, this does not necessarily mean that price rises will not actually be followed. Similarly, not all price reductions will be matched, although firms *believe* that they will be. Thus although the kinked demand curve theory can predict why an established price is likely to remain stable it cannot predict:

1.   what the initial equilibrium price will be, and
2.   how price will alter if the stability conditions are broken.

Despite these shortcomings this theory was thought by some to be an adequate explanation of firms' behaviour during the 1930s depression. The assumption that firms matched price cuts but not price rises was a realistic assessment of the situation in many markets at that time. However, in a more buoyant economic situation these assumptions are not likely to hold. Efroymson,[5] in fact, suggested that in boom conditions, when firms can sell everything they produce, they will believe that rivals will follow price increases and will not follow price reductions. He then showed how these assumptions would lead to a 'reverse kinked demand curve'.

In an empirical study, Stigler[6] observed that in a number of oligopolistic industries firms tended to match each others' price increases. It has been suggested that this evidence refutes the kinked demand curve explanation of oligopolies. However, these findings do not contradict the predictions of the kinked demand curve theory, only the assumptions about the way firms believe their rivals will react to price changes. The only predictions that the theory makes are that, within certain limits, cost and market demand changes will not cause price to alter. The theory does not say anything about what will happen when price does actually change and so the observation that firms changed their prices together neither contradicts nor provides any support for the kinked demand curve theory. A test of the predictions of the theory might involve, for example, an observation of a series of cost changes to see whether or not they induced any changes in price.

GAME THEORY

The theory of games, first set out by von Neumann and Morgenstern,[7] has been used by sociologists, political scientists and psychologists, as well as economists, to explain certain patterns of behaviour. Its application to

5.   C. W. Efroymson, 'The Kinked Oligopoly Curve Reconsidered', *Quarterly Journal of Economics*, vol. 69 (1954), pp. 119–36.
6.   G. J. Stigler, 'The Kinky Oligopoly Demand Curve and Rigid Prices', *Journal of Political Economy*, vol. 55 (1947), pp. 432–49.
7.   J. von Neumann and O. Morgenstern, *Theory of Games and Economic Behavior* (N. J.: Princeton University Press, 1953).

oligopoly is somewhat limited, however. Game theory is a method of trying to explain the behaviour of rival parties (the 'players') involved in decision-making situations. It is assumed that players have a finite number of possible courses of action, or strategies, open to them and will choose the strategy, or combination of strategies, that will benefit them best, given certain assumptions about the way rivals react. It is also assumed that each player knows what the outcome of each possible strategy will be for any given retaliatory strategy played by its rival(s).

The basic assumption about the behaviour of rivals is that each player believes that whichever strategy it chooses then its rivals will always chose the worst possible retaliatory strategy (from the original firm's viewpoint). Firms then choose the strategy that will yield the 'least worse' outcome, given this pessimistic assumption about how rivals will react.

Applied to oligopoly, the 'players' are the rival firms. Assume that an oligopoly consists of two firms, A and B (in other words, a duopoly) competing for sales in a market of given size. Firm A has three possible marketing strategies, A_1, A_2 and A_3, and firm B has the four strategies B_1, B_2, B_3 and B_4. These strategies may be a mix of advertising, special promotion schemes, or any other marketing methods. The outcomes of these different strategies, in terms of percentage share of the given market, are shown in Table 7.1. This is a pay-off table to firm A, that is, it shows the percentage of the market that A gets. (One could just as easily have drawn up the pay-off table to B by subtracting these numbers from 100.) This particular example is a zero-sum game, where what one player loses the other gains. If certain combinations of strategies caused the size of the whole market to change then it would be a non zero-sum game, and would necessitate the use of two separate pay-off tables for the two players.

It is assumed that A believes that B will always take the worst possible retaliatory action from A's viewpoint, and vice versa. Thus A thinks that if

TABLE 7.1   A zero-sum game with a saddle point

(Pay-off table for A)

		B's strategies				row min	
		B_1	B_2	B_3	B_4		
	A_1	50	90	18	25	18	← maximin
A's	A_2	27	5	9	95	5	
strategies	A_3	64	30	12	20	12	
	column max	64	90	18	95		

↑
minimax

it chooses strategy A_1 then B will respond with B_3. Similarly, strategy A_2 will be met with B_2, and A_3 with B_3. Firm A then looks at these minimum expected pay-offs, which are shown in the column headed 'row min', and chooses the strategy that yields the best of these pessimistically expected outcomes, known as the 'maximin'. In this example this means that A will choose strategy A_1. Whatever B then does, A can be assured of a market share of at least 18 per cent. To explain B's behaviour it must be remembered that in this zero-sum game the higher the figure in Table 7.1 the worse off B is, because its market share is 100 per cent minus A's share. Thus firm B believes that if it chooses strategy B_1 then A will respond with A_3. The expected outcomes for the other strategies open to B are shown in the row labelled 'column max'. Firm B will then choose the strategy that corresponds to the smallest of these, known as the 'minimax', which in this case is B_3. This game has an equilibrium or 'saddle point' because the maximin equals the minimax. If A chooses A_1 and B chooses B_3 then the market shares are 18 and 82 per cent, respectively, and neither firm can better its situation by changing to another strategy (assuming that the other player does not change its strategy).

Not all games, however, have a unique equilibrium. For example, in the game shown in Table 7.2 the maximin is 40, corresponding to strategy A_1, and the minimax is 50, corresponding to B_1. The combination of strategies A_1 and B_1 is not an equilibrium, though, because the maximin does not equal the minimax. If A plays A_1 then it would pay B to shift to B_2. A would then shift to A_2 and then B would go back to B_1. It would then pay A to return to the original strategy A_1, and so the same cycle of strategy switching would be repeated continually without ever settling at an equilibrium.

Games without a unique saddle point do have a solution, though, if mixed strategies are allowed. A mixed strategy means that a number of strategies are played with different probabilities, the total of the probabilities always

TABLE 7.2   **A zero-sum game without a saddle point**

		(Pay-off table for A)			
		B's strategies			
		B_1	B_2	row min	
A's	A_1	50	40	40	← maximin
strategies	A_2	30	60	30	
	column max	50	60		
		↑			
		minimax			

summing to one. For example, the mixed strategy solution[8] for the example in Table 7.2 is:

A plays A_1 with probability 0.75 and A_2 with probability 0.25

B plays B_1 with probability 0.5 and B_2 with probability 0.5

Although mathematically a game without a saddle point can be solved in terms of mixed strategies the applicability of this type of solution to oligopoly has been questioned. In the case of one-off business decisions, how many managers would resort to tossing a coin, which is what B's strategy amounts to in this example? In situations where the strategy decision is repeated a number of times, for example, on a weekly basis, then a firm could vary the frequency with which it plays different strategies so that over a period of time each strategy is played with a given probability. However over time the conditions under which the game is played can alter and a new pattern of possible outcomes may necessitate a new solution.

There also exist other criticisms of the applicability of game theory to economics. When a game is a non-constant sum the theory suggests that collusion may take place, but not how any mutual gains might be shared out. When there are more than two players, as is often the case in oligopolistic markets, game theory suggests that coalitions will be formed, but it is not able to predict which players will join forces.

The basic assumption of pessimism has also been challenged. Some people would argue that the essence of a dynamic business strategy is to take some risky decisions that have a chance of potentially high pay-offs. The assumption that firms have a finite number of strategies with all possible outcomes known can also be said to be unrealistic. However a theory is judged by the usefulness of its predictions, not the realism of its assumptions, and even though not all the assumptions of game theory may hold true it can give a useful insight into certain patterns of behaviour.

COLLUSION

In some industries firms may realise that, instead of competing against each other, their interests may be better served by colluding together. Collusion may be *explicit*, when firms formally agree on how they will operate together as a cartel, or *implicit*, when managers have informal agreements on price-fixing and other marketing strategies. Both forms of collusion are usually illegal in

---

8.   See Chapter 18 of W. J. Baumol, *Economic Theory and Operations Analysis*, 4th edn (Englewood Cliffs, N. J.: Prentice-Hall, 1977).

the United Kingdom. The 1956 Restrictive Trade Practices Act outlawed formal cartels and the 1968 Restrictive Trade Practices Act forbade informal agreements based on circulated information on each other's pricing policy. Both pieces of legislation, however, allowed for certain exceptional cases where there were other factors that outweighed the detrimental effect of collusion on the public interest.

Collusion may be *perfect* or *imperfect*. Perfect collusion is most likely to occur in formal cartels and involves the careful estimation of the joint profit maximising price. Imperfect collusion is most likely to occur in implicit informal price-fixing agreements and is, basically, anything less than perfect collusion. Although an economic model can be constructed that predicts what will happen under perfect collusion, the same cannot be done for the case of imperfect collusion. All that can be said is that the market will be closer to the situation predicted by the perfect collusion model the greater the degree of collusion. Numerous factors will affect the degree of collusion, many of which will be specific to particular industries. In general, though, the degree of collusion is likely to be affected, *ceteris paribus*, by:

1. The number of firms. The smaller the number of firms the easier it becomes to keep track of what rivals are doing, and to build up an element of trust, and so collusion will be more likely.
2. The degree of similarity between firms. The more similar firms are with respect to output levels, production costs and so on, the more likely they are to collude.
3. Age of the industry. One is more likely to find collusion in older established industries where managers have had time to learn about their rivals and how the market operates than in industries which have just been set up and where everyone is still learning about these matters.

Perfect collusion – cartels

The Two-Firm Cartel

The model of a two-firm cartel can also be used to explain the profit maximising behaviour of a two-plant monopoly. Assume that two firms in a cartel (or the two plants of a monopoly) have the two marginal cost schedules MC_1 and MC_2 shown in Figure 7.4. The market demand and marginal revenue curves are D and MR, respectively. The aggregate marginal cost curve MC_T is found by summing MC_1 and MC_2 horizontally (in an analogous manner to the price discrimination model where the marginal revenue curves are summed horizontally). The rationale for this is that, in order to minimise costs, production should be allocated so that the marginal cost of an extra unit of output is the same for both firms. If it were not, then it would be

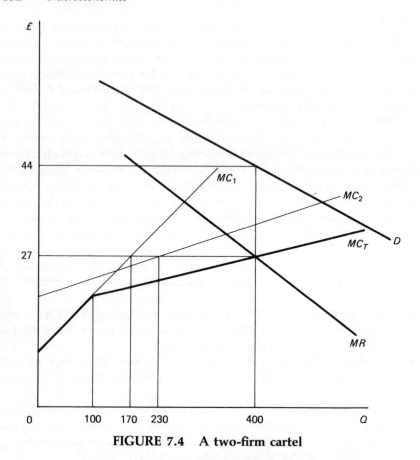

FIGURE 7.4   A two-firm cartel

possible to reallocate the production of any given amount and reduce the total cost of production.

In this example, up to an output of 100 units it is cheapest for firm 1 to produce everything. When production by firm 1 exceeds 100 units, though, the marginal cost of any extra units exceeds the marginal cost of the first few units produced by firm 2. Therefore, above a total output of 100 units, costs are kept to a minimum by sharing output between the two firms on the principle that MC_1 equals MC_2.

The profit maximising output is where MC_T equals MR, which is 400 units, and the corresponding price of £44 can then be read off the demand curve. To find out how this total production of 400 units is shared between the two firms, the value of MC_T where it intersects the MR schedule is found, namely, £27. Given that

$$MC_1 = MC_2 = MC_T$$

then production by firm 1 is that output that corresponds to a marginal cost of £27, that is, 170 units. Similarly, production by firm 2, when MC_2 is £27, is 230 units. As MC_T is by definition the horizontal sum of MC_1 and MC_2 then the outputs for the two individual firms found by this method must add up to the total output determined where MC_T equals MR.

Profit-Sharing

Up to this point the analysis of a two-firm cartel and a two-plant monopoly is the same. If the marginal cost curves in Figure 7.4 represented the two plants of a single monopoly producer then this would be the equilibrium profit maximising situation and total profit could be calculated from average cost (not shown here for the sake of clarity).

With a two-firm cartel, however, the problem of how to share out total profit still remains. Although the model explains how maximum total profits can be achieved it does not say how they are to be shared out between the firms. In practice firms usually only receive the profits that they earn from their own production, which could cause problems in situations such as that illustrated in the example above. If initially both firms had, say, both been producing the same output level, then firm 1 would not be likely to agree to reduce its output so that firm 2 could produce more unless it was recompensed in some way. It is difficult in practice, though, to arrange a system of transferring profits from more cost-effective firms to those who have a lower production quota and hence earn lower profits. Because of this difficulty, actual cartels usually allocate production quotas which diverge from the ideal joint profit maximising quotas derived in the above model and each firm receives only the profit from its own production.

The following are some common methods of allocating quotas:

1. According to pre-cartel market share.
2. By geographical area.
3. By non-price competition; that is, firms agree on a common price and then compete for sales through advertising, product design and so on.

The Multi-firm Cartel and Inherent Instability

Even if the problem of profit-sharing could be overcome (for example, if all firms had similar production costs and output was allocated equally) other problems of organising and policing a cartel would still remain. These problems increase with the number of firms involved and can be illustrated with the case of a large multi-firm cartel. Assume that 100 firms all have cost curves as shown in Figure 7.5(b) and that initially the market price is £23 and they all produce 270 units and make zero economic profit. This is similar to the case of perfect competition except that no new entry is allowed. The industry supply curve S in Figure 7.5(a) is, as in perfect competition, the horizontal summation of the individual firms' marginal cost curves. (It is assumed that there is no adjustment along the LAC curve.) If these 100 firms band together to form a cartel then the same principles as in the previous example are used to determine the joint profit maximising price and output. The horizontally summed MC curve (that is, S) cuts MR at an output of 16 000 units, which can be sold at a price of £35. If this total output is allocated equally to the 100 firms in the industry then each will be given a production quota of 160 units and will face average costs of £29. Thus each firm will make a profit of

$$(£35 - £29) \times 160 = £960,$$

clearly an improvement on the pre-cartel situation of zero profit.

Although they are better off than before, the firms now have an incentive to exceed their allocated quota in the pursuit of even greater profits. If all other firms kept to their production quotas then one individual firm considering exceeding its quota would perceive its demand curve as a horizontal line at the price of £35. As this would also be its perceived marginal revenue curve this firm would therefore wish to increase production to 380 units, where MC equals £35, and so increase its profits to £3420, given the new AC of £26. One firm might possibly manage to do this, but if more firms exceeded

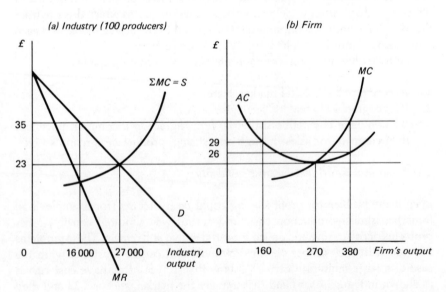

FIGURE 7.5   **A multi-firm cartel**

their quotas the industry supply curve would start to change from the vertical line at 16 000 units (which is what the quota system would mean) back towards its original position, thus causing price to fall. When they see the price fall eroding their profits, the rest of the firms will see no point in maintaining their quotas and eventually price will return to its original level and the cartel will be destroyed.

This inherent instability of cartels has meant that even where they have not been illegal they have usually not operated successfully for any length of time. Only cartels that have been able to enforce strict policing of member producers have had much success in the long term. A crucial factor in determining a cartel's success is the ability to observe what each firm is producing. A cartel will also have a greater chance of success if the following obtain:

1. There are a small number of firms in involved.
2. The product has an inelastic demand. If demand was very elastic there would not be much scope for increasing profits through price increases.
3. New entrants are barred. If they were not then extra profits would soon be eroded by new firms.
4. All or most of the major producers of the good join the cartel. If they do not then customers may buy from non-cartel members at a lower price.

The classic example of a successful cartel has been OPEC, where most of the above conditions are satisfied. However, the dramatic fall in oil prices in 1986 illustrates how even OPEC is susceptible to the problems of inherent instability that are faced by all cartels.

PRICE LEADERSHIP

If is often observed in oligopolistic industries that when one firm announces a price rise other firms soon follow. This does not necessarily mean that a cartel of some description is operating, although it is evidence that firms are aware of their interdependence. There are several forms that price leadership may take and some of these are described below.

The barometer firm

By convention, historical accident, experience or for some other reason, in certain industries one firm leads with price changes and then the others follow. This 'barometer firm' need not be the largest or most powerful firm in the industry. It may simply have proved to be a good indicator of market conditions in the past. If everyone follows the lead of this barometer firm when cost or demand conditions alter then price adjusts smoothly and there is not the risk of a damaging price war. The new price may not necessarily be the absolute optimum for maximum profits, but the removal of uncertainty and the threat of a price war every time price changes may compensate for this.

The low-cost firm

A firm which can produce at lower average cost than its rivals may wish to sell at a lower price than these rivals might choose. The low-cost firm has the capability of reducing price far enough to drive rivals out of business and it may use the threat of doing this to coerce the other firms into accepting the price that it wants. Anti-monopoly legislation may limit the extent to which it could actually drive out its competitors, however.

The dominant firm

This is really an extreme case of the low cost firm. In the dominant firm model it is assumed that there is one large firm and a number of smaller ones. The dominant firm decides the market price but allows the smaller firms to sell as much as they want to at this price. The small firms behave effectively as firms in a perfectly competitive market, except that new entry is not allowed. Anti-monopoly legislation may be the reason why the dominant firm does not drive the smaller rivals out of business completely. This model is illustrated in Figure 7.6.

Market demand is DD', the marginal cost curve for the dominant firm is MC and the small firms' supply curve is S. Above a price of £30 the small firms would wish to supply more than is demanded and the dominant firm would not be able to sell anything. Below £30 the small firms would not supply enough to meet the market demand, and below £10 they would not wish to supply anything. The dominant firm therefore faces the demand curve $dd'D'$, that is, between the prices of £30 and £10 it faces the market demand less the supply of the small firms and below £10 it simply faces the market demand. Corresponding to the demand curve dd' the dominant firm faces marginal revenue curve MR_d. It will maximise profits when MR_d equals MC, which occurs at an output of 320 units, and will set a price of £18. At this price the small firms will wish to supply 112 units and market demand will be 432 units. By definition the amount the dominant firm sells plus the quantity supplied by the small firms equals the market demand.

ENTRY-LIMITING PRICING

The oligopoly models considered so far look at the way existing firms may behave when there is no new entry into the industry. In the long-run, however,

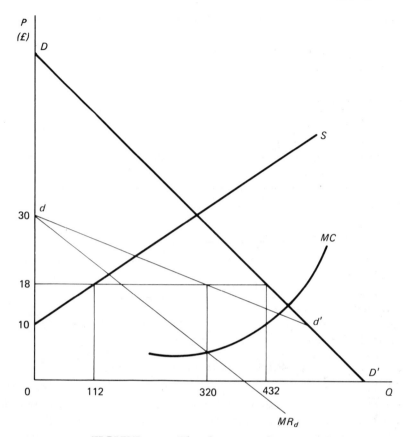

FIGURE 7.6   The dominant firm model

new firms may wish to enter and share any profits that are being made. In some oligopolies barriers to entry, such as those described in Chapter 6 with respect to monopoly, may completely block any new entry. In other industries, though, the barriers to entry may not be completely insurmountable and the possibility of new entry will depend on the pricing strategy adopted by existing firms, particularly when the main barrier to entry is economies of scale.

In Figure 7.7 it is assumed that existing firms have long-run average costs of LAC_E and that marginal cost is a constant at MC_E. If these existing firms collude to maximise joint profits then the optimum price is P_M. However, if the average production costs of a potential new entrant are as shown by LAC_N then a price of P_M will allow it to operate at a profit and thus break into the industry.

Should a new entrant manage to break into the industry it is not certain what the other firms will then do. They may possibly try a last ditch attempt

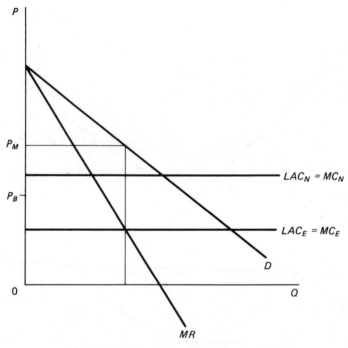

FIGURE 7.7   Entry limiting pricing

at forcing it out of business by price reductions. However, if the new firm has established itself and started to exploit economies of scale the other firms may come to the conclusion that a price war to drive the new entrant out will prove fruitless and will only lose them profits. If this is the case they may decide that they may as well accept it into the 'club' and negotiate a new joint profit maximising price. If, however, there are further potential new entrants the new price may be set at a level thought sufficient to deter their entry. Alternatively, the existing firms may permanently keep price below P_M, at P_B say, in order to block any new entry; in other words, short-run profits are sacrificed for future profits.

In practice the situation may not be as clear-cut as the above analysis suggests. It is not likely that there will be one single crucial price above which new entry will take place and below which it will not. Even if there was such a price, the existing firms would not necessarily know exactly what it was, and any entry-limiting pricing strategy would involve a certain amount of guesswork about potential competitors' production costs. If there are several potential new entrants the entry-limiting price may vary for each one. In effect then, existing firms are faced with a choice that involves a trade-off between current and future profits. The higher the price the more likely it is that new entry will take place. Their choice is thus between different time paths of profits, such as those shown in Figure 7.8. If a high price is initially chosen profits will follow path *AA'*, that is to say, high initially but soon eroded by new entry. If a lower initial price is chosen new entry will not be so rapid and path *BB'* will be followed. These are just two out of many different possible profit time paths, and the choice between them will depend on the time preferences of the firms involved.

Spence[9] has pointed out that excess capacity contributes to existing firms' ability to keep out new entrants. If a new entrant does initially break into the industry then the original firms will only be able to force it out by price reductions if they can actually produce enough to meet the extra demand that there will be at a lower price. Thus they must have the excess production capacity to do this, and Spence suggests that the excess capacity itself is a deterrent to potential new entrants.

Another possible entry-limiting strategy is the 'rationality of irrationality'. A new entrant is less likely to set up business in an industry if it thinks that existing firms are likely to start an all-out price war to drive it out. Such a price war could be very damaging to the profits of existing firms and so they would not wish to embark on such a strategy lightly. However, if a potential

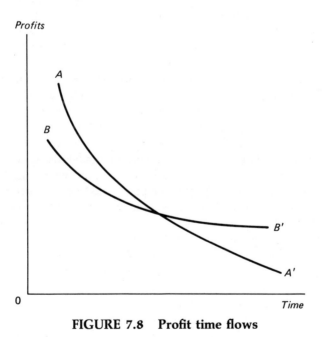

FIGURE 7.8   Profit time flows

9.   M. Spence, 'Entry, investment and oligopolistic pricing', *Bell Journal of Economics*, vol. 8, no. 2 (Autumn 1977), pp. 534–44.

new entrant believes that existing firms are reckless enough to risk their own profits in a price war then it may be deterred from attempting entry. Thus, if existing firms can make potential entrants believe that they are irrational enough to risk losing their own profits, perhaps by making the occasional threatening price cut, the potential entrant may be frightened off and the existing firms keep their profits. Hence the 'rationality of irrationality'.

Non-price competition

The use of advertising and other forms of non-price competition to create economies of scale, and hence make new entry difficult, is an important form of entry-deterring behaviour. One example is the washing powder industry.[10] Two firms, Proctor & Gamble and Unilever, produce most of the brands of washing powder on sale in the United Kingdom and vast amounts of money are spent advertising their different brands.

The principles behind this strategy can be explained with a fictitious example. Suppose that long-run average costs for the production of washing powder are as shown by LAC_P in Figure 7.9. This LAC schedule starts to flatten out at approximately 500 000 packets per year and so a new entrant able to produce this quantity might be able to compete on costs with larger established producers selling 2 500 000 packets per year. With this relatively easy new entry of competitors the existing firms would soon see their profits disappearing if they did not try to stop this happening by adopting some form of entry-limiting strategy.

Assume that the established firms spend £500 000 per annum on advertising and that any new entrant would have to spend a similar amount. (In fact in practice the cumulative effect of advertising usually means that new entrants have to spend more than existing firms.) Although total advertising costs are the same for all firms the average advertising cost curve will be AC_A, giving larger firms an advantage through lower average advertising costs. A new entrant producing only 500 000 packets per year would face average advertising cost of £1.00 per packet compared with the 20 pence per packet for the 2 500 000 packets per year producers. This strategy then creates artificial economies of scale and the total average cost curve becomes LAC_T. If the price per packet is 75p then the smaller new entrant facing average advertising costs of £1, plus production costs, cannot operate at profit. The larger established producers, however, still make 13 pence a packet profit. This is lower than the 33 pence a packet they might make at this price without the expense of the advertising campaign but this return would not be earned for very long because it would allow new entry.

10.   See pp. 141–53 of R. W. Shaw and C. J. Sutton, *Industry and Competition: Industrial Case Studies* (London: Macmillan, 1976).

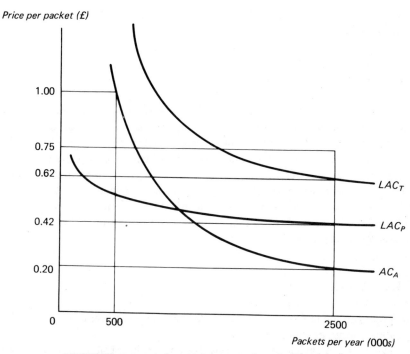

FIGURE 7.9   Advertising as a barrier to entry

Multiple branding

Alongside their heavy advertising campaigns, the producers of goods such as washing powder, toothpaste and chocolate bars produce a range of brands of basically the same product. This also has the effect of deterring new entrants who only have the production facilities to manufacture one brand. With goods that are bought on a fairly frequent basis a percentage of consumers buying the good in a given time period will switch brands. Although from the consumer's viewpoint the choice of the new brand is not always random, from the seller's viewpoint it is useful to assume that these 'floating customers' will choose from the other brands available on their supermarket shelves with equal probability when there is not a significant difference between the price or quality of different brands. Thus, if there are ten brands on display, a firm that produces five of them will have five times the chance of having its product bought as a firm that only has one brand on display. For each time period there are also a number of new consumers buying the product for the first time and again the firm with the largest number of brands available is more likely to get their custom. For example, at the start of every academic year there are a number of students who have just moved away from home and who for the first time will have to decide which brand of washing powder to buy.

CONCLUSION

As was said in the introduction to this chapter, there is no one theory of oligopoly. One has to choose the most appropriate theory, or theories, to explain and predict behaviour in a given industry. Each of the models considered in this chapter introduces a different aspect of possible behaviour, whereas in reality several forces may be working at the same time and some combination of different theories may be needed. In general one can say that, other things being equal, the fewer the number of firms and the older the industry the more likely it is that collusion will be present. However, there are always exceptions.

QUESTIONS

1. What can the kinked demand curve theory (a) predict, and (b) not predict, about firms' behaviour?
2. Two firms, A and B, have four possible advertising strategies: newspapers, TV, posters, or no advertising. The possible changes in A's profits (in £million) from their current level are given in the pay-off table below. Assume A's gains are B's losses; for example, if A advertises in newspapers and B on TV, then A loses £0.5 million and B gains £0.5 million.

TABLE 7Q.1

		B's strategies			
		Newspapers	TV	Posters	No Adverts
A's strategies	Newspapers	0	−0.5	0	2.5
	TV	1	0	1.5	5
	Posters	2	−2	0	3.5
	No Adverts	−2	−4	−3	0

What combination of strategies does game theory predict?

3. What conditions are necessary for a cartel to operate successfully? How do these apply to the case of OPEC?

4. Assume that it is only possible to have one size of plant and there are 100 firms in an industry, all with identical cost conditions. Each faces the marginal cost schedule $MC = 1.5 + 0.05q$ where MC is marginal cost (in £) and q is the firm's output. What would the equilibrium price (P) and the quantity produced by each firm be if they acted as firms in perfect competition (but with no new entry) and the market demand (Q_d) was given by the relationship below?

$$Q_d = 5000 - 1000P.$$

If they formed a cartel what would be the joint profit maximising price and how much would each firm produce assuming that they split the industry output equally? Under these cartel arrangements, what output would one firm be tempted to produce if it knew it could exceed its quota without the others' knowledge?

5. One firm is dominant in an industry and lets all of the other firms, which are much smaller, sell all that they want at the existing price. In other words, the smaller firms act as in perfect competition and the dominant firm sets the price, which the others accept. The industry demand is such that $P = 2100 - Q$ where P is the product's price and Q is total market demand.

The amount supplied by the smaller firms is

$$Qs = 0.5P.$$

The marginal cost curve of the dominant firm is $MC = Q_d$, where Q_d is its own output.

What will the price be?

How much will the dominant firm produce, and how much will the industry as a whole produce?

6. What is the relevance of the presence of excess production capacity for a group of oligopolists attempting to keep out new entrants?

CHAPTER 8

Monopolistic competition and contestable markets

This chapter covers two different approaches to the prediction of firms' prices and output: the theory of monopolistic competition and the theory of contestable markets. The theory of monopolistic competition considers a market structure that lies between the limiting cases of monopoly and perfect competition, the main feature distinguishing it from perfect competition being product differentiation. The theory of contestable markets tries to explain how output is determined by the cost structure of the industry and the pricing behaviour of firms, with particular emphasis being placed on the effect that potential new entrants may have. Its application is not restricted to any particular market structure. At the end of this chapter there is a table that summarises the main features of the different types of market that have been considered in Chapters 5 to 8.

MONOPOLISTIC COMPETITION

The theory of monopolistic competition is based on the ideas originally set out by Chamberlin,[1] and assumes that the following features are present in an industry.

1. Product differentiation. Each firm produces a product that differs in some way from competitors' products, for example, shoes, haircuts, or retailing of petrol (where the location of the filling station may cause the

---

1. E. H. Chamberlin, *The Economics of Monopolistic Competition*, 6th edn (Cambridge, Mass.: Harvard University Press, 1950) (first edition published in 1933).

differentiation). Since the products are differentiated, some customers may be prepared to pay a higher price if they prefer one particular firm's product to similar substitutes. Thus a price rise by one firm will not automatically reduce sales to zero, as in perfect competition. This means that a firm will face a downward sloping demand curve, although it may still be fairly elastic.

The differences in the product may be real or illusory. 'Real' differences are actual physical differences in the goods or services, such as quality, style, strength, location. 'Illusory' differences are entirely (or nearly so) created in consumers' minds by advertising and other marketing techniques. Some products sold by different firms are basically the same, apart from packaging and other cosmetic differences, but some consumers are convinced that there is some actual differentiation. However, for the purposes of the theory it does not matter whether the differentiation is real or illusory. If consumers behave as if they think there is a difference then that is sufficient.

2. Many sellers. The number of firms is sufficiently large for the actions of one individual firm to have an insignificant effect on the sales of the other firms.

3. Free entry and exit. New firms are free to enter if they think it will be profitable and existing firms can leave if profits are insufficient.

4. Similar cost and demand conditions. This assumption allows the behaviour of a typical firm in the industry to be analysed and the predictions then applied to other firms in the market. It can be questioned, however. If firms produce differentiated products then costs and demand might also be assumed to be different.

5. Firms operate on the assumption that when they change their prices the prices of other firms do not alter.

The product group

If all firms produce a different product then there is no clear-cut definition of the industry. The theory of monopolistic competition therefore assumes that a 'product group' can be defined, which is a group of producers of goods that are close substitutes. Exactly what may be considered a 'close' substitute cannot be precisely defined and when analysing actual markets a sensible cut-off point has to be defined, based on the nature of the market. For example, the market for footwear can be fairly clearly defined but if it is subdivided then the substitutability of different types of footwear can make it more difficult to define a product group. Leather fashion shoes can be substituted to an extent by synthetic material casual shoes, or sandals, or trainers and so on.

Because firms' products are differentiated it is not possible to analyse aggregate behaviour of the product group. Quantities of different goods cannot be added together and measured on the same axis and similarly there is no common price. The theory therefore explains the behaviour of a typical firm.

Price determination

From assumption (5) above, it follows that each firm will perceive that its demand curve is more elastic than it really is. Consider a firm that is operating at point A in Figure 8.1. It believes that if it tries to gain more sales by lowering its price then other firms will keep their prices constant and so quantity demanded will be shown by the demand schedule d_1. However, because each firm is assumed to face similar cost and demand conditions, if one firm considers it worthwhile to lower price then the rest will too. Note that this is not a retaliatory price change by other firms. (There are assumed to be a large number of firms so that price changes by one individual firm will not significantly affect the sales of others.)

If all firms lower price together then the actual demand schedule will be more inelastic than d_1, and is shown by D_1. Thus, if for example, a firm undertakes a price reduction that it thinks will take it from point A to point B it will, in fact, end up at C. After the move along D_1 to C the firm will, again, believe that it has a more elastic demand schedule which this time is d_1'. Thus every

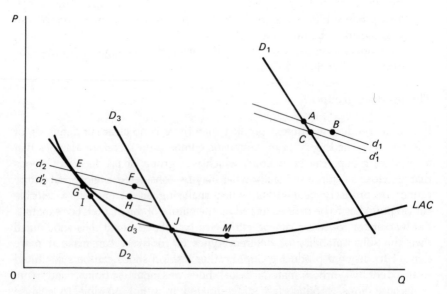

FIGURE 8.1   Price and output determination

time the firm changes price it only moves along D_1 although it believes that it faces more elastic demand schedules, such as d_1 and d'_1.

If a firm is assumed to be initially operating at the price and output represented by point A in Figure 8.1 then its profits will be greater than zero because price is greater than average cost. One of the assumptions of this model is that there is free entry and exit and so these profits will attract new entrants into the industry. If more competitors enter the industry then at any given price each individual firm will be able to sell less than before, even though there is product differentiation. This means that the effective demand schedule will move to the left, say from D_1 to D_2. At point E on D_2 zero profits are made and so there will be no further new entry. If it were not for firms' misconceptions about their demand schedules then E would also be an equilibrium.

A firm at point E will believe that it faces the demand schedule d_2. It will also think that it can improve on this zero profit situation by moving to point F where price will exceed average cost. However, if it lowers price accordingly all that happens is that it moves along D_2 to G, and consequently makes a loss because price is below average cost. It may still think that it can rescue the situation by moving along d'_2 to H where, again, it appears profits can be made. This merely results in a movement to I, though, and the firm's losses are even greater than before. Further similar attempts to make profits by reducing price will also fail and, sooner or later, firms will leave the industry because they cannot perpetually keep running up losses. This will cause the demand schedule facing an individual firm to shift to the right, to D_3 for example.

Eventually the combined effects of price changes and entry and exit will lead to the establishment of a long-run equilibrium at point J. Zero profits are made and so there is no incentive for any further new entry or exit. Also, as the perceived demand schedule d_3 is tangent to the LAC curve at this point, firms believe that if they try to decrease or increase price they will make a loss and will therefore not wish to alter price.

Excess capacity

The main prediction of the theory of monopolistic competition is that firms will operate under conditions of excess capacity, which means that they will produce below the output level at which average costs are at a minimum. Because each firm's perceived demand curve slopes down from left to right, in long-run equilibrium this demand schedule will be tangent to the LAC curve to the left of its minimum point. This excess capacity can be split into two components, as shown in Figure 8.2. If the equilibrium output is Q_1 then Q_0Q^* is the excess capacity due to operating a sub-optimal size of plant and

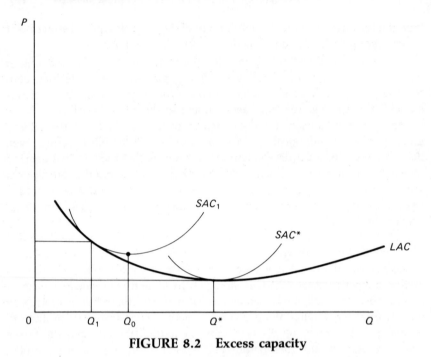

FIGURE 8.2   Excess capacity

Q_1Q_0 is the excess capacity due to operating this plant below its optimal capacity.

The predicted excess capacity is easily observable in the different branches of retailing which could be considered examples of monopolistic competition, that is, where the product group is made up of the retail outlets rather than manufacturers of the goods sold. For example, many shoe shops or petrol stations could serve more customers without expanding their premises.

Product choice

In perfect competition in long-run equilibrium price is equal to the value of average cost at the minimum point on the *LAC* curve, but in monopolistic competition price will be higher than this because equilibrium is to the left of the minimum point of the *LAC* curve. Chamberlin suggested that this relatively higher price was a 'sort of ideal' because in a monopolistically competitive industry for this higher price consumers get a greater choice than they would in perfect competition, where every firm is assumed to produce an identical product. This, of course, is a value-judgement and cannot be proved one way or the other. Opinions will differ among consumers as to whether they think greater variety of choice would justify a higher price for a given type of product. Their opinion will be influenced by the size of this price differential as well as their preferences for particular varieties of the good. In some cases where monopolistic competition results in a very wide range of choice one could argue that this may make it more difficult for consumers to use all the available information to make the choice that best satisfies their needs.

Another aspect of monopolistic competition that can be taken into account in this debate is the fact that in some cases advertising and other costs involved in differentiating the product will shift firms' average total cost curves upwards, as shown in Figure 8.3. The curve LAC_0 shows the average cost of producing a particular good excluding the cost of the advertising and marketing that is necessary to differentiate it from other firms' products, whereas LAC_1 includes these additional costs. In perfect competition there is usually assumed to be no advertising and marketing expenditure and so price would be determined at the equilibrium point B. The monopolistically competitive equilibrium at A corresponds to a price, P_1, which is relatively higher than the perfectly competitive price P_0, not just because it is not at the minimum point of LAC_1, but also because LAC_1 lies above LAC_0. This means that some of the higher price that the consumer pays in monopolistic competition may just go on more advertising rather than increased variety of choice but, again, one cannot prove that this is necessarily a good or a bad thing.

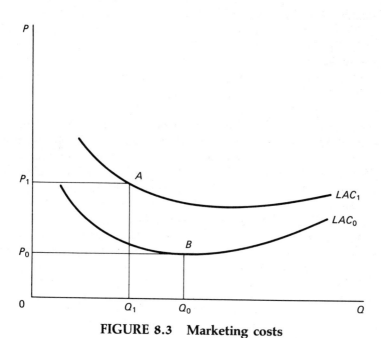

FIGURE 8.3   Marketing costs

CONTESTABLE MARKETS

The theory of contestable markets is a relatively recent development in microeconomics, stemming from work by Baumol.[2] Its central theme is the effect of potential new entrants on price and output decisions, but it is not simply another theory of entry-limiting pricing under oligopoly and it can be applied to other market structures.

A contestable market is defined as one in which entry is free and exit is costless. Free entry means that new entrants can set up production and operate with the same cost structure as existing firms and without any disadvantage with respect to consumers' product preferences. Costless exit means that firms leaving the industry can get back the money they have invested in the necessary production facilities, less an amount for depreciation during the period of production, by selling all their capital. A firm that only operates in the industry for a short time period will, therefore, not suffer any cost disadvantage compared with a firm that remains for a relatively long time. This makes contestable markets vulnerable to 'hit and run' entry. If at any time economic profits can be earned in such an industry, even on a temporary basis, new entrants will swiftly seize the opportunity to move in to grab a share and then depart just as quickly when the opportunity to earn these profits disappears. The condition of free entry and exit is also assumed in the theory of perfect competition and so perfectly competitive markets are, by definition, perfectly contestable. The reverse is not true, however. In a contestable market it is possible that there may only be a handful of firms and so the large number of producers condition for perfect competition will not always hold.

There are several predictions that can be made about perfectly contestable markets:

1. In equilibrium profits will be zero. If positive profits were earned this would mean that a new entrant would be able to break into the market. The new entrant would face the same average cost as existing firms, if it produced the same output level, and even if it slightly undercut the original price it would still make economic profits. Free entry will ensure that all economic profit is eroded away.

2. Output will be produced by the most efficient method and firms will operate at the optimum scale of output. If inefficient firms were able to cover their costs and operate in a break-even position then the opportunity would exist for new entrants to make economic profits by selling at the same price but with lower costs due to improved efficiency.

---

2. W. J. Baumol, J. C. Panzar and R. D. Willig, *Contestable Markets and the Theory of Industry Structure* (San Diego: Harcourt Brace Jovanovich, 1982).

3. Price will never be less than marginal cost. If firms were able to break even at a price below marginal cost then a new entrant that produced a slightly lower output than the original firms would face lower average costs and thus be able to make economic profits, even if it slightly undercut the existing price.

4. Price will not be greater than marginal cost when there are two or more sellers. If price is above marginal cost the opportunity for earning economic profits will attract new firms. There will be the opportunity for new entrants to sell one more unit than existing firms and still be able to slightly undercut the previous price, unless the industry was previously a monopoly. The only way that more output can be sold when there was previously only one seller is by moving along the market demand curve. Thus marginal revenue may fall rapidly and wipe out any potential for making profits. However, when there are two or more sellers a new entrant can steal, at least temporarily, sales from existing firms without causing a substantial movement along the market demand curve.

Predictions (3) and (4) together ensure that price will equal marginal cost, unless there is only one seller. The presence of economies of scale can mean that marginal cost pricing will cause losses (see Chapter 12) but evidence suggests that long-run average costs are often L-shaped, or U-shaped with a flat section in the middle. If a firm operates on the flat section of its average cost curve then marginal cost pricing and zero profits will be compatible.

In a contestable market the optimum size of firm and the optimum number of firms in the industry will be determined by market forces. This is an important proposition from a policy viewpoint. Economies of scale in the production process may mean that the most efficient way of satisfying a given market demand is for production to be organised in the hands of a few large oligopolists and that perfect competition will not necessarily be the most efficient market structure (see Chapter 12). Thus any regulations that a government brings in to control monopolies, or near monopolies, in the interests of the consumer will in fact have a negative impact on consumer welfare in a contestable market. Free entry and costless exit keep price equal to marginal cost and ensure that production is organised in the most efficient way. If firms are forced by the government to change the scale of their production, or alter their prices, they will therefore move away from this optimum situation. However, it is also important to remember that the conditions of contestability are not satisfied in every market and so government intervention may still be required to protect the consumer from monopoly exploitation. Baumol suggests that the nearer to a perfectly contestable market an industry becomes the more closely its behaviour will match the predictions outlined above which apply to the limiting case. He also explains how the contestable markets approach can be applied to the

TABLE 8.1 Summary of market structures

Market model	Number of firms	Type product	Control over price	Entry conditions	Non-price competition	Examples
Perfect competition	Very many	Standardised	None	Easy	None	Agricultural products, commodity markets
Monopolistic competition	Many	Differentiated	Some	Relatively easy	Yes	Garment manufacture, shoe shops, petrol stations
Oligopoly	Few	Standard or differentiated	Some, depends on rivals' behaviour	Often difficult	Usual	Petrol, tobacco
Monopoly	One	Unique – no close substitutes	Considerable	Blocked	Sometimes	Gas, telephones, (usually regulated by the government in the UK)

more realistic situation of an industry that produces a multiplicity of commodities.

The theory of contestable markets is unique in that it does not specify the number of firms in the industry and then predict pricing behaviour. Instead it explains how pricing behaviour, together with the cost structure of the production process, can affect the number of firms in the industry.

QUESTIONS

1. If all firms produce different products under monopolistic competition how can an industry be defined?
2. If the assumption of firms' 'myopia' did not apply and all firms realised what their true demand schedule was, then in monopolistic competition each firm's output would be lower than that predicted when this assumption did hold. Explain why.
3. 'The relatively higher prices, compared with perfect competition, predicted by the theory of monopolistic competition can be justified because there is greater variety of choice'. Comment.
4. Why are perfectly contestable markets vulnerable to 'hit and run' entry?
5. Why does the theory of contestable markets predict that markets will always adjust to the most efficient structure?

CHAPTER 9

Consumer theory

Consumer theory attempts to provide an economic model that can explain how the demand for a good will be affected by variables such as its price, consumers' incomes, and the prices of other goods. This chapter analyses more fully some basic principles of demand theory which were presented in Chapter 1. The model of consumer behaviour developed can also be applied to other aspects of individual decision making, such as the labour supply decision.

Since market demand is the sum of individuals' demands, consumer theory is based on an analysis of the consumption decision of individual consumers. It does not, however, involve a psychological probe into the motives underlying consumer purchasing patterns. All it does is to analyse how a rational 'average' consumer would allocate his or her limited income so as to maximise the satisfaction derived from the goods purchased, and then to predict market demand on the assumption that all consumers behave in the same manner as this typical rational consumer. Of course in reality all consumers are different and the same consumer can behave differently at different times. No one actually plans their consumption decisions along the lines suggested by the models of consumer behaviour set out in this chapter.

Although the assumptions made about individual consumer behaviour may be unrealistic, they do allow a model to be developed that can be used to explain aggregate market demand. What must be remembered is that economics can only explain the behaviour of large groups, and the purpose of this analysis is to make predictions about market demand and not individual demand. The more realistic proposition that market demand is made up of the demand of millions of different individuals, about which very little can be said, does not yield any useful predictions.

CARDINAL UTILITY

Some early economists worked on the idea that satisfaction from the consumption of goods and services could be measured in some way. This measurable concept of satisfaction was given the name 'cardinal utility' (the cardinal numbers are 1, 2, 3 and so on). One suggestion was that there could be interpersonal comparison of utility, that is, the comparison of different individuals' satisfaction levels, but as different people get different satisfaction from the same amounts of the same goods such comparisons cannot objectively be made. Cardinal utility theory therefore assumes that there is a separate scale of measurement for each individual. To understand how cardinal utility is related to consumption, consider the example of an individual who consumes several cups of tea each day. Some hypothetical values of the utility she might derive are shown in Table 9.1. Total utility *TU* measures the total satisfaction from all the tea that is drunk. Marginal utility *MU* measures the increase in utility from each additional, or marginal, cup.

This example illustrates the *hypothesis of diminishing marginal utility*, which states that, as an individual consumes increasing amounts of a good, after some point additional units will add less utility than preceding units, that is, after some point *MU* will decline. In the above example this occurs after the second cup of tea. One cannot 'prove' this law, although it does lead to certain predictions about aggregate consumer demand that can be empirically tested. It also seems a reasonable proposition from an introspective viewpoint. Extra units of most goods do not usually give as much pleasure as the first few do.

Note, however, the following:

1. It is assumed that goods are consumed within a given time period. This

TABLE 9.1   Total and marginal cardinal utility

Cups of tea per day	TU	MU
0	0	—
1	20	20
2	45	25
3	60	15
4	70	10
5	75	5
6	72	− 3

excludes the possibility of saving them for consumption in future time periods. Resale is also assumed not to take place.

2. Marginal utility may possibly increase for the first few units of a good that are consumed, but this need not always happen.

3. Marginal utility may eventually become negative but, again, this is not inevitable in all cases.

Measuring marginal utility

Marginal utility can be quantified by relating it to what a consumer is prepared to pay for successive units of a good. People will only buy something if its value to them is *at least as great as* the money that is exchanged for it. If it is not then the transaction will not take place because individuals only voluntarily engage in trade if they gain some benefit from it. Thus if someone buys a loaf of bread for 50p it must give them more satisfaction than the 50p they part company with, otherwise they would not make the purchase. Consider another hypothetical example, this time of a consumer who drinks coffee. Assume that when the price of coffee is 30p a cup this consumer buys 4 cups a day. This means that the fourth cup, and the previous three, must be worth at least 30p to her. It also means that a fifth, and any subsequent cups of coffee, are valued at less than 30p. If the price falls to 20p and she then consumes five cups the fifth cup must be worth somewhere between 20p and 30p. If it is assumed that her valuation of the fifth cup is exactly 20p (and her valuations of the fourth, third, second and first cups are 30p, 40p, 50p, and 60p, respectively) this individual's demand schedule, *D*, can be plotted as shown in Figure 9.1.

A monetary value has been put on the worth to the consumer of each extra unit of the good and so, effectively, a measure of *MU* has been derived. This method of measuring individual consumers' utility can be used as a basis for the consumer surplus approach to the measurement of aggregate consumer welfare. Consumer surplus is defined as the difference between what a consumer would be willing to pay for a unit of a good and the price that is actually paid. The way that this concept can be used to try to assess the relative merits of different economic policies is explained in Chapter 12.

There is also a rather obvious prediction that can be deduced from the relationship between *MU* and willingness to pay for additional units of a good. If *MU* declines as more units of a good are consumed consumers will be willing to pay less for these extra units. Thus individual consumers' demand schedules will slope downwards and consequently so will aggregate demand.

Free goods

In the above example the individual's demand curve cuts the axis at seven

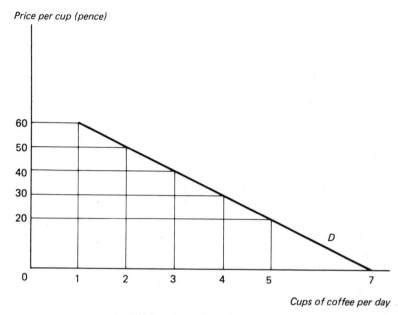

Price per cup (pence)

Cups of coffee per day .

FIGURE 9.1   Individual demand

cups of coffee. Thus, even if coffee was free, no more than seven cups would be consumed because any further cups would have a negative *MU*, that is, they would actually make the consumer worse off. Any free good will only be consumed up to the point where *MU* is zero.

The same principle applies to goods that are not free but where there is a lump sum payment that is not related to the quantity consumed, assuming that the decision to pay this fixed charge has been made; an example is domestic water consumption. Although water metering is possible, most householders still pay a fixed rate for all water authority services. Water is therefore consumed as if it was a free good and is used in quantities and for purposes that might be different if it had to be paid for by the gallon; for example, someone washing their car might not leave their hosepipe on when not absolutely necessary.

The optimum allocation of income

Most goods are not free and so consumers face the resource allocation problem of how to use their limited income to best satisfy their unlimited wants. According to the cardinal utility theory, a consumer achieves the highest possible level of utility when the marginal utility of the last penny spent on each good equals the marginal utility of the last penny spent on every other good that is consumed. The rationale for this rule is best explained with an example.

Assume that a consumer is faced with the limited choice of bread or beer on which to spend her income. If her initial spending pattern is such that the last penny spent on bread adds 10 units of utility and the last penny spent on beer adds 5 units then this is not the optimum method of allocating her income. If marginal utility does not change for small increases or decreases in the amounts of the goods she consumes one more penny spent on bread will add 10 units of utility and one less spenny spent on beer will mean a decrease of 5 units. She will therefore enjoy a net gain of 5 units of utility if she switches one penny of expenditure from beer to bread. If more expenditure is transferred from beer to bread then the marginal utility of bread will fall and the marginal utility of beer will increase, assuming that both *MU* schedules slope downwards. As the prices of the goods do not change, this switching of expenditure from beer to bread will eventually result in equal utility being gained from the last penny spent on each of the goods. When this is achieved the consumer will not be able to achieve a higher level of utility by any further reallocation of expenditure.

Note, however, that in most cases the change in marginal utility as expenditure changes does not simply involve a movement along each good's *MU* curve. This is because the utility derived from one good often depends on the amounts of other goods that are consumed with it. For example, the utility one gets from a bowl of cornflakes will alter if one also has a portion of milk to consume with it. This means that the whole *MU* schedule for one good may alter its position when the amount of the other good consumed changes (in the same way that, in production theory, the marginal product schedule of a variable input will shift its position if the amount of the fixed input that it it used in conjunction with changes).

The example above considered a consumer's allocation of income on only two goods, but the same principles determine the optimum allocation of income over any number of goods. Maximum utility is obtained when a consumer allocates income over goods 1, 2...*n*, such that

$$\frac{MU_1}{P_1} = \frac{MU_2}{P_2} = \ldots = \frac{MU_n}{P_n}$$

Two applications of cardinal utility theory are considered below.

1.   The water–diamond paradox

If water is a necessity for life and diamonds are a luxury then why are diamonds more expensive than water? This was the famous 'water–diamond' paradox that troubled some early economists. It can be resolved if one considers the cardinal utility proposition that the price of a good only reflects what consumers are willing to pay for the last unit that is consumed, in other words, that price reflects marginal utility. If a consumer was faced with the choice of having one extra pint of water or one more diamond then she would most likely choose the diamond. However, if the same consumer was given the choice of being able to consume water or being able to consume diamonds then she would choose water because it is a necessity for life. The relative scarcity of diamonds ensures low consumption levels and contributes to their high marginal utility. Thus, although the marginal utility from one extra pint of water is less than the marginal utility of one more diamond, the total utility from consuming water is greater than the total utility from consuming diamonds.

2.   Insurance

Many people are prepared to pay an insurance premium in order to be sure that they will be recompensed in the event of a loss due to some unforeseen and uncontrollable circumstance, even though the probability of such an event happening might be quite small. This can be explained using the total utility of money (TU_M) schedule in Figure 9.2. Its shape is based on the assumption that as a person gets richer the marginal utility of money declines. Thus the rate of increase of TU_M becomes smaller as wealth increases. This seems a reasonable proposition (although alternatives have been put forward). An extra pound will usually mean more to a poor person than to a rich person.

Assume that the individual whose TU_M schedule is illustrated in Figure 9.2 has £1000 worth of property and that there is a 0.1 probability that in the next year it will be destroyed in an accident leaving her with nothing (and therefore a 0.9 probability that it will not). If she does not take out insurance the expected value of her wealth will be

$$(0.1 \times 0) + (0.9 \times £1000) = £900.$$

Her expected total utility will be

$$(0.1 \times 0) + (0.9 \times U_3) = U_1 \qquad \text{(corresponding to point } Y\text{)}.$$

If she does take out insurance then she will have to pay a premium to an insurance company. An insurance company insuring 10 similar properties would expect to pay out one claim of £1000 although, of course, in any given year there might be more than one loss or no losses at all. The premium will be based on this estimated loss of £100 per property owner, plus an extra charge to cover the company's administrative expenses of, say, £50.

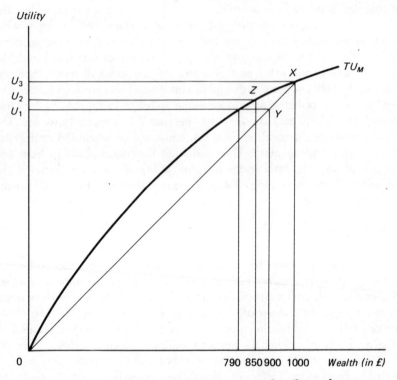

FIGURE 9.2   Insurance and the marginal utility of money

(Note that in practice insurance companies also make money by investing their premium income, which is usually paid at the start of the period of cover whereas claims are spread out over this period and sometimes settled even later.)

The individual in this example is faced with the choice of paying for insurance, and being left with a certain £850, or of not insuring, and risking losing all of her property. The total utility from a certain £850, at Z, is U_2. This is greater than the expected utility of U_1 from taking the risk of not insuring and so she will prefer to pay for insurance. In this example the individual concerned would prefer to insure for premiums of up to £210. This would leave her with a certain income of £790, which yields the same total utility as the expected utility of not insuring, U_1.

ORDINAL UTILITY THEORY

Instead of assuming that utility is some quantifiable concept, the ordinal utility theory just assumes that consumers can put different consumption choices in some order of preference.

More specifically, it is assumed that consumers:

1. have perfect knowledge of all possible consumption choices open to them;
2. try to maximise the satisfaction that they get from consumption, subject to a given budget constraint;
3. have a preference ordering, that is, they can rank different consumption choices in order of preference.

This preference ordering is assumed to have the following properties:

(a)   Completeness. This means that a consumer is always able to make some judgement about the relative preferences of any two combinations of goods. If X and Y are two bundles of good then one of the following three statements must hold:
(i) X is preferred to Y.
(ii) Y is preferred to X.
(iii)   The consumer is indifferent as to the choice between X and Y.
Indifference is a conscious decision that two choices are of equal preference. It is not the same as a consumer saying, 'I cannot make up my mind about this choice.'
(b)   Transitivity (or rationality). This means that if X is preferred to Y and Y is preferred to a third choice, Z, then X must be preferred to Z.
(c)   Divisibility. There is complete divisibility of commodities.
(d)   More of a good is preferred to less of it. This property applies in most cases, but there are a number of exceptions. If a good's MU become negative then less of it would make the consumer better off. Some commodities always make the consumer worse off (pollution, for instance) and, for want of a better word, are sometimes called 'bads'.

INDIFFERENCE CURVE ANALYSIS

Indifference curves can be used to illustrate certain concepts in both cardinal and ordinal utility theory when the consumer's choice only involves two goods. On a graph where the axes measure the quantities of the two goods consumed in a given time period, indifference curves join combinations that yield the same level of satisfaction. In cardinal utility theory they are assumed to represent some measurable level of utility (in the same way that isoquants represent production levels), but in ordinal utility theory they are just assumed to link points of equal preference. The following analysis is based on the latter assumption.

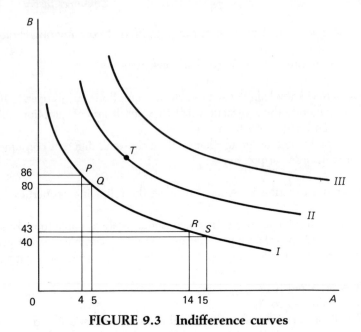

FIGURE 9.3   Indifference curves

In Figure 9.3 the lines I, II and III are indifference curves which represent successively higher levels of preference. The combinations of the two goods *A* and *B* represented by the points *P* and *Q* are equally preferred because they are on the same indifference curve, and *T* is preferred to both *P* and *Q*.

Properties of indifference curves

Certain properties of indifference curves can be deduced from the assumptions made above with respect to consumers' preference orderings:

1. Indifference curves are 'everywhere dense'. There must be an indifference curve through every possible combination of the two goods *A* and *B*. This follows from the completeness assumption (a) which ensures that every single combination of the goods must lie somewhere in a consumer's order of preference. Obviously only a few representative indifference curves can be drawn on indifference curve maps such as Figure 9.3, otherwise the whole diagram would be a solid black mass.
2. Indifference curves do not intersect. This property follows from the transitivity assumption (b) which makes it impossible to have the situation illustrated in Figure 9.4. In this example, *X* and *Y* are on the same indifference curve, and so are *Y* and *Z*. Thus *X* is indifferent to *Y* and *Y* is indifferent to *Z* and so, according to the transitivity assumption, *X*

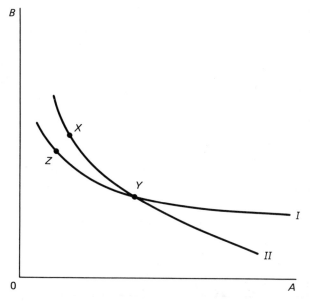

FIGURE 9.4 Rationality and intersecting indifference curves

should be indifferent to Z. However, Z is not on the same indifference curve as X and is, in fact, less preferred to X. Thus intersecting indifference curves contradict one of the assumptions on which ordinal utility theory is based and so they cannot exist.

3. Indifference curves slope down from left to right. This follows from the assumption (d) that more of a good is preferred to less. Consider the combination of goods represented by point X in Figure 9.5. Any combination to the north-east of X (area M) has more of both goods and is therefore preferred to X. Any point to the south-west of X (area L) has less of both goods and is therefore less preferred to X. (Along the vertical and horizontal lines that go through X and define these areas either more, and less, of one good is consumed than at X.) Point X can, therefore, only be equally preferred to points to the north-west and south-east (areas E_1 and E_2). Thus the indifference curve that goes through X must slope down from left to right. In cases where assumption (d) does not hold, 'bads' for example, indifference curves may slope in other directions.

4. Indifference curves are convex to the origin. This property of indifference curves does not follow from any of the assumptions above. It is based on certain assumptions about the way in which consumers are willing to exchange one good for another, as explained below.

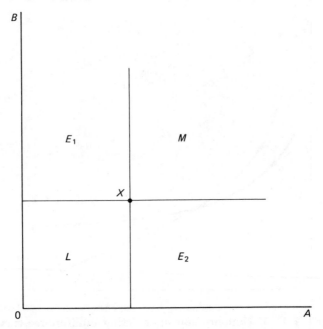

FIGURE 9.5   Indifference curves sloping down from left to right

The marginal rate of substitution

The rate at which a consumer is willing to exchange one good for the other is known as the marginal rate of substitution. The marginal rate of substitution of B for A (MRS_{BA}) is the amount of good B needed to compensate for the loss of one unit of good A. Thus in Figure 9.3, above, the MRS_{BA} is 6 between points P and Q and, further along the same indifference curve, it declines to 3 between points R and S. It is this fall in the MRS_{BA} that causes the indifference curve to be convex to the origin.[1]

In Figure 9.6 the MRS_{BA} between X and Y is XZ/ZY, which is the negative of the slope of the line XY. If Y was nearer to X then the slope of XY would be closer to the slope of the tangent TT', which represents the slope of the indifference curve at X. Therefore, for an infinitesimally small distance between X and Y the MRS_{BA} is equal to the negative of the slope of the indifference curve at X. Thus at any point on an indifference curve the negative of its slope equals the MRS_{BA}.

If the two goods A and B were perfect substitutes then the MRS_{BA} would be a constant and the indifference curve would be a straight line. If the two

---

1. Sometimes the notation used for this concept is MRS_{AB}, but this text sticks to the notation MRS_{BA}, which is more intuitively obvious to students and is also consistent with the way that the $MRTS_{KL}$ is defined in Chapter 2.

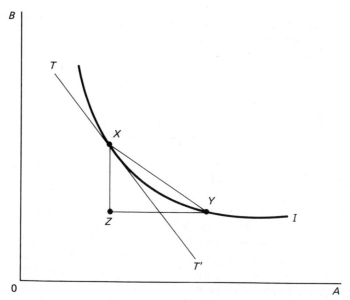

FIGURE 9.6   The MRS_{BA} and the slope of an indifference curve

goods were perfect complements the indifference curves would be a series of right angles. (Analogous properties of isoquants were explained in Chapter 2.) Given that most pairs of goods lie somewhere between being perfect substitutes and perfect complements then most indifference curves are expected to be something between a straight line and a right-angle, that is, a curve convex to the origin. In ordinal utility theory it is just assumed that the MRS_{BA} declines along an indifference curve as more of B and less of A is consumed. In cardinal utility theory, however, it can be shown that, when A is measured on the horizontal axis and B on the vertical axis, the slope of an indifference curve at any point is equal to

$$- MU_A / MU_B.$$

(As an exercise, see if you can prove this result for yourself after referring back to the section on the $MRTS_{KL}$ in Chapter 2.)

According to the hypothesis of diminishing marginal utility, if more of A is consumed then MU_A will fall, and if less of B is consumed MU_B will rise. Thus moving along an indifference curve from left to right will cause the negative of its slope to decline, that is, it will be convex to the origin.

The budget constraint

In the same way that a budget constraint can be constructed for a firm using two inputs (see Chapter 3) a budget constraint can be drawn which shows the feasible choices available to a consumer. With a given income M, and given prices P_A and P_B for the two goods A and B, respectively, this budget constraint's slope will be

$$-P_A/P_B.$$

Thus a change in the relative prices of A and B will alter its slope and a change in income will cause a parallel shift in its position.

OPTIMAL CONSUMER CHOICE

Consumers are assumed to purchase the combination of goods that will yield the greatest level of satisfaction subject to the constraints of a limited income and given prices for the goods bought. They will thus try to reach the highest indifference curve that the budget constraint allows. In Figure 9.7 this optimal consumer choice occurs at X, the point of tangency between the budget constraint and indifference curve II.

This result could have been deduced without actually drawing an indifference curve map. It follows from the condition that the marginal rate of substitution between two goods must always be equal to their price ratio when a consumer is optimally allocating income. If P_A/P_B was 0.5 and the

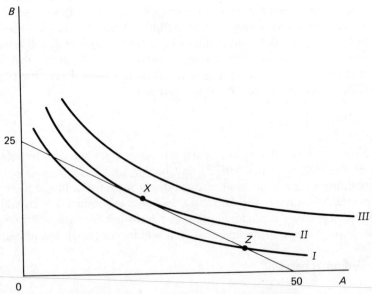

FIGURE 9.7   Optimal consumer choice

MRS_{BA} was 0.2 it would mean that 0.5 more units of B could be bought if one less unit of A was bought, but only 0.2 units of B would be needed to compensate the consumer for the loss of one unit of A. Thus by switching expenditure from A to B the consumer would be better off. She should keep reallocating expenditure until MRS_{BA} equals P_A/P_B. When this is achieved further reallocation of expenditure cannot make her any better off. It thus follows that a consumer is maximising satisfaction when the slopes of the budget constraint $(-P_A/P_B)$ and the relevant indifference curve $(-MRS_{BA})$ are equal.

The adjustment towards this optimal position is made by moving along the budget constraint. In Figure 9.7 the original situation is at Z, where the indifference curve has a slope of -0.2 compared with the budget constraint's slope of -0.5. At the optimum, X, the indifference curve and the budget line both have a slope of -0.5. Note that it is because of this general condition for consumer optimisation that the tangency condition occurs in indifference curve analysis, not the other way around.

An exception to this tangency optimisation rule occurs when there is a corner solution. It is also necessary for the indifference curve to be convex to the origin at the tangency point with the budget constraint to ensure that the consumer is maximising, not minimising, satisfaction. (Go back to Chapter 3 if you do not understand these two points.)

Changes in income

If income changes then the budget constraint will shift and there will be a new equilibrium. The change in the optimal amount consumed of each good will depend on whether it is a normal good (quantity demanded increases when income rises) or an inferior good (quantity demanded decreases when income rises). Figure 9.8 illustrates three possibilities.

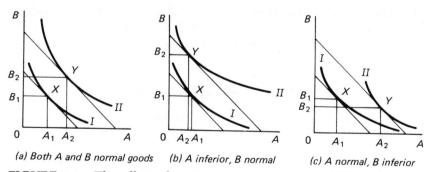

(a) Both A and B normal goods   (b) A inferior, B normal   (c) A normal, B inferior

FIGURE 9.8   The effect of an increase in income on optimal consumer choice

Note that when a consumer can buy only two goods they cannot both be inferior goods. The quantity demanded of an inferior good only falls when income rises because more of another (normal) good is demanded.

Changes in price

A change in the price of one good will cause the slope of the budget constraint to alter and a new equilibrium will thus be established. In Figure 9.9 it is assumed that consumer income is £64, the price of B remains constant at £4, and that the price of A is initially £16 and then falls successively to £8, £4 and £2 per unit. The four equilibrium positions corresponding to these four prices are W, X, Y and Z, respectively, and the amount of A demanded increases from 2 to 3.2, 6, and 9.5 units, successively. This information allows the demand curve for A to be plotted in the bottom section of Figure 9.9. As the price of A falls the quantity demanded increases and so the demand schedule, D, slopes downwards, as is the usual case.

In this particular example the demand curve for A is inelastic (within the price range shown). This could have been determined by calculating the change in total revenue resulting from the increase in output, but it can also be deduced by observing the slope of the price expansion path PEP. The PEP is a line that joins the different equilibrium points on an indifference curve map corresponding to different prices for one good, assuming that income and the price of the other good are held constant. If the PEP slopes upward when the price of the good measured on the horizontal axis falls then this good's demand schedule must be inelastic. To prove this it is necessary to look at what happens to expenditure on the good measured on the vertical axis.

If the PEP slopes upward then more of B is demanded as a consequence of the fall in A's price. Given that the price of B does not alter then this must mean that total revenue spent on B increases. The consumer's income is unchanged and so, if more is spent on B out of a fixed budget, the total revenue spent on A must fall. If the total revenue spent on A falls when its price falls then its demand must be inelastic. Similarly, it can be shown that if the PEP slopes downward then the demand for A is elastic, and if the PEP is horizontal then the price elasticity of demand is unity.

The income and substitution effects of a price change

A price change can be split into two components:

1. The substitution effect. If the relative prices of two goods change then a consumer will demand more of the good that becomes relatively cheaper and less of the good that becomes relatively more expensive.
2. The income effect. A change in the price of one good will alter a consumer's real income and may consequently affect the demand for all

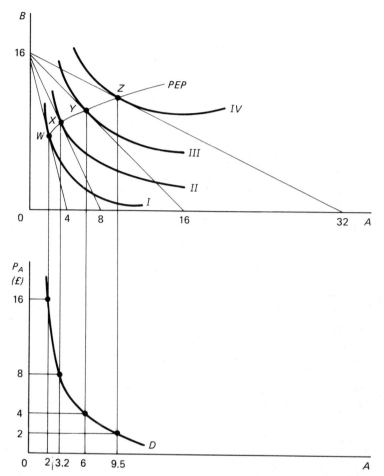

FIGURE 9.9 **Changes in price and optimal consumer choice**

goods consumed. The direction of the income effect with respect to the good whose price changes will depend on whether it is a normal or an inferior good.

Economists have suggested different methods by which these two concepts might be analysed. It must be pointed out, though, that it is impossible actually to measure the income and substitution effects of a price change. Only the net effects of any price change can be empirically observed and, in any case, predictions are only tested for a large number of observations and not at the level of an individual consumer.

Hicks's method of splitting a price change into its income and substitution effects is explained using Figure 9.10 (p. 200). Assume that a consumer is initially in equilibrium at X on indifference curve I and budget constraint CD, and that

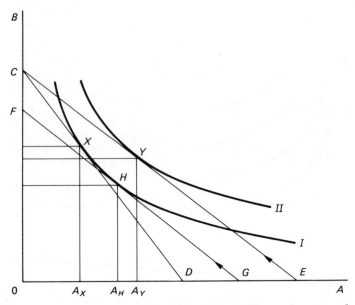

FIGURE 9.10   The income and substitution effects of a price decrease for a normal good

the price of *A* then falls causing the budget constraint to change to *CE*. The new equilibrium will be at *Y*, on the higher indifference curve II, and the amount of *A* demanded will increase from A_X to A_Y. To separate the income and substitution effects of this price change, consider what the consumer's expenditure pattern would be if there was the same change in the price of *A* relative to the price of *B*, but the consumer could still only achieve the same utility level as before the price change; in other words, keeping the consumer on the same indifference curve is assumed to be equivalent to keeping real income unchanged. To do this, a new 'ghost' budget line *FG* is drawn which has the same slope as *CE*, representing the new relative price ratio, but is tangent to the original indifference curve, I, at *H*. The substitution effect is thus from *X* to *H*, the new tangency point, and the income effect is from *H* to *Y*.

The substitution effect is always negative, that is, the change in quantity demanded is in the opposite direction to the change in price. If a new, flatter, budget constraint, corresponding to the lower relative price of *A*, is drawn tangent to the same indifference curve that the original budget constraint is tangent to, then the new tangency point must be to the right of the old one. In Figure 9.10 the relative fall in the price of *A* produces an increase in quantity demanded from A_X to A_H.

The increase in real income that the fall in the price of *A* causes is shown by the parallel shift outward of the budget constraint from *FG* to *CE* and the

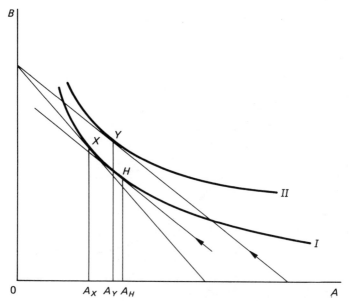

FIGURE 9.11 **The income and substitution effects of a price decrease for an inferior good**

move from H to Y. This causes an increase in demand for A from A_H to A_Y and so in this example A must be a normal good. Point Y is higher than point H and so the increase in real income has a positive effect on the demand for B, that is, B is also a normal good.

Figure 9.11 illustrates a situation where the price of A falls and A is an inferior good. In this case the substitution and income effects work in the opposite directions. The substitution effect causes an increase in demand, from A_X to A_H, but because A is an inferior good the increase in real income provokes a fall in demand from A_H to A_Y. The net effect, however, is still an increase in the demand for A, from A_X to A_Y. Thus the demand schedule for A will still slope down from left to right, but it will be inelastic, given the upward sloping *PEP*.

Giffen goods

It is conceivable that in extreme cases the income effect of a price change for an inferior good may totally counteract the substitution effect, with the result that the amount of the good demanded actually drops when its price falls, that is, its demand schedule slopes up from left to right. Such cases are known as Giffen goods. Economists still dispute whether or not there is empirical evidence that proves the existence of any Giffen goods, but explaining the rationale for their possible existence is still a useful exercise to see if the analysis of income and substitution effects has been properly understood.

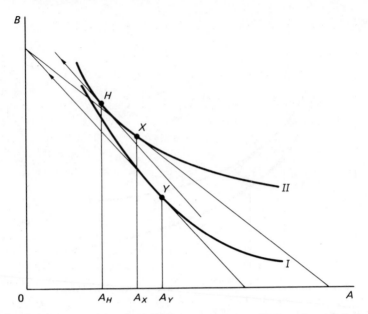

FIGURE 9.12   The income and substitution effects of a price increase for a Giffen good

If a poor section of the community spend a very large proportion of their income on one staple food (such as potatoes at the time of the Irish famine) then a rise in the price of this basic food would mean that less money is available to buy other types of food. If these other types of food are substitutes for the staple good, and less are bought due to the fall in real income, then more potatoes will be demanded to ensure a sufficient diet. In the case of a Giffen good this reduction in real income produces such a significant increase in the demand for the inferior good, potatoes, that it outweighs the fall in demand resulting from the substitution effect. In other words the demand for potatoes rises when price increases. This is illustrated in Figure 9.12, where A represents consumption of potatoes per time period and B represents other types of food.

Note that the explanation above assumes an increase in the price of a good whereas the previous examples assumed a fall in price. The income and substitution effects of a price rise can be analysed using the same method, although care should always be taken to make sure that the 'ghost' budget line represents the new relative price ratio. (It helps if an arrow is always put on the second budget line as soon as it is drawn, as a reminder of which line represents the new relative price ratio, and the same notation is kept to denote the income and substitution effects. In the examples above, X to H always represents the substitution effect and H to Y always represents the income effect.)

THE THEORY OF INDIVIDUAL LABOUR SUPPLY

Until now it has been assumed that a consumer's income has been exogenously given. However, many individuals receive income in the form of a wage and can alter their income by changing the number of hours that they work. The basic microeconomic theory of labour supply assumes that an individual gets satisfaction from both leisure and income (or rather the goods and services that income can be used to buy). If the hours worked each time period can be varied, up to a given maximum (determined by the necessity to have some time to sleep, eat, travel to work and so on) then the hourly wage rate determines the income and leisure choices open to the individual.

The way that the optimum combination of income and hours of leisure is determined is shown in Figure 9.13. It is assumed that an individual's preferences between income and leisure can be represented by indifference curves such as I, II and III. It is expected that the marginal rate of substitution of income for leisure will fall as the individual moves along an indifference curve and more leisure, and less income, is chosen. Thus the indifference curves are assumed to be convex to the leisure–income origin.

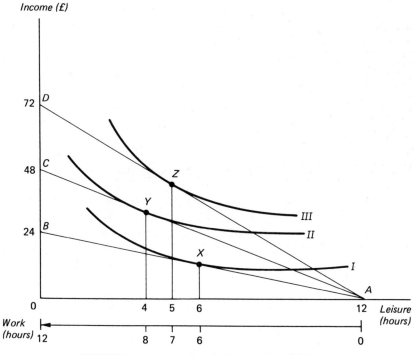

FIGURE 9.13   Individual supply of labour

The more leisure that is taken the less time there is available for working. Thus hours of work are measured on the same axis as leisure hours, but in the opposite direction. Zero work hours corresponds to 12 hours of leisure, which is assumed to be the maximum working day. If the hourly wage rate is £2 then if the maximum 12-hour day is worked an income of £24 is earned and if zero hours are worked then income is zero.

Between these two extremes there are numerous other possible combinations of hours of work (and thus hours of leisure) and income, illustrated by the budget constraint *AB*, for example 8 hours' work (and 4 hours' leisure) yields an income of £16. If the wage increases to £4 an hour the budget constraint becomes *AC*, and at £6 an hour it becomes *AD*.

If the hourly wage rate is £2 then the optimal leisure–income choice is at *X*, where indifference curve I is tangent to budget constraint *AB*. Thus income is £12, for 6 hours of work and the individual has 6 hours of leisure. An increase in the wage rate to £4 increases the number of hours the individual wishes to work to 8. However, when there is a further increase in the hourly wage, to £6, the optimal choice of *Z* signifies a reduction in the desired working day, to 7 hours. Why should anyone wish to work less hours if they can earn more per hour? This can be explained in terms of the income and substitution effect of the wage change, but first consider an intuitive explanation.

Suppose that you could choose the number of hours worked each day and that this decision was fixed for the foreseeable future (that is, you could not work flat out for a short period and then retire to spend your earnings). If you could earn £2 an hour how many hours would you work? At £5 an hour? At £20? At £100? At £1000? At some point you are likely to realise that if the wage rate increases you can work less hours and still have more income. Above a certain hourly wage most people would decide to cut down on their hours of work in order to have more leisure time in which to spend this increased income.

The income and substitution effects of a wage rise

Consider the increase in the hourly wage that causes an individual's optimum leisure–income combination to move from *Y* to *Z* in Figure 9.14. The rise in the hourly wage effectively makes each hour of leisure taken more expensive. There will thus be a substitution effect causing less leisure to be taken and more income to be earned; in other words, hours of work will increase. Using Hicks's method, the substitution effect is determined by drawing a new budget line representing the new relative price ratio but tangent to the original indifference curve and is shown by the move from *Y* to *H*. This rise in the hourly wage rate also effectively increases the individual's real 'income' in the sense that she can now enjoy more of both leisure and income if she wishes. Both leisure and income are normal 'goods' and so the income effect

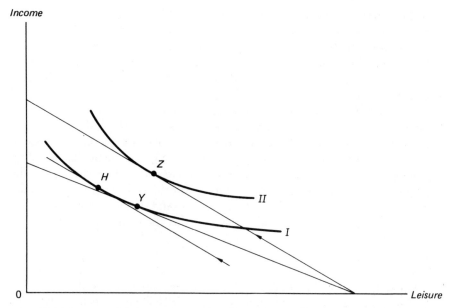

FIGURE 9.14   The income and substitution effects of a wage rise

of the wage rise causes more of both to be taken, shown by the move from *H* to *Z*.

The income and substitution effects of a wage rise work in opposite directions and so it is possible that the income effect may completely outweigh the substitution effect and reduce the desired number of hours of work. This is the case in Figure 9.14, and also in Figure 9.13 when the wage rises from £4 to £6 an hour. Note, however, that although an increase in the wage may eventually cause less hours to be worked it will always cause an increase in the individual's income.

Extensions of the basic labour supply model

The model above assumes that there is freedom of choice over the number of hours worked and that income is zero if no work is done. In reality many workers have a fixed working week and can only vary the number of hours of overtime work done. They can, however, attempt to change jobs to find one that has working hours that suit them. In the last few decades the significant growth of part-time working has also contributed to a greater variation in average hours worked. In 1985 approximately one in five of all workers in Great Britain worked part-time and between 1971 and 1985 the number of part-time employees in employment grew by 33 per cent while the number of full-time employees in employment fell by 12 per cent. Most (90 per cent) of these part-time workers are female and in 1985 just over 50 per cent of all married women in employment worked part-time.[2]

It is also true that a large number of people will not have a zero income if they work zero hours, particularly if they live in households with another person in employment. The basic model can be extended to incorporate some of these features.

In Figure 9.15 the budget constraint of someone who has an unearned income of £10 and can work at £3 an hour is *AB*. If this individual is in a job where there is a fixed working day of 8 hours then the income–leisure choice is between *C*, working, or *A*, not working (assuming that no other employment is available). With a set of preferences as illustrated by the indifference curves I, II and III, *A* is preferred to *C* and so zero hours would be worked. This individual's optimum income–leisure is at *D*, which corresponds to 4 hours of work a day, but this choice is not possible.

Overtime work

If workers are near the point where their labour supply curve starts to bend backwards an increase in the hourly wage rate will cause them to want to work less hours. To get round this problem employers usually pay for overtime

2. For further explanation of these changes see A. T. Mallier and M. J. Rosser, *Women and the Economy: A Comparative Study of Britain and the USA* (London: Macmillan, 1987).

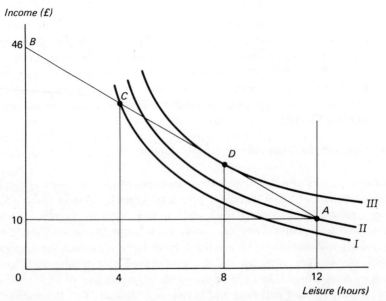

FIGURE 9.15   Individual labour supply with a fixed working week and unearned income

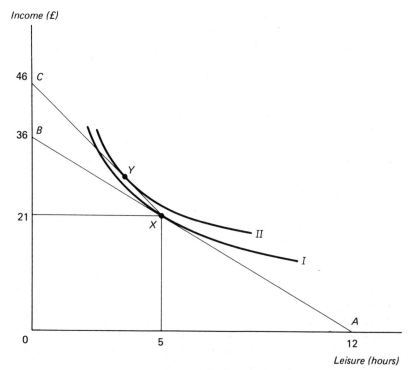

FIGURE 9.16   Overtime work and the labour supply decision of an individual

work at a higher rate than for the basic working week when they want their existing workforce to put in more hours. By paying a higher rate just for the overtime hours the employer effectively allows the substitution effect of a wage rise to operate but not the income effect.

Assume that when faced with an hourly wage rate of £3 a worker is initially at an optimum at point X in Figure 9.16, supplying 7 hours of work. If a wage of £5 is paid for any extra hours the budget line then becomes the kinked line AXC and the new optimum at Y corresponds to an increase in hours worked. In fact any overtime premium on the wage rate that causes the budget constraint to the left of X to become steeper must result in a new tangency point to the left of X; that is, it will always result in an increase in the amount of work supplied by an individual.

Further developments in the theory of individual labour supply, which are not pursued here, include the consideration of non-market (that is, domestic work) and the recognition that in households with more than one person of working age there is usually a joint labour supply decision.[3]

---

3.   See C. Joll, C. McKenna, R. McNabb and J. Shorey, *Developments in Labour Market Analysis* (London: George Allen & Unwin, 1983).

QUESTIONS

1. 'If someone spends 30p on a bar of chocolate then the value to them of the bar of chocolate is 30p.' True or false?
2. Assume that an individual is currently spending all of her income on two goods, A and B, whose prices are 8p and 6p, respectively, and currently enjoys a marginal utility of 72 units from the last unit of A that she consumes and a marginal utility of 40 units from the last unit of B. How should she adjust her expenditure in order to increase total utility?
3. Using indifference curve analysis, illustrate the difference between the two following explanations of the increasing share of coffee in the market for beverages in the last few decades.

    (a) 'Consumer preferences have not changed. The share of coffee has risen because incomes have risen and tea is an inferior good.'
    (b) 'Consumer tastes have changed, with the help of marketing. If they hadn't then tea and coffee would still have unchanged market shares despite the rise in incomes.'

4. Assume that a consumer spends all her income on two goods, A and B, and when the price of A falls the amount of B consumed does not change. What can be said about (a) price elasticity of demand for A, (b) price elasticity of demand for B, (c) income elasticity of demand for A, (d) income elasticity of demand for B and (e) cross elasticity of demand between A and B?
5. Suppose that the government is considering whether to give an income supplement or food vouchers to a certain group of the population who are currently on low incomes. A survey reveals that a typical household in this group has a net weekly income of £48 and spends £16 on food and £32 on other goods. Using an indifference curve map between food and other goods, show that a £20 income supplement may possibly give greater satisfaction than £20 worth of food vouchers, but not vice versa. Assume that vouchers cannot be traded and can only be used in the week for which they are issued.
6. Using the basic income–leisure model of individual labour supply, explain what would happen to the number of hours of labour supplied by an individual if there was an increase in unearned income.
7. 'An increase in the hourly wage rate may reduce the average number of hours of work that individuals would wish to supply, but it would never reduce the number of people who would wish to work.' Explain.

CHAPTER 10

Factor markets

In a market economy consumers derive their income by selling the resources that they own to firms, to be used as factors of production. Incomes will therefore depend on the prices paid for these factors and the amounts sold. This chapter explains how the markets for factors of production operate and how these prices and quantities will be determined. The markets for the different factors of land, labour and capital have several common features, but special attention will be paid to the market for labour. As Table 10.1 shows, income from employment is clearly the main source of income in the United Kingdom.

Just like prices in other markets, factor prices are governed by the interaction of supply and demand. The analysis of factor prices is made more complex, though, as one has to take into account the degree of competition in both the factor market and the market for the finished good that a factor is used to produce. There is also the possibility that the buyer's side in a factor market, as well as the seller's side, may be monopolistic.

Although an understanding of the way factor prices are determined may be used to help formulate income redistribution policies, it is the task of positive economics to explain how the market system determines the prices and employment levels of factors of production and not to comment on the fairness of this system. Some people would argue that a system which pays some popular entertainers millions of pounds a year, while many other workers' earnings are below the official poverty line, is unjust. On the other hand, there are people who think that the way that the market system determines incomes is satisfactory. Any support for either viewpoint would involve value-judgements, which cannot be objectively tested. Value-judgements concerning income distribution still have to be made, however, when it comes to making actual policy decisions.

TABLE 10.1   Functional distribution of income in the UK, 1985

	% *share of total domestic income*
Income from employment	63
Income from self-employment	10
Gross trading profits of companies	17
Gross trading profits of public corporations	2 .
Rent	7
Total domestic income*	100

* Does not include Social Security and other personal transfer payments which totalled approximately 15 % of GDP at market prices.
(Figures do not add exactly to 100 because of rounding and other minor adjustments.)
Source: UK National Accounts (The CSO Blue Book), 1986 edition, HMSO Table 1.3.

THE DERIVED DEMAND FOR LABOUR

Although consumers purchase goods and services because of the satisfaction that they get from consuming them, firms do not see the employment of labour as an end in itself. In private industry firms will only employ workers if profits can be increased by selling the goods that they produce; in other words, the demand for factors of production is a derived demand.

Although this criterion forms the basis for the theory of factor demand by profit maximising firms, which is explained in this chapter, it does not apply to public sector workers such as the police, the armed forces, or teachers. The demand for labour in the public sector is, nevertheless, still a derived demand. Public sector workers are only employed when the state decides that it wishes to provide the goods and services that they produce, and the state's decision will reflect the public's demand as expressed through the ballot box instead of the cash till.

In a mixed economy like the United Kingdom, even though the profit criteria may not underlie the demand for all public sector workers, the state still has to buy its labour services in the market (given that there is no compulsory conscription to the armed services) and compete with the private sector for different types of workers. In determining its labour demand, the state may decide either on the number of workers it wishes to employ, which will be related to the desired level of output produced by these workers, or on the total revenue it is willing to spend on certain types of workers, but economic theory cannot explain the levels that it will decide upon.

THE SHORT-RUN DEMAND FOR LABOUR

The demand for labour is a flow per time period, for example worker hours per week. In the short-run it is assumed that the amount of capital that a firm uses is fixed and that the quantity of labour employed can be varied. To maximise profits, the amount of labour employed should be increased as long as the revenue generated by the sale of the output produced by an additional unit of labour exceeds the marginal cost of employing it, that is, as long as extra units of labour add more to revenue than to costs.

The addition to revenue resulting from the employment of one more unit of labour is called the marginal revenue produce of labour (MRP_L). It can be calculated from the formula

$$MRP_L = MP_L . MR_X.$$

That is to say, it is the extra output produced by an additional unit of labour multiplied by the marginal revenue that the sale of one extra unit of output X would generate. The relationship between marginal revenue and output will depend on the nature of the demand schedule that a firm faces and so the two cases of perfectly competitive and monopolistic goods markets will be considered separately.

THE SHORT-RUN DEMAND FOR LABOUR IN PERFECTLY COMPETITIVE GOODS MARKETS

The firm's demand

Assume that a firm sells good X in a perfectly competitive finished product market where the current price of X is £5 per unit. In perfect competition marginal revenue equals price and so the MRP_L is simply the output generated by a marginal unit of labour times the price for which it can be sold. If output increases with extra units of L as shown in Table 10.2 then the MRP_L can be calculated simply by multiplying MP_L by £5.

Assume also that the firm buys labour in a perfectly competitive factor market. This means that the price of labour, in this case assumed to be the weekly wage rate W, is determined by supply and demand in the factor market. Thus an individual firm effectively faces a horizontal supply of labour at this wage. If a firm can employ any amount of labour that it wishes at a given wage then its marginal cost of labour schedule will also be a horizontal line at this wage.

Given the figures in Table 10.2, how much of L will a profit maximising firm employ if W is £300? The first five units have a MRP_L greater than

TABLE 10.2   Marginal revenue product for a perfectly competitive firm

L	X	MP_L	MRP_L
0	0	–	–
1	63	63	£315
2	130	67	£335
3	199	69	£345
4	267	68	£340
5	332	65	£325
6	392	60	£300
7	445	53	£265
8	490	45	£225
9	524	34	£170
10	547	23	£115
11	557	10	£50

Note: L is measured in worker weeks; X and MP_L are measured in units of output. Price of X is £5 a unit.

£300 and so would definitely be employed. The seventh, and subsequent, units of L would add less than £300 to revenue and so would not be taken on. Because Table 10.2 considers whole unit changes in L then it appears that the sixth unit would add the same to revenue as to costs and so it would not matter if it was employed or not. However, if L and X are assumed to be divisible into small units then the relationship between MRP_L and L will be continuous, as shown by the graph in Figure 10.1. This assumption of divisibility is reasonable as units of L can be divided up, by employing some workers part-time, for example. Thus, to maximise profits the firm should expand its usage of labour up to the point where L equals 6 units. Any fractionally lower level of L would offer the opportunity for further increases in profit.

If the wage was reduced to £225 then 8 units of L would be demanded. In a similar fashion the amount of L that a profit maximising firm would employ for other possible wage rates can be determined from its MRP_L schedule. An individual firm's demand for labour schedule is, therefore, the same thing as the downward sloping section of its MRP_L schedule. Any initial upward sloping section can be ignored. In this example, if W was £300 then, although MRP_L equals to W at both 0.8 and 6 units of L, a firm would clearly expand L past 0.8 units because MRP_L is greater than W for any further increases in L.

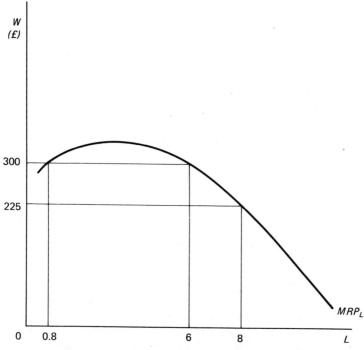

FIGURE 10.1   The firm's demand for labour

The industry demand for labour

Although the industry demand for labour at any given wage is the sum of the amount demanded by the individual firms in the industry, it is not simply the horizontal summation of the individual demand curves. This is because when all firms expand output at the same time the price of the finished product is likely to fall and hence shift the position of their MRP_L schedules.

Suppose that an industry consists of a hundred similar firms, each facing the schedule MRP_L^0 shown in Figure 10.2(a). If the wage is initially given as £390 then each firm will employ 26 units of labour and the industry demand will be 2600 units. If the wage paid by an individual firm fell to £200 then, given the demand for labour schedule MRP_L^0, it would wish to employ 42 units of labour. However, if, in response to this drop in the wage rate, all firms simultaneously attempted to employ more labour, and hence expand output, there would be an outward shift of the supply curve for the finished product. Simple supply and demand analysis predicts that this would cause a fall in the price of the finished product. Thus the marginal revenue product of labour would have to be recalculated using the new, lower, price. If each

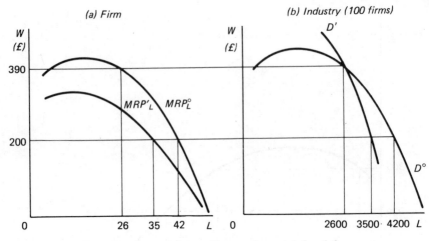

FIGURE 10.2   The industry demand for labour

firm's marginal revenue product of labour schedule falls to MRP'_L then at the new wage of £200 it would demand 35 units of L and the industry demand would thus be 3500 units. Further changes in the wage would bring about further shifts in the firms' MRP_L schedules and so the industry demand that would be traced out would be D'. This is more inelastic than D^0, which is the simple horizontal sum of the individual demand for labour curves (when the product price remains constant at £5).

THE SHORT-RUN DEMAND FOR LABOUR IN MONOPOLISTIC GOODS MARKETS

A monopoly has to lower the price of its product if it wishes to sell more because it directly faces the downward sloping market demand schedule. Marginal revenue is therefore less than price at any given output level and so a monopoly's MRP_L schedule cannot simply be calculated by multiplying marginal product by price. To derive the relationship between MRP_L and L one has, instead, to use the formula

$$MRP_L = MP_L . MR_X.$$

When data is only available for the effect on output of whole unit increases in L it is, however, not actually necessary to calculate MR_X or MP_L to derive approximate values of the MRP_L for these whole unit increases. In the example shown in Table 10.2 the change in total revenue caused by a unit increase in L is calculated directly. The first unit of L increases output from zero to

TABLE 10.3   **Marginal revenue product for a monopolist**

K	L	X	MP_L	Price	Total revenue	MRP_L
12 units	0 units	0	—	—	—	—
12 units	1 units	40	40	£1.00	£40.00	£40.00
12 units	2 units	90	50	£0.85	£76.50	£36.50
12 units	3 units	130	40	£0.70	£91.00	£14.50
12 units	4 units	160	30	£0.60	£96.00	£5.00
12 units	5 units	180	20	£0.50	£90.00	− £6.00
12 units	6 units	190	10	£0.45	£81.50	− £8.50

Note: X and MP_L are both measured in units of output.

40 units. These can be sold at a price of £1 each and so total revenue is increased from zero to £40. Thus the MRP_L of the first unit of L is £40. When L is then increased to two units, output expands to 90 units, price falls to £0.85 and total revenue changes to £76.50. The increase in total revenue caused by the unit increase in L is therefore £76.50 − £40.00 = £36.50. The same method can be used to calculate the MRP_L for other unit increases in L. Note that when marginal revenue becomes negative then the MRP_L also becomes negative.

SHIFTS IN THE SHORT-RUN DEMAND FOR LABOUR SCHEDULE

A change in the price of labour will just cause a movement along the demand for labour curve but the whole MRP_L schedule will shift if MP_L or MR_X, or both, alter. Possible causes of such changes are:

1. a change in the demand for the finished product, which would alter the MR_X schedule;
2. changes in technology, which would alter the production function and hence the MP_L schedule;
3. a change in the usage of other factors of production which, again, would alter the MP_L of the factor in question.

THE LONG-RUN DEMAND FOR LABOUR

The long-run demand for labour is the amount of labour that will be demanded at any given price when other factors of production are allowed to adjust in response to any change in the price of labour. There are several analytical problems involved in explaining the long-run demand for labour that are not encountered in short-run analysis.

The change in a consumer's demand for a good in response to a fall in its price can be analysed on an indifference curve map by drawing a new budget constraint corresponding to the new set of prices and then finding the highest feasible indifference curve. However, the same principle cannot always be used in isoquant analysis because the size of the budget may change in response to an input price change. Even if the budget is held fixed, an input price change will have income and substitution effects which may work in opposite directions and so the net effect on the demand for the input still cannot be unambiguously predicted.

An example of an input price change with a fixed budget is shown using the isoquant map in Figure 10.3. It is assumed that the prices of the two inputs K and L are initially £50 and £20, respectively, and that the firm has a budget of £600. The corresponding budget constraint is AB and the optimal input combination is at X. If the price of L falls to £12, then the budget constraint becomes AC. Given this isoquant map the new optimum will be at Y and so there is no change in the demand for L. Although L is cheaper relative to K, the firm can now afford to have more of both inputs and so

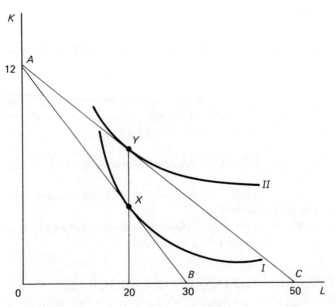

FIGURE 10.3   The long-run demand for labour

the income effect of this price change works in the opposite direction to the substitution effect and, in this particular example, completely cancels it out. It is also possible for the net result of these income and substitution effects to be an increase or a decrease in the demand for L.

An example showing how an input price change may warrant a change in a firm's budget is illustrated in Figure 10.4, which shows the revenue and cost curves facing a monopoly producer of good X. If this firm initially faces the average and marginal cost curves AC_0 and MC_0, respectively, then it will maximise profits by producing output X_0 and selling it at price P_0. Total costs will be represented by the area AX_0OC_0. Now assume that a fall in the price of L causes the marginal and average cost schedules to shift to MC_1 and AC_1, respectively. The profit maximising output increases to X_1, price falls to P_1, and total costs change to BX_1OC_1. Although in this particular example the relative sizes of these areas indicate that there is a fall in total costs, the

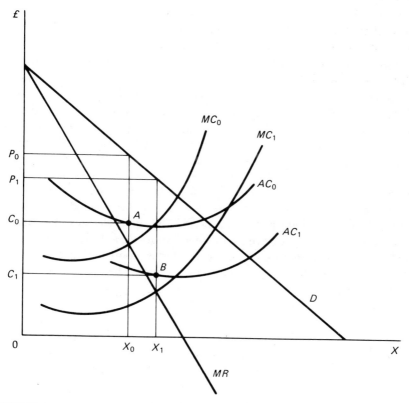

FIGURE 10.4   Changes in a firm's budget as a result of an input price change

direction and amount by which total costs change will vary from case to case and in general cannot be predicted.

If information is available about the form that a firm's production function takes then the changes in the relative size of the total payments to the inputs of capital and labour in response to a change in the relative input price ratio may be predicted, allowing for long-run adjustments of both inputs. To do this it is necessary to know how the K/L ratio will change in response to a change in the $MRTS_{KL}$, and this rate of responsiveness is called the *elasticity of substitution*.[1] This effectively measures how quickly the slope of an isoquant alters along its length; in other words, it is a measure of the curvature of an isoquant whereas the $MRTS_{KL}$ only measures its slope at one point. There are several problems encountered in trying to estimate empirically a value for the elasticity of substitution. In particular, it can be difficult to establish whether any observed changes in input usage are the result of input price changes or the result of changes in technology.

THE SUPPLY OF FACTORS OF PRODUCTION

It is assumed that the owners of factors of production will wish to sell them where they will get the best reward. This often means the best monetary return but, particularly in the case of labour, non-monetary factors, for example the type of work involved and its location, can also be important. Although owners of land and capital do not usually consider influences other than monetary return, there can be instances where land or capital owners might forgo the best monetary return because of non-monetary influences. For example, some landowners may not like to see certain industrial activities carried out on their land because it would destroy a beautiful landscape.

The supply of factors of production is a flow per time period and, as with factor demand, the longer the time period the more elastic is the supply schedule likely to be. However, individual factors cannot be separated into fixed and variable components and so the terms 'short-run' and 'long-run' cannot be used in the same sense as they are used when considering firms' demand for factors of production.

Land

Although the total acreage of land in the economy is fixed, the amount supplied for different uses will depend on the return that can be earned (in

---

1. See p. 74–6, 468–72 of A. Koutsoyiannis, *Modern Microeconomics*, second edn. (London: Macmillan, 1979).

the absence of laws restricting the usage of land). An increase in the return earned may cause a switch in usage; for example, a farmer may change from growing potatoes to carrots if the price of the latter increases, or it may bring into use otherwise unused natural resources; for example, only the increases in oil prices by OPEC in the early 1970s made it worthwhile to exploit the North Sea oilfields (and the oil price fall in the mid-1980s consequently brought a halt to many off-shore oil drilling ventures).

When the supply of land cannot be changed any increase in demand will only cause prices to be bid up, as has happened to rents in city centres, particularly in London. The longer the time period under consideration, the more elastic will supply become. This is particularly relevant to land which is built on. The cost of construction will not make it worthwhile to continually change buildings in response to short-run fluctuations in the rewards to different activities. However, relatively new buildings are sometimes demolished to make way for more profitable ventures. The theory of factor prices considers the prices paid for the flow of factor services each time period from individual factor owners to firms, as opposed to the sale of the ownership rights of the factors themselves. However, the actual ownership of the resources of land and capital can be sold (but obviously not labour, as slavery is illegal). In particular, with respect to the market for land it is the price paid for the land itself rather than the annual rental on it that is often the most relevant figure for resource allocation purposes. The price paid for a plot of land will still reflect the demand for its usage in relation to the available supply, though, and the implicit expected return will be 'capitalised' into its price.

Capital

Items of capital are produced and sold by firms trying to make a profit just like those firms supplying consumers directly. One would therefore expect the supply curve for capital goods to slope upwards in the same way that the supply schedules for other goods would do.

Labour

Even when the total population does not change, the supply of labour in total and to individual industries and occupations can alter. Higher wages will induce new workers to enter the labour force as well as changing the supply to specific types of employment. As Table 10.4 shows, although the population of working age only increased by 2.14 per cent between 1971 and 1981, the number of people in the workforce (that is, those in work plus those seeking work) grew by 3.86 per cent. The main reason for this was an increase in the proportion of females of working age who were economically active, from

TABLE 10.4   Labour force changes in Great Britain, 1971–81

	1971	1981	% Change 1971–81
Population of males aged 16–64 years	16 435 320	16 773 964	+ 2.06
Economically active males aged 16–64 years	15 282 395	15 158 588	− 0.81
Proportion economically active (%)	92.99	90.37	
Population of females aged 16–59 years	15 048 930	15 383 759	+ 2.22
Economically active females aged 16–59 years	8 334 060	9 368 857	+ 12.42
Proportion economically active (%)	55.38	60.90	
Total population of working age	31 484 250	32 157 723	+ 2.14
Total economically active	23 616 455	24 527 445	+ 3.86
Proportion economically active (%)	75.01	76.27	

Note: Working age is defined as 16–64 years for males and 16–59 years for females. A number of economically active persons aged under 16 in 1971 (when minimum school leaving age was 15 years), and above the usual retirement age in both years, are therefore not included.
Source: Census of Population 1971, Economic Activity Tables Part I, Table 1, p. 1. Census of Population 1981, Economic Activity Great Britain, Table 2, pp. 16–17.

55.38 per cent to 60.9 per cent, contributing to a 12.42 per cent increase in the number of females in the labour force. In comparison, male employment actually fell, both in absolute numbers and relative to the size of the male population of working age. Although movements in wage levels can partially explain these changes in the labour force there were also a number of other contributory factors.

In Chapter 9 it was explained why an individual's labour supply schedule is expected to 'bend backwards', that is, above a certain wage the amount of labour supplied will start to decrease. The supply of labour to an industry, however, will not usually slope backwards because new workers will be attracted from other industries, or from outside the workforce, even if existing workers may wish to work less hours when the wage rate rises. The elasticity of the supply of labour depends on how quickly workers will change jobs in response to any movement in the wage rate. There is not always an immediate rush of workers from one industry, or firm, to another when wages alter because any such move may be moderated by a number of influences, including:

1.   Geographical immobility. If taking up a new higher paid job necessitates moving to another geographical area then the cost of moving house, social ties, the disruption of children's education and the rest may make such a move less likely.
2.   Occupational immobility. Lack of training or insufficient natural ability may prevent workers changing occupations.
3.   Man-made barriers. Non-transferable pension schemes, union 'closed-shop' agreements and so on will slow down any job transfers.

FACTOR PRICES

If it is assumed that there is perfect competition among buyers and sellers in a factor market (some other possible market structures are considered below) then the equilibrium factor price is simply determined where supply and demand intersect, as shown by W^* in Figure 10.5.

If all workers were identical then all wage rates would tend to equalise out as workers moved from lower paid to higher paid jobs. However, people are different and wage differentials do exist. It is possible to distinguish between (1) dynamic and (2) static reasons for the existence of wage differentials.

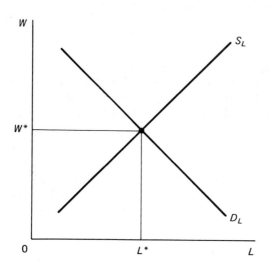

FIGURE 10.5   **Factor price determination in a perfectly competitive factor market**

1. In some cases the influences itemised above, such as moving costs, retraining and so on may temporarily delay rather than completely stop any move to higher paid employment. These dynamic influences will produce temporary wage differentials.

2. For some people the non-monetary benefits of living in a particular area or doing a certain job will always compensate for a lower wage and they will never wish to move to higher wage jobs that do not offer these benefits. In other cases it is impossible for some workers ever to acquire the skills and strengths required for certain jobs. Static factors such as these will cause permanent differentials in wages. Note, however, that even though some existing workers may never change occupation or area of residence in pursuit of higher wages, they will eventually retire, or leave the labour force for other reasons. The school-leavers and other new entrants who replace them will tend to try to enter the relatively better paid jobs. Thus over a long period of time as the composition of the labour force changes the supply of labour to specific areas of employment will not remain static.

Transfer earnings and economic rent

The total payment received by a factor of production can be split into the two components of transfer earnings and economic rent. Transfer earnings *TE* are the minimum payment that a factor must receive in order to prevent its transfer to another use. Economic rent *ER* is any payment in excess of *TE*. Two examples illustrate the use of these two concepts.

1.   The Market for Land

Consider a farmer who owns a plot of land on which she currently grows cabbages which yield an annual income of £1000. The next best return, £800, could be got from growing carrots. Other possible uses for the land are grazing, yielding an annual income of £600, or letting campers use it for £500. If cabbages are grown then *TE* are £800, because the land would be transferred to carrot growing if the return from growing cabbages fell below this figure. *ER* is the balance of £200, given the current income of £1000. If one is talking about growing crops in general *TE* are £600, and for agriculture as a whole the *TE* of this piece of land are £500. It can thus be seen that the *TE* of a factor are relative to the use that is under consideration.

2.   High Incomes

The extremely high incomes that are received by some popular entertainers, actors and so on are nearly all economic rent with respect to their current occupation. A successful entertainer earning £100 000 a year might have transfer earnings of only £3000 a year. These *TE* may not necessarily be the same as the income that could be earned in the next best paid possible source of employment. People may prefer to remain in a particular occupation because of its non-monetary benefits even though they might earn more elsewhere.

The above discussion refers to *TE* with respect to an occupation, but the *TE* of a successful entertainer with respect to other employers may be much higher. This is illustrated in Figure 10.6, where S_L is the supply curve of the individual's labour services. It soon becomes vertical because the amount of work one person can do is obviously limited. The MRP_L is the usual downward sloping shape which cuts S_L at a salary of £100 000. Nearly all of this income is *ER* and the individual would still be willing to do the same job for a much lower income as long as her *TE* of £3000 are covered. So why do employers pay this entertainer such a high salary instead of just paying something slightly higher than the *TE*? The reason is that in a market economy the salary will be bid up by competing potential employers. Each will have seen that it is worthwhile paying anything up to the salary which equals the extra revenue

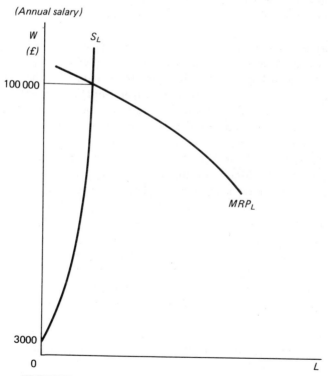

FIGURE 10.6   **Economic rent and high earnings**

generated from using this individual's labour services. Thus, from the individual's viewpoint, *TE* with respect to one employer are much higher than the *TE* for the occupation. In some centrally planned economies where there is only one state-run film company top actors are paid much less than in the West. Because there is no competition from other employers the state company only has to pay them slightly more than their *TE* for the occupation to get them to work for it.

WAGES AND EMPLOYMENT UNDER IMPERFECT COMPETITION

The above analysis of factor price determination assumed perfect competition on both sides of the factor market. Three other possible market structures will now be considered:

1. Monopsony – one buyer and many sellers.
2. Monopoly – one seller and many buyers.
3. Bilateral monopoly – one buyer and one seller.

Many other possible market structures exist where the state of competition lies somewhere between the limiting cases of perfect competition and monopoly. As with the case of oligopoly (see Chapter 7) there are many possible different solutions to these intermediate situations, where wage and employment levels will depend on the strategies adopted by the different parties involved as well as on the degree of monopoly present. In general all that can be said is that the greater the degree of monopoly then the closer the factor price will be to that predicted in the case of pure monopoly.

Another limitation of the following analysis of imperfect factor markets is that only the short-run demand for labour, based on the MRP_L, is considered.

1. Monopsony

A monopsonist, or single buyer, will face an upward sloping labour supply schedule such as S_L in Figure 10.7. Unlike a perfectly competitive firm, which can employ as much labour as it wishes at the market wage, a monopsonist has to pay a higher wage to attract more labour, whether from other occupations or as new entrants into the labour force. When the labour supply schedule slopes upward the marginal cost of labour (MC_L) schedule will slope up even more steeply. This is because an employer who wishes to take on more labour will have to pay any increase in the wage rate to the existing labour force as well as the wages of the additional workers. In Figure 10.7 it

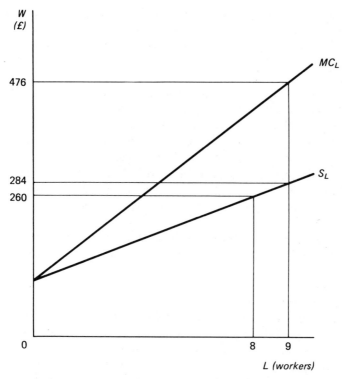

FIGURE 10.7   The marginal cost of labour schedule

can be seen that 8 workers will be willing to work for this monopsonist at a wage of £260 and 9 at a wage of £284. Thus:

The total wage bill for 8 workers = 8 × £260 = £2080.
The total wage bill for 9 workers = 9 × £284 = £2556.

Therefore the marginal cost of the ninth worker is £476. Another way that this figure could have been calculated is:

Additional payment to existing workers = 8 × £24 = £192.
Payment to ninth worker   = £284.
Thus total extra cost of ninth worker   = £476.

It can be shown that the MC_L schedule will have the same intercept on the vertical axis as the supply schedule but will have twice the slope.
* Proof

Assume that $W = a + bL$ where a and b are parameters
Total cost of labour $(TC_L) = W.L = (a + bL).L = aL + bL^2$

Marginal cost of labour (MC_L) is the rate of change of TC_L and thus by differentiating:

$$MC_L = dTC_L/dL = a + 2bL$$

The monopsonist's demand for labour schedule will be its MRP_L schedule, which will take the usual downward sloping shape as shown in Figure 10.8. One would normally expect that a monopsonistic buyer of a particular type of labour would also be the only producer of the finished product, and that D_L would also be the industry demand for labour, although this is not inevitable.

A profit maximising monopsonist will employ labour up to the point where the marginal revenue of one extra unit of labour equals its marginal cost. In Figure 10.8 the optimal amount of labour is therefore L^* and so the monopsonist must pay a wage of W^*. Thus under monopsony less labour will be employed and the wage will be lower than in the case of a perfectly competitive factor market where these variables would take the values L_C and W_C, respectively.

2. Monopoly

A labour market may become monopolistic if workers form a trade union, which is an organisation of workers formed to protect their own interests. A

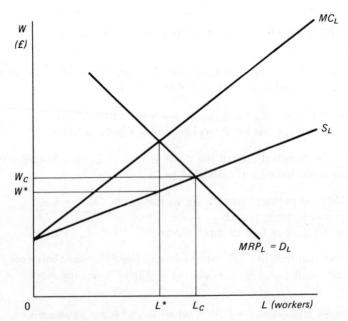

FIGURE 10.8   Factor price determination under monopsony

trade union may concern itself with wages, employment levels and working conditions, including matters such as health and safety, but only the possible effects on the wage rate and employment level are considered here. There are different methods by which trade unions may try to achieve their objectives, for example, collective bargaining, strikes, working to rule and so on. Their success will depend on their bargaining power, the ability to sustain a strike, the proportion of the workforce that is in the union, and other influences that fall into the realm of industrial relations rather than microeconomics. It is just assumed here that a trade union can enforce a minimum wage below which none of its members would be prepared to work.

Assume that a trade union is formed in a factor market that was initially perfectly competitive with wage and employment levels at W_0 and L_0, respectively, as shown in Figure 10.9. If it is assumed that the trade union sets a minimum wage of W_1, which is greater than W_0, then the amount of labour that firms will wish to employ will fall to L_1 and the amount of labour supplied will increase to L_2, that is, there will be L_1L_2 excess supply of labour. Note that the excess supply of labour L_1L_2 is not necessarily made up of unemployed workers. Those workers who wish to work in this industry but cannot do so may currently be employed elsewhere in less preferred jobs.

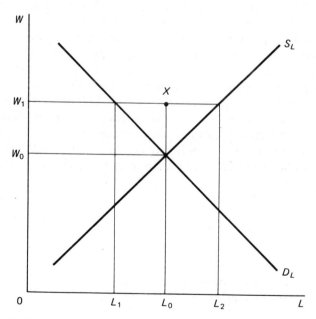

FIGURE 10.9   Factor pricing with a unionised workforce and many buyers of labour

The above analysis assumes that, although the trade union sets the wage rate, employers decide on the amount of labour that is employed. This is not always the case, though, and a trade union may try to force a firm off its demand for labour curve. Just as there may not be jobs for all workers who may wish to have one at a particular wage rate, so firms may not be able to employ exactly the amount of labour that they would wish. For example, a trade union may try to achieve a wage of W_1 and also force employers to employ L_0 of labour, in other words, try to attain the wage employment combination shown by X in Figure 10.9. Whether or not such a position may be attainable will depend on, among other things, the profits that the firm is making initially. If it was making some economic profit then the extra wage costs might be absorbed from it. However, if the firm was only just breaking even then any further cost increases might force it out of business.

Another way in which a trade union may be able to increase its members' incomes without causing some of them to lose their jobs is to combine an increase in the hourly wage with a reduction in the working week. This method will only work if the demand for labour is inelastic over the relevant wage range, that is, an increase in the wage will increase the total wage bill. If the demand for labour is elastic then an increase in the price of labour will lead to a reduction in the wage bill and there will be no way of sharing it out so that all workers receive more.

Assume that the demand for labour, D_L, is as shown in Figure 10.10, and that initially the wage for a 40-hour week is £200 and 400 workers are employed. If a trade union insists on a minimum weekly wage of £272 then the employers will only wish to employ 360 workers (still on the basis of a 40-hour week). The trade union can avoid 40 of its members losing their jobs if it can arrange a work-sharing agreement to absorb this drop in the demand for labour. This can be explained if the example in Figure 10.10 is analysed in terms of worker hours instead of workers. The initial weekly wage of £200 for a 40-hour week corresponds to an hourly wage of £5, and a weekly wage of £272 would correspond to an hourly rate of £6.80.

Thus, at an hourly wage of £5.00, the demand for labour would be

$$400 \times 40 = 16\,000 \text{ hours}$$

and, at an hourly wage of £6.80, the demand would be

$$360 \times 40 = 14\,400 \text{ hours.}$$

If this 14 400 hours was equally divided among the 400 workers who were initially employed it would mean a 36-hour week and the weekly wage would then be

$$£6.80 \times 36 = £244.80.$$

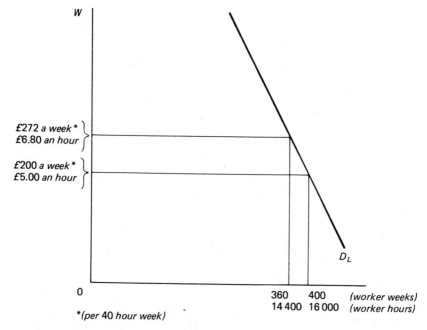

FIGURE 10.10   **Work sharing and the effects of a wage increase**

Thus, although the weekly wage does not rise as much as it would do if there as no reduction in the working week, this system means an increased weekly wage as well as no reduction in the number of workers employed. Whether or not such a work sharing agreement could be implemented in practice would depend on a number of other factors not mentioned above, such as fixed training and equipment costs for each worker, which would vary according to circumstances.

3. Bilateral monopoly

To explain some of the possible solutions to a bilateral monopoly situation, assume that a factor market is initially monopsonistic and that labour is competitively supplied by a non-unionised workforce. This situation is illustrated in Figure 10.11 where the monopsonist's MC_L and MRP_L schedules intersect at I, L is 22 units and the corresponding wage is £160. If a trade union is then formed which enforces a minimum wage of £180 the employer will effectively face the labour supply curve ABS_L. This supply schedule is horizontal at a wage of £180 up to 26 units of L, but to attract any more labour the employer will again face the original supply schedule and will thus have to increase the wage. The MC_L schedule will also be constant at £180

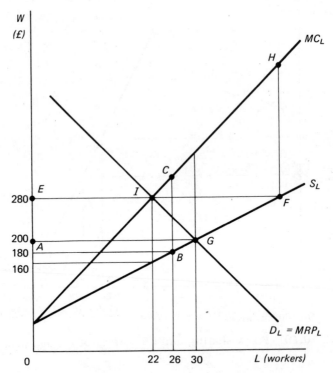

FIGURE 10.11   Bilateral monopoly

up to the 26th unit of L and then, as the employer reverts to the original supply schedule, so the original MC_L schedule also applies again. The employer therefore faces the discontinuous marginal cost of labour schedule $ABCMC_L$. This MC_L schedule cuts the MRP_L schedule at 26 units of L, which would be the employer's optimum employment level in these circumstances. Thus the union succeeds in increasing both the wage and the level of employment. If the union enforced any other wage above the original £160 there would be a similar effect on the labour supply and MC_L schedules. For example, with a minimum wage of £280 the supply curve would become EFS_L and the relevant MC_L schedule would be $EFHMC_L$. This cuts the MRP_L schedule at the original employment level of 22 units of L. If a minimum wage above £280 is enforced the firm will reduce the amount of L it uses below the original monopsonistic employment level.

The theory cannot predict what the wage and employment levels will be under bilateral monopoly but it can explain what the feasible choices open to the union are. A union would wish to be somewhere on the section GI of the employer's demand for labour schedule but the actual solution will depend on all the other factors that affect the bargaining powers of the two parties involved. It must also be remembered that the analysis is a greatly simplified model that illustrates certain basic principles that can be applied to labour markets in general. Employers and unions do not have these little diagrams in front of them when they sit round a table to discuss wage negotiations!

QUESTIONS

1. A firm uses two inputs, K and L, and only L can be varied. The table below shows the output that can be obtained by using additional units of L with a fixed amount of K.

TABLE 10Q.1

Units of Output	0	40	100	150	190	220	240	250	255
Units of L	0	1	2	3	4	5	6	7	8

The firm sells its output in a perfectly competitive market where the ruling price is 20p. How much of L will be used if the cost per unit of L is (a) £4.00, (b) £2.00, (c) £8.00? What would the cost per unit of L be if the firm found the optimal usage of L to be 6?

What is likely to happen to the amount of L employed if (a) the demand for the finished product increases and (b) the amount of K used is increased?

2. In the absence of compulsory conscription, what economic criteria should be employed in determining the pay of the Armed Forces?

3. A firm uses the inputs L and K to manufacture product X, and can vary the amount of L, while K is fixed. It buys L in a perfectly competitive factor market, but is a monopoly seller of X. Table 10Q.2 shows how much of X can be produced with varying amounts of L, and the price at which these quantities will be sold.

How much L will be employed if the firm is maximising profit and the price of L is £315 a unit?

4. What shape do you think the supply curve for North Sea Oil is?

5. A firm is a monopsonistic buyer of labour, and the relationship between the MRP_L and L, the amount of labour employed, is given by

$$MRP_L = 100 - 0.8L$$

TABLE 10Q.2

L	X	Price of X (in £)
0	0	—
1	12	84
2	30	66
3	45	51
4	57	39
5	67	29
6	76	20
7	84	12
8	92	4

The supply of labour to the firm is such that

$$L = 2.5w - 50 \qquad \text{where } w \text{ is the wage rate.}$$

Answer the following questions, either by drawing a graph or mathematically. What amount of labour will the firm employ to maximise profit, and what wage will be paid? If the workers form a trade union and can force a minimum wage rate, what is the maximum amount of L that they can cause to be employed? If they try to maximise the wage paid to those at present employed what will this be?

6. In what circumstances will the wage rate that a firm pays its workers *not* be equal to the marginal revenue product of labour?

7. How could the theory of factor pricing account for the fact that before the 1970 Equal Pay Act came into force in 1975 a number of women were paid less than men for doing the same work? What would this theory predict would be the effect of the legislation that made sex descrimination in pay illegal?

8. From an individual worker's viewpoint, which will usually be the higher: (a) her transfer earnings with respect to her current employer, or (b) her transfer earnings with respect to her current occupation?

CHAPTER 11

The Marxian theory of the firm and the market economy

Some readers may be surprised at finding a chapter on Marxian economics in a book that is mainly concerned with the behaviour of firms and consumers in a market economy. It is not as widely realised as perhaps it should be that most of what Marx wrote was in fact concerned with the operation of a market economy. He said relatively little about the operation of a socialist economic system and, of course, his main work *Capital*[1] was first published half a centry before the Russian revolution and the coming into being of the first planned economy.

Marx's work was a mixture of positive and normative concepts. His most important economic prediction was that the capitalist system was inherently unstable and would eventually collapse, and the main concern of this chapter is to explain the reasons he gave for this prediction. His main normative proposition was that workers were exploited under capitalism and that they would be better off under a socialist economic system.

Ideological bias

Given the sometimes controversial attitudes toward Marxian theory it is perhaps appropriate to say a few words about ideological bias in the study of economics. Although some people would argue that economics, or positive

---

1. K. Marx, *Capital* (London: International Publishers, 1970) (originally published in German in 1867; first English translation in 1886).

economics at least, is a value-free analysis of how the economy operates, any study of limited length must be selective in the ideas that are considered. The inclusion or exclusion of any particular theories is itself a form of bias. Some studies of the operation of free market economies do not attempt to consider Marxian theory because it is thought that Marx's explanation of the operation of capitalism is incorrect. However, another reason sometimes given for not considering Marxian theory is that it is thought that a state-planned economic system is undesirable. From an analytical viewpoint this latter reason is rather illogical and is an example of ideological bias. The way to assess a theory is to examine the logic of the analysis and the accuracy of its predictions, as opposed to ignoring it because one does not like what might happen if it were correct. If one accepts Marx's prediction that capitalism will collapse it does not necessarily mean that one believes that state planning is the best way of organising an economy. Given that a sizeable proportion of the world's population lives in economies that base their objectives on what Marx wrote, and some of the most important economic and political arguments of our time relate to Marx's ideas, it is amazing how little is known about these ideas by many students of economics.

Having said all this it must be admitted that this book itself is biased. Out of twelve chapters only one tackles the Marxian line of analysis. It does, however, go a little way towards redressing the balance between the Marxian and the mainstream neo-classical approaches to the analysis of the firm and the market economy that are usually taught in microeconomics courses.

AN OVERVIEW OF MARXIAN ANALYSIS

Marx's ideas span many disciplines and in one chapter it is only possible to present a summary of certain main threads in his analysis. The interested reader can refer to other more detailed introductions to this subject, for example, Junankar,[2] Hunt and Sherman,[3] Burkitt.[4]

Marx's explanation of the decline of capitalism must be seen in the context of how he interpreted historical change in general.

Historical materialism

As societies have developed, their productive capacities have improved and enabled them to produce a surplus over and above a basic subsistence standard

---

2. P. N. Junankar, *Marx's Economics* (Oxford: Philip Allen, 1982).
3. E. K. Hunt and H. J. Sherman, *Economics: An Introduction to Traditional and Radical Views*, 4th edn (London: Harper & Row, 1981).
4. B. Burkitt, *Radical Political Economy* (Brighton: Harvester Press, 1984).

of living. According to the theory of historical materialism, the history of mankind can be interpreted in terms of the struggle between different groups within society to win a greater share of this surplus and so increase their living standards. Marx argued that throughout each stage of economic development since the primitive community a certain group has taken this surplus and left the rest of the population with only enough for a subsistence standard of living. One interpretation of this approach suggests that a society would pass through five stages.

1. The primitive community – where everyone lived at subsistence level.
2. Slavery – where the slave-owners took the surplus.
3. Feudalism – where land-owners took the surplus.
4. Capitalism – where the owners of capital took the surplus.
5. Socialism – this would be the final stage where exploitation would be eliminated and the surplus would be shared out over the whole community. Marx did not say much about how such a system would be organised. He did, however, suggest that there would be two stages in its evolvement:

(a) The first stage of socialism would entail the elimination of private ownership of the means of production and greater equality in the distribution of what was produced. There would still be a need to offer wage incentives to induce people to work and in this transitionary stage political controls would be necessary to avoid disruption by groups who opposed this system. It could be argued that most of today's communist countries are still at this stage.

(b) In the second or 'higher form' of socialism, when all the transitionary problems were overcome, pure communism would be achieved. The state would have managed to improve the productive capacity of the economy. Everyone would willingly work for the good of society, and would not be alienated from their work; the role of the state would wither away, and society would operate on the principle: 'From each according to his ability, to each according to his needs.'[5] There are controversial views on the questions of whether or not the final, or higher, stage of socialism is feasible or desirable, but these are not issues that this chapter attempts to tackle.

The transition from one stage of economic development to the next, it is argued, results from the operation of natural economic forces, whereas the social system, or 'social base' is more rigid. This is because society's culture, laws and social and political institutions will tend to reflect the 'economic

---

5. K. Marx, 'Critique of the Gotha Programme', in L. S. Fleur (ed.), *Marx and Engels: Basic Writings on Politics and Philosophy* (London: Fontana, 1969). (Written in 1875, but not originally published until 1891, in German.)

base' of the current stage of development. The priviliged groups who receive the surplus will try to mould the social system to their own advantage and to maintain their position. The transition from one stage of economic development to the next therefore involves a conflict between those who wish to maintain the existing system and those who believe that they will benefit under the new system. This might involve violent revolution but such a development is not inevitable. The transition from feudalism to capitalism in Britain, for example, was relatively peaceful. However, it could be argued that the French Revolution and the American Revolution were part of the struggle to throw off the yoke of the aristocratic land-owners and to free individuals to pursue their own fortunes in a free market capitalist system. Given that the United Kingdom is currently in the fourth stage, capitalism, it is Marx's conclusion that this system will collapse that is our main interest.

The question is sometimes asked, 'If Marx thought that the decline of capitalism was inevitable then why did he not sit back and wait for it to happen instead of devoting most of his life to writing about it?' The reply to this is that although Marx believed that man could not alter the path of history it was possible to alter the speed at which any changes might take place and the way in which they might happen. Given that he thought that most of the population were unfairly exploited under capitalism he wished to point the way to the changes that would be necessary if they were to improve their lot.

THE INSTABILITY OF CAPITALISM

Marx predicted that a capitalist economy would undergo a series of economic booms and slumps. Each recession would be more severe than the previous one and eventually the economy would enter a recession so severe that it would never recover and the system would collapse. A long-term decline in the rate of profit would underlie this cyclical pattern of economic activity. The reasons for these predictions are spelt out below. These are followed by some interpretations of the way Marxian economic theory can be used to explain more recent events. It must be remembered that Marx's original ideas were based on the way he saw the capitalist system operating in Britain over a hundred years ago.

The structure of capitalism

A capitalist society is made up of two main groups, capitalists and workers, together with other groups such as sole traders and merchants and the unemployed. Capitalists own the means of production, or capital. They employ workers to produce goods using this capital. Workers are paid less than the value they add to the goods that they produce and the capitalists then take the surplus value as profit. The only resource that workers own is their own labour, which they have to sell to capitalists in order to survive.

Accumulation

Capitalists can either take their profits as income, and spend them on consumption, or reinvest them. Marx termed this reinvestment the 'accumulation' of capital. Capitalists who reinvest their profit will gain an advantage over those who do not. The existence of economies of scale, particularly in manufacturing industries, means that the capitalists who invest in large-scale production facilities will be able to reduce average production costs. In addition, as technical progress brings down the cost of production, so those capitalists who invest in the latest plant and equipment will be able to produce more cheaply than rivals who do not. In a competitive industry reinvestment therefore becomes a necessity for survival. Those who do not reinvest sufficiently will find their prices undercut by those who have reaped economies of scale and have installed the latest labour-saving technology through reinvestment. The smaller firms who lose out in this battle to survive will be driven out of business and their owners will be forced to join the ranks of the workers or the unemployed. The end result of this process of accumulation is the centralisation of production in the hands of a few large monopolistic producers.

Business cycles

According to Marx there would not be a smooth progression towards the monopolisation of industry. In the early stages of industrialisation shortages of labour would cause hold-ups in economic growth. These labour shortages would then cause wages to be temporarily bid up until sufficient numbers of new workers were attracted. These additional workers were drawn mainly from the agricultural sector in the case of Britain during the Industrial Revolution.

   Once the process of industrialisation was under way a large pool of industrial labourers would be established. Labour-saving technical progress and the concentration of production in the hands of a few large firms would mean that there would not be jobs for all who wanted one and a 'reserve army of unemployed' would come into being. Even in times of economic expansion, the existence of this reserve army would usually prevent further labour shortages developing and thus allow capitalists to keep down wages. This keeping down of wages is a central factor in causing the business cycles that Marx predicted would take place in an industrialised economy.

   In a period of economic expansion firms find their sales increasing and so order more plant and equipment to cope with the anticipated increased production. This helps fuel the economic boom as the firms producing capital equipment take on more workers who then create further increases in the demand for final goods by spending their incomes. In this expansionary phase of the business cycle the owners of firms will be doing all they can to reap the greatest possible profits. Not being content with some of the extra income from increased sales going to their workers, they will try to hold down wages to try to secure a greater proportion of this extra revenue for themselves. This, however, contributes to the end of the boom. When workers' wages are held down their spending power diminishes. Thus the expansion of demand for goods is stifled unless the capitalists spend the same amount on the consumption of goods out of their increased profits as workers would have if they had had this income paid as wages. This is not likely to happen and so a 'realisation crisis' occurs, that is, the expected profits do not actually appear because there is insufficient effective demand for the goods that are produced.

It is important to understand that this theory argues that it is the collective action of all firms that causes the boom to end. Individual firms are acting in the best way from their own viewpoint in trying to increase profits by holding down wages while sales are booming. If one capitalist said 'I can that see holding back wages will be our downfall and so I will pass on the benefits of this growth in sales to my workers in higher wages' he would be throwing his own money away. His own workers would not necessarily buy the goods that his firm produced and he would still not prevent the collapse of the boom. If all firms collectively agreed to pay more in wages it might help the boom to continue, but in a competitive environment this would not be likely.

In the trough of a depression high unemployment and lack of demand will tend to lower the cost of both labour and capital. This fall in costs increases profits and starts to stimulate further investment, the economy starts to climb out of the recession and so the 'boom–slump' cycle continues.

The 'accelerator' effect compounds the fizzling out of the economic boom as well as helping to generate enough demand to break out of an economic slump. The accelerator effect is due to the demand for capital goods being more reliant on the rate of expansion of consumer demand than its absolute level. When consumer demand is growing at its fastest rate the demand for new capital equipment to produce these goods is at its highest. Once the growth in consumer demand slows (not falls), for whatever reason, less new capital goods will be demanded. Workers will then be laid off in the capital goods industries. This will lead to a reduction in their spending power and lead to further cut-backs in the demand for capital goods. Eventually these forces will cause the demand for final goods to stop growing and lead to the onset of another economic depression. In a depression there is still a certain amount of industrial production and eventually the wearing out of machinery will mean that new capital equipment will be bought. The extra employment thus generated in the capital goods industries will stimulate the demand for goods and start to lead the way out of the depression. Successive slumps are more severe than earlier ones because of the changes that the structure of industry is going through.

Monopoly capitalism

In the early stages of capitalism the firms that grow and prosper steal the markets of the firms that are driven out of business. However, in the later states of capitalism, when there are only a few large monopolies who have survived, this avenue for increasing sales no longer exists. There will be the opportunity for these remaining firms to increase profits using their monopoly position to exploit the consumer, but the potential of this strategy is also limited. When profits are reinvested they will generate even greater productive capacity but the only way that these monopolies can sell any increased output is by reducing price, which would reduce their profits. If, on the other hand, they chose not to spend their profits on investment then, unless they compensated for this with sufficient increased consumption demand out of their profits, which would be unlikely, aggregate demand would fall and profits would still decline. Thus, in its final stages, capitalism is seen to stagnate and start to crumble.

Individual firms may see their route out of this crisis through increased investment in the latest labour-saving technology. However, although this may appear to be a sound business decision from an individual firm's viewpoint, if all firms pursue the same strategy then the total workforce is reduced and consequently there are less customers for the goods that are produced. Thus the collective action of all firms contributes to their own downfall via underconsumption.

Alienation

Although this chapter's main concern is the economic aspects of Marxian analysis it is important to realise that Marx also provided a sociological analysis of the changes that society would go through under capitalism. In this context, one of the most important themes is the concept of alienation. Under capitalism, Marx argued, workers lose all sense of identity with their work. They just become like machines and have no control over what work they do or even whether they work or not. The only reason they work for the capitalists is to earn wages. He put forward the view that work is part of life and is a means through which men and women can fulfill their potential to contribute to society and gain self-respect and personal satisfaction.

Ideally, he argued, workers should have control over how they work and what they produce and that everyone should have the right to work.

The final collapse of capitalism

Marx predicted that the 'increasing misery of the proletariat' under capitalism would eventually lead to their rising up and destroying the system. There are different forces working towards this, however, and there is some disagreement as to what will actually bring about the final collapse.

Unemployment will rise as production becomes concentrated in the hands of a few large monopolies fighting a losing battle to keep up the rate of profit. In addition to the discontent of the growing pool of unemployed, the degree of inequality between the incomes of capitalists and workers will increase. Although the rate of profit may fall, as explained below, the total amount of profit may still increase, given that there is a greater investment on which this rate is earned. Thus profits will take up a greater share of national income at the expense of wages. It is also argued that increased alienation among workers will add to the discontent created by these other factors, eventually bringing about the ultimate collapse of capitalism.

THE LABOUR THEORY OF VALUE

The labour theory of value is a formal analysis of the way in which labour is exploited under capitalism and why there will be a long-term decline in the rate of profit. Marx introduces several different meanings to the word 'value' and the analysis below is only a simplified version intended to convey the main ideas involved.

According to Marx, it is the labour input that gives a commodity its value. Without the labour of workers a capitalist cannot use his capital to manufacture commodities and to make profits. The value of a commodity can be defined in terms of the number of hours of labour that are necessary to produce it. Marx recognised that differences in skills and the intensity of work effort can affect what is produced in an hour but assumed that each commodity required a given 'socially necessary' number of hours of 'average' labour.

He also recognised that in some cases, even though a number of hours of labour may have been expended in producing it, a manufactured item has no value if no one wants it. An example of this might be a picture painted by someone with no artistic talent. Capitalists only make profits from producing commodities with a final 'use value'.

The manufacture of commodities requires other inputs as well as labour.

A 136

2 (a) Indicor a longitudinal than . FC

(b) Is it necessary the normal or spherical rate of voltage .

These other inputs, such as raw materials and capital equipment, will themselves have required a labour input in their production. Thus to determine the labour value of a particular commodity one has to take into account the labour value embodied in other inputs as well as the direct labour input. It is only labour that confers value, however, not machines. The labour value of a good is not the same as its price. Marx said that prices depended on the exchange value of different goods, which would vary according to market forces. However, the labour value of commodities as a whole is related to the average wage, and it makes the analysis simpler to understand if, in some illustrative examples, the labour value is thought of as the price of commodity in terms of the average hourly wage. Consider first an example where there is no capitalist and where workers receive the full value of their labour.

Assume that two hours of direct labour and one unit of corn are required to produce one unit of bread and that the production of one unit of corn requires four hours of labour only. Using Marx's terminology:

variable capital $(v) = $ the value of the direct labour input;
constant capital $(c) = $ the value of labour embodied in other inputs
used up in production.

The labour value u of each commodity is calculated from the formula

$$u = c + v.$$

For one unit of corn

$v = 4$ and $c = 0$ (there are no other inputs) and so

$u = 0 + 4 = 4.$

For one unit of bread

$v = 2,$

$c = 4$ (the labour value of one unit of corn).

Thus $u = 4 + 2 = 6,$

that is, it takes a total of 6 hours to manufacture one unit of bread.

If the standard working day is 12 hours then workers would be paid enough to buy commodities that have 12 labour hours embodied in them. If the whole wage was spent on bread then a worker would be able to afford two units given its labour value of 6 per unit.

Now the capitalist is introduced and some further terms defined:

Surplus value s is the value of the profit taken by the capitalist.
The rate of surplus r is defined by the formula $r = s/v$
and so

$$s = r.v.$$

Continuing with the example above, assume that $r = 2$. This means that surplus value equals $2.v$, that is, the actual amount of surplus created is relative to the input of direct labour.

The formula for the value of a commodity now becomes

$$u = c + v + s.$$

Thus for corn

$$u = 0 + 4 + (2 \times 4) = 12$$

and for bread

$$u = 12 + 2 + (2 \times 2) = 18.$$

In this situation a worker will only be paid enough to be able to buy 2/3 of a unit of bread for 12 hours work. This means that a worker receives what can be produced in 4 hours as payment for a 12-hour working day. The value of the other 8 hours of work is expropriated by the capitalist as profit.

Capitalists can increase their profits by increasing the rate of surplus value. By increasing the rate of surplus value the relative extraction of surplus value changes and the capitalists take a greater share of what is produced. This can be distinguished from the increasing of profit through the absolute extraction of surplus value, where production is increased by getting workers to work longer hours, or by other methods of increasing productivity, but the same proportion of the total value created is taken by the capitalist.

Consider an increase in the rate of surplus value to 3 in the example above. This would mean:

for corn

$$u = 0 + 4 + 12 = 16;$$

for bread

$$u = 16 + 2 + 6 = 24.$$

Thus for a 12-hour day a worker would only be paid enough to buy half a unit of corn, which requires 3 hours of labour to produce. The fruits of the other 9 hours of work would be taken as profit by the capitalist. The extent to which capitalists can increase the rate of surplus is limited by the requirement that workers must be paid at least a minimum subsistence wage. In this example, if the subsistence wage is enough to buy two-thirds of a unit of bread a day then the maximum rate of surplus that can be extracted is 2.

Exactly what Marx meant by a subsistence wage has been the subject of dispute. Certainly it means more than barely enough to keep a worker alive from one day to the next. Workers must have a living standard that allows them to do their job and also to raise a family that will provide the next generation workers. Marx termed this wage the value of a worker's labour; that is to say, the subsistence wage can be expressed in terms of the labour value of the commodities necessary for subsistence. Critics of the Marxian school of thought have pointed to the average wages in Western industrialised countries, which are well above a subsistence level in this sense, as evidence that Marx was wrong. Others, however, have argued that the subsistence wage is a relative concept and that as living standards have generally improved so has the minimum wage. What a worker in the United Kingdom today would require as the minimum wage to do a job would be far greater than the wage a worker of a hundred years age would have required, even when inflation has been allowed for. Another view is that workers in Western industrialised countries themselves indirectly exploit workers in the third world, through the unequal patterns of international trade and finance that exist, and it is these third-world workers whose wages are at a subsistence level.

Even if wages have risen above a minimum subsistence level this does not necessarily invalidate Marx's main predictions. Although perhaps Marx did not foresee the growth in trade union power that has helped increase workers' wages in the twentieth century, it has been argued that this phenomenon only delays the eventual collapse, as explained later.

The declining rate of profit

Marx defined the rate of profit as

$$p = s/(c + v)$$

and the organic composition of capital as

$q = c/v.$

Taking the formula for the rate of profit and dividing top and bottom by v, this formula becomes

$$p = \frac{s}{c+v} = \frac{\dfrac{s}{v}}{\dfrac{c}{v}+1} = \frac{r}{q+1} \qquad (1)$$

As firms reinvest their profits the organic composition of capital changes and q increases. Once r has reached its maximum, determined by the subsistence wage, it can rise no further. Therefore, as q rises and r remains constant, there is a tendency for p, the rate of profit, to decline over time.

Factors counteracting the long-term decline in the rate of profit

Several factors may work towards reversing the decline in the rate of profit, although according to Marxian theory they can do no more than temporarily delay its long-term downward trend.

1. Technological Change

If productivity can be improved through technological improvements then output per worker hour will increase. If workers are still paid the same subsistence wage then there will be extra output that can be sold to make more profits. This means that the rate of surplus r can increase in equation (1) above. A rise in r may counteract the effect of the rise in q so that the rate of profit p increases. The extra profit, however, will then be reinvested, causing q to increase even further. Thus the long-term decline in the rate of profit will still prevail unless advances in the state of technology allow the rate of surplus perpetually to rise faster than the rate at which the reinvestment of profits increases the organic composition of capital, q.

2. Imperialistic Expansion

When capitalists can no longer extract any more surplus from the domestic workforce they may be able to maintain the rate of profit by exploiting other countries. They may invest directly (for example, by building factories) or indirectly (by lending). Cheaper inputs in these countries, particularly low wages and low raw commodity prices, can help maintain profits.

Foreign markets may also provide sales opportunities. The increased output that is produced with reinvested profits may not all be able to be sold in the home market. The international expansion of capitalism extends into both industrialised Western economies as well as poorer third world economies. Marxian economists would argue, though, that even overseas opportunities for cheap inputs and sales outlets are limited and thus the same forces that make an individual capitalist system unstable will also work on a global scale towards the eventual collapse of capitalism.

3. Mergers and Monopoly Power

In a competitive environment there is not much scope for increasing profits through higher prices. Any firm attempting this strategy would soon lose sales to rivals that undercut its prices. However, a monopoly, or a group of oligopolists acting in collusion, may successfully increase profits through price increases. Marxian theory predicts that, in an attempt to reverse the fall in the rate of profit, firms will strive to achieve a monopoly position through natural growth or take-over and merger. Although the elimination of competitors may allow profits to be increased initially, when it comes to reinvesting these profits it becomes a problem for these monopoly capitalists to find a way of selling the resulting increased production, as has already been explained.

4. Exploitation of The Family

The minimum subsistence wage is sufficient to allow workers to raise a family to provide a future generation of workers. Thus, if a capitalist is paying a male worker enough to maintain his whole family, profits can be increased if some of the labour of the other family members is utilised for the same total wage. The widespread employment of women and children in manual industrial occupations at very low rates of pay at the start of the last century is cited as an example of this method being used by capitalists to increase the absolute extraction of surplus value.

RADICAL INTERPRETATIONS OF THE TWENTIETH CENTURY

During the Great Depression of the 1930s many people thought that the collapse of capitalism was imminent. They believed that this was the most severe and thus the last of the business cycles that Marx had predicted. By the Second World War II, however, a recovery had started. After the war, with a few minor fluctuations, this recovery continued into the 1950s and 1960s in the United Kingdom and most other Western economies. Many people saw this as evidence which proved that Marx was wrong and that the collapse of capitalism was not inevitable. Marxian economists, though, have argued that, basically, Marx was correct and that the post-war recovery of capitalism was just another temporary phase in the boom–slump cycle that Marx predicted. In the same vein, the depression of the 1980s has been seen by some as another phase leading towards the ultimate collapse. The privatisation of public industries, attempts to keep down wages, and the installation of the latest labour-saving technology, can all be seen as methods of trying to maintain the rate of profit in the face of an unfavourable economic climate.

A number of explanations for the post-war recovery have been put forward by radical economists. There is some disagreement, however, concerning the extent to which these different factors have contributed to the survival of the capitalist system.

1. State intervention

Keynesian demand management policies implemented in the 1950s and early 1960s smoothed out the troughs in aggregate demand that would otherwise have been created by the business cycles of an unfettered free market and thus kept down unemployment. This meant that, at least temporarily, producers were able to find markets for their commodities.

Government intervention, through the emergence of the Welfare State, also helped remove some of the extremes in income inequalities produced by a free market economy. Marx foresaw the growth of a penniless army of unemployed who would have nothing to lose and everything to gain from overthrowing the capitalist system. The provision of a basic social security payment to those with no other income has helped to control this discontent.

2. Technical progress

Rapid advances in technological progress have at times allowed productivity to increase faster than wages although, as explained above, this can only temporarily halt the long-term decline in the rate of profit. Most progress was made in countries like Japan and Germany where productivity growth exceeded the growth in wages and thus allowed profits to increase. In Britain trade unions forced wage increases to match productivity growth more closely and so the recovery in profits was not so marked.

3. Trade union power

The increased wages won by trade unions have helped keep up the demand for firms' products, although high wage costs can make exports uncompetitive and contribute to the loss of overseas markets. Some people see the growth of trade union power as a step along the path to socialism but, paradoxically, the higher wages won by unions may have helped to prop up the system by keeping up the demand for manufactured goods and by preventing widespread discontent with the capitalist system spreading among poorly paid workers.

4. Imperialistic expansion

Although Western nations no longer march into third-world countries, hoist a flag and then call it part of their empire, economic exploitation still continues. While it was Britain in Marx's time, since the Second World War it has been suggested that it has been mainly the USA which has benefited from economic expansion into many parts of the third world. These nations have provided sources of cheap labour and raw materials and sales outlets for expensive manufactured goods.

5. Monopolies and marketing

In the last stages of monopoly capitalism firms face problems in selling the output that is produced with the capital equipment bought with reinvested profits. As has already been explained, they cannot increase sales by taking them from rivals because there are none left, or they are close partners in collusion. If they attempt to increase sales by lowering prices profits will fall, and if they do not reinvest their profits then aggregate demand in the economy will fall and provoke a realisation crisis.

Baran and Sweezy[6] contended that monopoly capitalists have managed, at least temporarily, to keep up sales through advertising and marketing, including product innovation. New products, or modified and redesigned existing products are continually launched. Advertising has the effect not only of increasing demand for the specific product being advertised but of inducing a generally more materialistic consumer society which is forever spending on the products of capitalism. Another line of argument is that governments are manipulated into a situation of perpetual rearmament, thus propping up demand through ever-increasing defence expenditure.

6. Female and part-time workers

The significant growth of the female labour force in the post-war era is seen by some as the use of female workers as part of a reserve army of labour, brought into the labour force at a time of economic expansion to prevent a

---

6. P. A. Baran and P. M. Sweezy, *Monopoly Capital* (London: Penguin, 1968).

labour shortage developing and wages rising. According to this cyclical theory of female employment, when a downturn in economic activity comes these additional workers are no longer needed and so female employment falls back. However, as Table 11.1 shows, female employment continued to grow in the post-1966 era when male employment fell back and unemployment rose significantly above the comparatively low level that had been experienced in the 1950s and early 1960s. It has been argued that this continued growth of female employment during a slack period in economic activity has been a result of employers substituting female for male workers, particularly at times of technological and organisational change, because they are relatively cheaper to employ. Although legislation has made sex discrimination illegal there are still substantial differentials between male and female workers' earnings in many industries. Also, nearly half of all females in employment are part-time workers, many of whom do not enjoy earnings and other employment benefits comparative with those received by full-time workers, and whose employment protection is also weaker.

Evidence exists to support both the cyclical and the substitution explanations of the growth in female employment. Marx did not identify specific demographic groups in his definition of the reserve army of workers and it is not necessary to try to explain all of the growth of female employment in terms of one or other of these two theories. Both forces may have operated, to a greater or lesser extent, in different industries.

7. The division of the workforce

When Marx was writing *Capital* he saw workers and capitalists as two clearly

TABLE 11.1   Male and female employment in Great Britain, 1955–1985

	Males		Females	
	Employed	Unemployed	Employed	Unemployed
1955	15.2	0.1	7.81	0.06
1960	15.5	0.3	8.25	0.09
1965	16.0	0.2	8.84	0.06
1970	15.3	0.4	9.01	0.08
1975	14.7	0.7	9.49	0.15
1980	14.3	1.1	10.05	0.5
1985	13.9	2.2	9.94	0.95

Note: Mid-year estimates, all figures in millions.
Source: *Annual Abstracts of Statistics*, nos. 97 (1960 edn) to 123 (1987 edn), Table 6.1, HMSO.

identifiable groups. There was a vast difference between the incomes and lives of the mass of manual workers and the wealthy factory owners. Today, however, the dividing line is not so clear-cut. Many workers, particularly those in management and skilled non-manual jobs, do not see themselves as part of the 'lumpen proletariat'. A number have some share in the ownership of capital in one form or another, such as pension funds or life assurance policies. The decline of the manual occupations in manufacturing industry since the mid-1960s has reinforced this trend. Some radical economists see this as an example of the 'divide and rule' strategy. If some workers are given higher incomes and better conditions of employment they tend to identify themselves with the side of the capitalists. They will support a system that gives them better rewards than other workers. In reality, however, they are all in the same boat. They sell their labour to the capitalists and most only get a small fraction of their income from investment in capital. In the long-run they too are likely to lose their jobs or suffer a reduction in income as the system starts to crumble.

POLITICS AND ECONOMICS

How relevant is Marxian economics to current political debates about economic policy? Most of the world's Marxian economies have not gone through the stages of economic development that Marx described. Some, such as the USSR, have passed from basically feudal agricultural societies straight to socialism, without experiencing fully-fledged capitalism. Others, such as East Germany, have entered the capitalist stage but the transition to communism has been the result of war rather than the internal collapse of the capitalist system. This observation in itself does not prove that Marx was wrong. The only true test is to wait long enough to see if the economies of the older industrialised nations, such as the United Kingdom, survive or collapse if left to the mercies of unfettered market forces. Marx argued, in fact, that it was necessary to pass through capitalism for an economy to build up an industrial base ready for the transition to socialism. Not all Marxists think that a violent revolution is necessary to change the economic system. Many believe that the economy can be changed gradually into a state-planned system through the process of parliamentary democracy and government intervention. These people must be distinguished from those in the centre of the political spectrum who believe that government intervention is needed to correct some of the shortcomings of the system but that basically the capitalist market system should be retained.

There is a view held by some Marxists that 'tinkering about' with a basically unsound economic system only prolongs the agony of those bearing the brunt of capitalist exploitation. They believe that if a right-wing government were to allow a market economy to operate free from any state interference the collapse of the system would come sooner than if it were propped up by state interventionist policies. This is why, for profoundly different reasons, there are some supporters on the left of the political spectrum, as well as on the right, for an economic policy of non-interference in the market economy.

QUESTIONS

1. Is Marxian economic theory more relevant to market economies than to centrally planned economies?
2. Assume that it requires 2 hours of labour to produce 1 unit of corn and it requires 1 hour of labour plus 2 units of corn to produce 1 unit of bread. If the working day is 12 hours and the minimum subsistence wage is 1 unit of bread a day, is it possible for a rate of surplus (s/v) of 2 to be extracted?
3. Marx defined the rate of profit as $p = s/c + v$, where $s =$ surplus, $c =$ constant capital and $v =$ variable capital.

    (a) Why is it argued that p will decline over time?
    (b) What may delay or counteract a fall in p?
    (c) Is there a difference between this definition of the rate of profit and the definition usually employed in company accounts?
    (d) If this *rate* of profit does decline what can be said about the *share* of profit in national income?

4. Why is it sometimes argued that monopoly capitalism is bound to stagnate?
5. What reasons have been put forward by radical economists for the recovery of capitalism after the 1930s depression?
6. To what extent have Marx's predictions proved correct with respect to the British economy?

Welfare economics

It was stated in Chapter 1 that it is usually accepted that the role of economists is to explain how the economy operates and that is the government's responsibility to decide what the objectives of economic policy should be. The reality of the situation, however, is that, although the government may decide the broad principles of economic policy, in order to actually implement these policies economists are often called upon to suggest more specific guidelines. For example, a government may decide that private monopolies exploit the consumer by charging too high prices, but it is left to economists to suggest exactly what a 'fair' price might be.

Welfare economics is the branch of economics where these guidelines for economic policy are considered. Its main area of application is microeconomic policy. At a macroeconomic level the main objective of economic policy is to increase the standard of living, although income distribution also has to be taken into consideration. The control of certain economic indicators, such as the balance of payments or the rate of inflation is not an end in itself, although one sometimes gets the impression that, reading in the newspaper that a certain number has gone down or up, should make one feel better. These indicators are important, but only inasmuch as they may tell us what is happening, or may happen, to living standards and income distribution.

Any proposals as to how the economy should operate must be based on value-judgements. Economists have tried to base their proposals on value-judgements acceptable to most people. This is a difficult thing to do, however, and whatever set of value-judgements is chosen there will almost inevitably be criticism from some quarter. If one cannot be sure that welfare economics provides the best set of guidelines then why should students try to master the basic principles of the present state of the art? One reason is that many government economic policies are actually based on proposals derived from welfare economics and it is important to understand the reasoning behind these proposals whether they are right or wrong.

There are two main approaches to the assessment of the welfare implications of economic policy:

(1)   the theory of Pareto optimality, and
(2)   the theory of consumer surplus.

Both approaches basically boil down to the recommendation that economic welfare will be maximised when price is equal to marginal cost, although there are a number of criticisms of the grounds on which this proposal is made. Before examining these issues some of the value-judgements that underlie these methods of assessing welfare are considered.

In the past the view was sometimes held that the theory of Pareto optimality was a 'scientific' approach to welfare economics based on a self-evident set of axioms. But, of course there is no such thing as a self-evident value-judgement and it is now recognised that an unproveable set of value-judgements underpin the whole of Paretian welfare economics. Although many people might agree with them as value-judgements they are still open to dispute. Four of these value-judgements (which are also common to the theory of consumer surplus) are:

(1)   All individuals should count. This principle means that the welfare of all individuals in the economy should be taken into account. Should then the effects of economic policies on the citizens of other economies and on future generations be ignored?
(2)   Individuals are the best judges of their own welfare. As explained in Chapter 1, there are a number of reasons why complete freedom of choice in consumption may be considered undesirable. This is why, for example, the state imposes age restrictions on the consumption of alcohol and tobacco and make some other addictive drugs completely illegal.
(3)   Only goods and services bought in the market place affect welfare. What about the environment, health, culture, social relationships?
(4)   The more one consumes the better off one is. Apart from the influences of non-economic factors on one's welfare, another criticism of this value-judgement is based on the view that well-being depends on one's relative living standards rather than one's absolute level of consumption; in other words, one's level of satisfaction depends on how one's present material consumption compares with what one has been accustomed to in the past and how one sees the consumption levels of other people. Thus, although some unemployed people today may have a materially better living standard than the unemployed (and some of the employed) had in the 1930s depression they do not feel better off because in comparison to the majority of people currently in employment their living standards are still relatively low.

THE PARETO PRINCIPLE

Most economic policies affect more than one person. There is, however, no objective method of measuring and comparing the welfare of different individuals. Giving everybody the same goods will not necessarily make everyone equally happy because needs and preferences differ. The Pareto optimality principle is used to try to overcome this problem. If two situations, *A* and *B*, are compared and in situation *B* at least one person is better off than in situation *A*, and no one is worse off, then *B* is said to be Pareto superior to *A*. A situation where no one can be better off without someone else being made worse off is a Pareto optimum. This might appear to be a reasonable proposition to most people but in itself its usefulness is rather limited. Most economic policies usually involve some people becoming better off and others worse off and so the Pareto principle cannot be directly used to assess them. Nevertheless, it can still be used to derive a set of rules for the efficient allocation of resources in an economy.

The attainment of Pareto optimality – a simplified analysis

The usual graphical derivation of the conditions necessary to achieve a Pareto optimal allocation of resources is set out separately in an appendix to this chapter. Students should try to master this analysis, but an understanding of the simplified explanation below is all that is necessary to follow the rest of the material in this chapter. The author has adopted this approach with the hope of generating a better understanding of the fundamental principles of welfare economics. Students often pay so much attention to the intricacies of the Pareto optimality analysis that they do not really grasp some of the more fundamental principles of welfare economics or realise its importance.

Even if it is not possible objectively to choose between two Pareto optimal situations, at least an attempt can be made to eliminate those situations that are inefficient in the sense that a Pareto improvement is possible. The combinations of goods that it is Pareto efficient to produce can be illustrated, for the two-goods case, by a production possibility frontier (*PPF*) such as that shown in Figure 12.1. The *PPF* shows the maximum amounts of each of the two goods *X* and *Y* that it is possible to produce for a given quantity of the other good. For example, if production of good *X* is given as X_1 then a maximum of Y_1 of good *Y* can be produced. All points along the *PPF* are Pareto efficient. A movement from *A* to *B*, for example, means that more of *X* and less of *Y* is produced. At *A* or *B* it is not possible to produce more of either good without reducing production of the other. On the other hand, the production combination *C* is not Pareto efficient because further Pareto improvements are possible. It is possible to increase production of *X* or *Y*, or both, by moving out towards the section of the *PPF* between *A* and *B*.

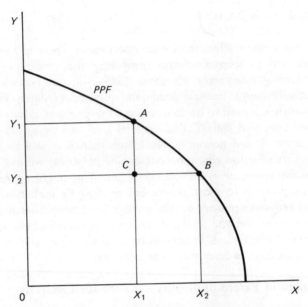

FIGURE 12.1   The production possibility frontier

When the distribution of goods among consumers is Pareto optimal it is not possible to make one consumer better off without making at least one other worse off. To achieve this situation it is necessary for all consumers to have the same marginal rate of substitution between the goods, that is, to be willing to exchange marginal units of the goods at the same ratio.

Consider this simple example. Assume that there are only two individuals, A and B, who consume only two goods, bread and beer. They both start off with a given initial allocation of both goods and have sets of preferences such that:

A would be willing to exchange 3 pints of beer for 1 loaf of bread;
B would be willing to exchange 1 pint of beer for 2 loaves of bread.

The two individuals have different marginal rates of substitution between the two goods and so a Pareto improvement must be possible. One way that this might be achieved would be for A to give B one pint of beer in exchange for two loaves of bread. A would be better off, since she values the two extra loaves as equivalent to six pints of beer but has only lost one pint, and B's satisfaction level would be unchanged. If the two individuals had valued the two goods in the same ratio then no further unambiguous gains in welfare would be possible through trading.

Another condition necessary for Pareto optimality is that the relationship between production and trade should be such that the rate at which consumers are willing to exchange two goods for each other is equal to the rate at which society can transform the production of one good into the other. For example, if consumers valued one pint of beer as equivalent to one loaf of bread and it was possible to reorganise production so as to produce four more loaves of bread if one less pint of beer were to be produced, then there would be a net gain in welfare if such a reorganisation of production was to take place. Consumers would only require one loaf to compensate for the one lost pint of beer and so an extra three loaves would be available to increase welfare.

As the amount of a good consumed increases consumers tend to put a lower value on additional units of it, and as more of an input is used the extra output that additional units will generate declines. Thus by altering patterns of production and trade it is possible to achieve a state where no further Pareto improvements of any kind can be made. It can also be shown (see Appendix) that if all markets are perfectly competitive and in equilibrium then the conditions for Pareto optimality will be satisfied. Because price equals marginal cost in perfect competition in equilibrium the rule for the achievement of Pareto optimality is also that price should equal marginal cost.

Criticisms of the Pareto optimality criteria

1. There can be an infinite number of Pareto optimal allocations of resources in an economy and the theory does not tell us how to choose between them. Perfect competition will not necessarily bring about the 'best' Pareto optimal organisation from the viewpoint of society. Arrow[1] proved that it is impossible to derive a consistent and rational ordering of different states of society through voting, but a social preference ordering does not necessarily have to be based on the special conditions that Arrow specified.

2. Income distribution is ignored. The theory of Pareto optimality assumes that consumers have some initial allocation of resources which they can then trade, but the possibility that this initial allocation might be unfair is not considered. What might be considered a 'fair' or an 'unfair' distribution is, of course, a normative question but in actual policy decisions value-judgements on such issues have to be made. When assessing the merits of different policies economists usually differentiate between the two principles of efficiency in the allocation of resources and equity, or the 'fairness' of this allocation, and it is sometimes argued that the question of reallocation of resources on grounds of equity should

1. K. J. Arrow, 'A Difficulty in the Concept of Social Welfare', *Journal of Political Economy*, vol. 58 (1950), pp. 328–46.

be kept distinct from the question of whether or not resources are efficiently allocated.

3. Until Lipsey and Lancaster[2] published their 'theory of second best' it was commonly thought that even if it was not possible to satisfy all the conditions necessary for Pareto optimality the 'second best' solution was to satisfy these conditions in as many markets as possible. However, Lipsey and Lancaster proved that if the conditions for Pareto optimality are not met in one market (for example, if price is not equal to marginal cost) then there will be an entirely different set of conditions for a 'second best' optimum allocation of resources in other markets. Since in practice there are always going to be some markets where the Pareto optimality conditions are not met, this means that resource allocation will not necessarily be made more efficient by ensuring that price is equal to marginal cost in other markets.

Lipsey and Lancaster's actual proof is rather complex, but a simple example can illustrate the principles involved. Suppose that a motorway is built to bypass a congested town. One possibility would be to charge motorists to use this stretch of motorway and to base the charge on the marginal cost per vehicle of maintaining the motorway. However, if a charge was imposed then some through traffic might continue to drive through the town, to the detriment of the local residents. The socially optimum solution would be for all through traffic to use the bypass, but it is not a practical proposition to charge motorists for driving on the ordinary roads through the town in order to induce them to use the bypass. Therefore, the second best solution might be for there to be a zero charge for using the bypass.

4. Technological advances are ignored. Although it is not possible to fully explain what causes technological advances, the devotion of resources to research and development is one contributory factor. If all firms were forced to keep price equal to marginal cost they might not earn sufficient profits to finance the research and development of new products and the improvement of existing ones. There would also be less incentive for such investment if firms knew that there would be constraints on the prices they could charge for any new or improved products. Thus in the long-run marginal cost pricing may be detrimental to consumer welfare if it hampers product improvements.

5. The welfare of future generations is ignored in the basic Pareto optimality model, which considers only one time period. The analysis has been extended to incorporate consumer preferences for future time periods but

---

2. R. G. Lipsey and K. Lancaster, 'The General Theory of Second Best', *Review of Economic Studies*, vol. 24 (October 1956), pp. 11–32.

there is some scepticism over the validity of this approach. Although existing consumers can express their preferences for the future through their willingness to borrow or lend money at different rates of interest, it is not possible for future generations to express their preferences through the market system if they are not yet born. If everyone acted purely in their own interests then in a private enterprise economy the current population would have property rights to all existing resources which they would be free to consume if they wished and so leave nothing for future generations. Thus one view is that the government should take into account the welfare of future generations in its economic policies, given that the market does not adequately do so.

6. The theory of Pareto optimality is based on an unrealistic set of assumptions. In Chapter 1 it was explained that one judges a theory by the accuracy of its predictions, not the realism of its assumptions. This principle, however, refers to positive economics. In welfare, or normative economics, one is not trying to predict anything and so one cannot use this argument to justify the use of unrealistic assumptions. If one's assumptions about what makes people better off are incorrect then any policies based on such assumptions may not be particularly successful in improving welfare.

Pareto optimality and the free market

There is something of a paradox in the way that the theory of Pareto optimality is used in welfare economics. On the one hand there is the argument that the theory of Pareto optimality shows that a free market economy provides the most efficient allocation of resources and, on the other hand, it is only used when the government thinks that the free market economy is not functioning adequately and there is a need for intervention.

Some people who support the idea of a free market economy sometimes argue that there is an economic 'proof' (that is, the theory of Pareto optimality) that the free market provides the most efficient allocation of resources. It has been demonstrated that there are various flaws in this 'proof' and, of course, the whole issue is a normative one where there cannot be a conclusive proof in either direction. Even if there was agreement on the normative propositions on which the desirability of Pareto optimality is based, it is unlikely that in reality all the conditions for a Pareto optimal situation would be met.

This does not necessarily mean that the free market economy is not the most desirable economic system, however. One could argue that the profit incentive, competition (including advertising and product quality competition, which are absent from the restrictive perfect competition model on which the Pareto optimality theory is based) and freedom of choice make it better than any other system, but there also exists a set of counter arguments to be weighed against these views.

CONSUMER SURPLUS

The theory of consumer surplus is a method usually employed to assess welfare changes in individual markets whereas the theory of Pareto optimality considers the efficient allocation of resources over the economic system as a whole. It is based on the idea that the welfare that an individual derives from a unit of a good can be measured in terms of her willingness to pay for it. (This approach to the measurement of marginal utility was explained in Chapter 9.) Consumer surplus is defined as the difference between the price that a consumer would be willing to pay and the price that is actually paid for any unit of a good that is consumed. Thus from the individual demand curve D_i in Figure 12.2 it can be seen that when the price of good Q is £1 the consumer surplus on the first unit bought is

$$£4 - £1 = £3.$$

Similarly the consumer surplus on the other units can be calculated as £2 on the second unit, £1 on the third unit and zero on the fourth unit. The total

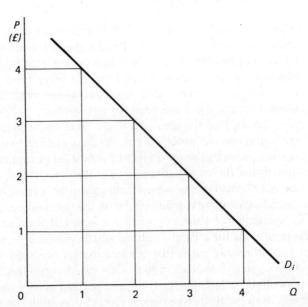

FIGURE 12.2   Consumer surplus and individual demand

consumer surplus is therefore

$$£3 + £2 + £1 = £6.$$

Turning to the market demand schedule D in Figure 12.3, if price is P_1 the total consumer surplus of all consumers is equivalent to the area ABC, that is, consumer surplus is the area above price and below the demand curve. If price is reduced to P_2 then the increase in consumer surplus is area $CBFE$.

The benefits that might be derived from public projects where no price is directly paid by those enjoying their benefits, for example, a new road, can also be assessed using the theory of consumer surplus. When price is zero then consumer surplus is the total area under the demand curve, that is, AOG in the example in Figure 12.3.

In order to derive some guidelines for optimal resource allocation it is also necessary to introduce the concept of *producer surplus*. This is defined as the difference between the price that a firm receives from the sale of a unit of a good and the minimum price that this unit would be supplied at, that is, its marginal cost. Thus in Figure 12.4 if price was P_1 and output was Q_M then the total producer surplus would be equivalent to area F.

Assume that initially the market illustrated in Figure 12.4 is perfectly competitive and that the supply curve S is determined in the usual way by horizontally summing the marginal cost curves of the individual firms that

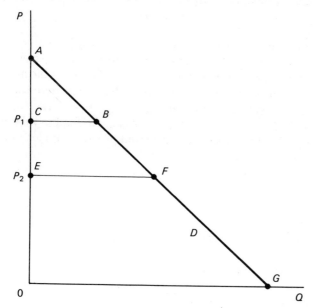

FIGURE 12.3　Consumer surplus and market demand

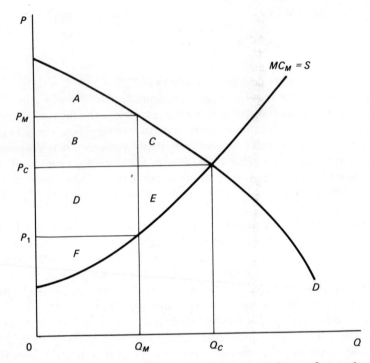

FIGURE 12.4   Consumer surplus, producer surplus and marginal cost pricing

make up the market. Equilibrium price and quantity will then be P_C and Q_C, respectively. Now assume that these small firms merge together to become one large monopoly producer and that this single firm faces the marginal cost curve MC_M, which is the same as the perfectly competitive supply curve. Price and quantity will then be P_M and Q_M, respectively. The MR schedule, which intersects MC at output Q_M, is not shown, for the sake of clarity. Now consider what happens to consumer and producer surplus in these two situations.

Under monopoly:

consumer surplus $= A$;
producer surplus $= B + D + F$.

Under perfect competition:

consumer surplus $= A + B + C$;
producer surplus $= D + E + F$.

Thus under perfect competition there is a net increase in the total of producer surplus and consumer surplus of C plus E. (There is also a distributional change of B from producer surplus to consumer surplus.) There is no other price at which the total of consumer surplus and producer surplus would be greater, and so the result is arrived at that welfare will be maximised when price equals *MC*.

The theory of consumer surplus can be criticised from both (1) analytical, and (2) normative, viewpoints.

1.   Analytical criticisms

Although the approach of considering one market at a time has the advantage of simplicity over the theory of Pareto optimality, it can mean that the total welfare effects of policies are not taken into account. For example, if price is reduced in one market then any repercussions in other markets are ignored. Three types of such 'knock on' effects can be demonstrated using the example of a reduction in public transport prices.

(i)   Income effects. Those individuals who use public transport will find their real incomes increased by a reduction in its price. This increased real income may mean that expenditure patterns in other markets may change. For example, there may be an increase in the demand for clothes. A shift outward in the demand curve for clothes will cause consumer surplus in the market for clothes to alter which, by definition, causes a change in welfare. Although economists have extended the theoretical analysis of consumer surplus to take such income effects into consideration,[3] it is in practice extremely difficult to do this. In actual policy assessment exercises income effects are usually ignored, or at best only a few of the most obvious income effects are taken into account.

(ii)   Price effects on substitutes. If more people use public transport because it is cheaper then the demand for other modes of transport may fall. A shift inward of the demand for private cars, for example, would result in a change in consumer surplus in the car market.

(iii)   Price effects on complements. There may, for example, be an increase in demand for magazines and books for reading while travelling by public transport which, again, would alter consumer surplus in these other markets.

2.   Normative criticisms

The principle that willingness to pay should be used as a measure of the benefit that someone gets from the provision of a good can be criticised for

---

3.   See Chapter 4 of Y.-K. Ng, *Welfare Economics: Introduction and Development of Basic concepts,* revised edition (London: Macmillan, 1983).

a number of reasons (such as imperfect information, paternalism, external effects, inequitable income distribution) which were spelled out in Chapter 1. One could argue that consumers' willingness to pay determines their allocation of goods through the market system and so criticisms of the use of this principle for measuring welfare is a criticism of the fundamental principle on which the whole market system is based. However, the state usually intervenes when it considers that the market system fails to allocate resources efficiently and so its policies do not necessarily have to be based on the same principles upon which the market system operates.

Even if the willingness to pay principle is accepted, one could argue that one cannot simply aggregate different individuals' preferences to obtain an aggregate market indicator of social welfare, as is done when using the consumer surplus measure, because one cannot make interpersonal comparison of welfare. However in practice such interpersonal comparisons have to be made and, although this simple aggregation is not necessarily the best method of doing this, no obvious alternative methods spring to mind.

MONOPOLY PRICE CONTROL (NATIONALISED AND REGULATED PRIVATE INDUSTRIES)

Because monopolies restrict output and charge a price greater than marginal cost they contribute to an inefficient allocation of resources according to both the Pareto optimality and the consumer surplus criteria. Monopolies are also sometimes accused of being inefficient in terms of keeping down costs and product improvement because of the lack of competition. On the other hand, when there are economies of scale there may only be room in an industry for one firm producing above minimum efficient scale and able to keep average cost to a minimum. (This does not necessarily mean that these lower average production costs will be passed on to the consumer, however.) A single producer can also avoid the wasteful duplication that would arise through competition in some industries. In particular, it would be wasteful to have several distribution systems for utilities like gas, water, electricity, telephones and cable television, although it may be possible for there to be competition in what is sold through the distribution system. In other cases, wasteful advertising and marketing campaigns between competitors may be avoided.

These, and other, arguments for and against monopolies all rest on value-judgements and it is not possible to weigh them all up objectively and come down conclusively in favour of or against monopolies. This is reflected in the stance taken in the United Kingdom competition policy,[4] where each

---

4.   See J. R. Cable, 'Industry', in M. J. Artis (ed.), *The UK Economy: A Manual of Applied Economics*, 11th edn (London: Weidenfeld and Nicolson, 1986), pp. 215–44.

case is decided on its own merits. Although a monopoly that restricts output and earns excessively high profits is in itself usually considered undesirable, other possible redeeming factors are also taken into consideration such as its positive contribution to the balance of payments or local employment.

It should be noted that if a monopoly is considered to be against the public interest and broken up, or a merger is prevented from taking place, then the resulting market form will usually be an oligopoly. Thus it can be misleading to compare monopoly with the case of perfect competition for the purposes of analysing the case for monopoly controls.

The government may consider that a monopoly is the most efficient way of organising production in an industry but that its pricing policy should be regulated to ensure that consumers are not exploited. One way to do this is by nationalising the industry, which was the policy adopted in the United Kingdom in the decade following the war. In the 1980s this pattern was reversed and privatisation took industries out of state ownership, but the private monopolies that were created still had their prices regulated by the government.

There have been attempts to apply marginal cost pricing in some nationalised industries. However, when economies of scale are present marginal cost is below average cost and hence a loss is made if price is set equal to marginal cost. This problem is illustrated in Figure 12.5. Note that in this example it is long-run marginal cost (LMC) that is being considered. Long-run and short-run marginal cost pricing are compatible given that SMC equals LMC when the firm is operating with the most efficient size of plant for any given output (see Chapter 3). As the market demand curve D cuts the LAC schedule when it is still falling, marginal cost, and hence the price P_1, will be below average cost. Thus the firm will make a loss, equal to P_1C_1 on each of the Q_1 units that it produces.

The fact that a nationalised industry makes a loss and has to be subsidised does not necessarily mean that this policy should not be implemented. There are no widely accepted alternatives to the marginal cost pricing rule for ensuring an efficient allocation of resources and there may also be unpriced benefits to society from the provision of goods or services by a subsidised nationalised industry. For example, the presence of a railway line may reduce road accidents and the cost of road repairs. This is a separate argument in favour of state assistance in the provision of these external benefits, though, rather than part of the case for marginal cost pricing *per se*.

Another suggestion is that the marginal cost pricing rule should be modified and that consumer surplus should be maximised as long as a loss is not incurred, that is, that firms should operate at a break-even position, such as B in Figure 12.5. This, however, still ignores the need to make profits for reinvestment in new plant and equipment, and research and development into product improvement. Thus in the 1960s the United Kingdom government

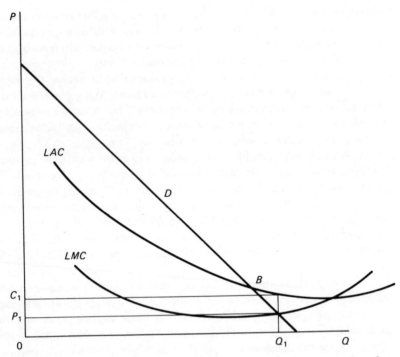

FIGURE 12.5   Marginal cost pricing and economies of scale

instructed nationalised industries to break even and to earn a specified rate of return on capital invested. The newly privatised monopolies in the 1980s were told to keep price increases below the rate of inflation, but otherwise they basically operated along the same lines as profit maximising firms.

One fact that is sometimes overlooked when considering the merits of marginal cost pricing is that not all the customers of nationalised industries have been private individuals. Some of the output of nationalised industries, such as rail freight, or industrial electricity supply is sold to private firms. Thus price controls on what is sold to these customers would not necessarily benefit consumers because there is no guarantee that any input price reductions would be passed on to consumers in the form of lower prices instead of being taken as profit. Thus different pricing policies have been adopted with respect to private and industrial customers. (Bulk buying and different distribution systems also contribute to the different prices paid by these two groups.)

EXTERNALITIES AND POLLUTION

An externality occurs when one party is affected by the actions of another party and no payment is made by either. A negative externality occurs when this effect is to the detriment of the party that is affected, for example, when someone plays music loudly in the middle of the night and keeps neighbours awake. A positive externality occurs when the effect benefits the affected party, as when neighbours enjoy listening to music coming from next door. An area of major concern with respect to negative externalities is pollution of the environment. Positive externalities may be the result of government policy with respect to the provision of public goods, which are considered later.

Externalities cannot be dealt with by the market mechanism. The main reason for this is that no one has clearly defined property rights over certain resources, such as the air, and the market system only allocates resources through trade and exchange between owners of goods and resources. One obvious reason for the lack of property rights is the difficulty of measurement. Sophisticated scientific instruments may be necessary to detect the presence of certain types of pollutants in the air, and even with these instruments it may not be possible to attribute the pollutants in a given portion of air to their different originators. Even if the problem of measurement can be overcome, the problem remains of deciding who is entitled to the resource in question. If people are annoyed by smoke caused by a factory this does not necessarily mean that it does not have the right to use the atmosphere to get rid of waste fumes. The question of the allocation of property rights is a matter of value-judgements and within an economy it is the state that is the final arbiter. On an international scale, though, such disputes are more difficult to settle because it is not always possible to enforce international agreements. For example, if one country wishes to extend the limits to coastal fishing around its shores then this will cause an externality because the amount of fish caught by trawlers from other countries will fall without a payment being made for this loss. If another country wishes to dispute this extension of fishing rights there may not be a straightforward way of resolving the problem.

Pollution control

In the United Kingdom, government policy with respect to the externality of pollution has developed as the need has arisen. It is recognized that he environment is useful for disposing of waste materials, and controls are usually only introduced when pollution is considered harmful or a nuisance. The perceived need to introduce controls has been influenced by the growth of industry and the development of new products and processes that create new types of pollution, scientific knowledge of the possible harmful effects of pollution, and public and governmental opinion as to the relative merits of a clean environment and industrial growth. Since the last century numerous pieces of legislation have extended and amended the laws governing pollution, and the Pollution Control Act 1974 provided a comprehensive revision and update of pollution controls in a range of different areas.[5]

The optimal level of an externality

Assume that a firm causes levels of pollution that are directly proportional to its output level, as measured along the X axis in Figure 12.6. Assume also that each extra unit of pollution causes increased suffering for people living near the firm and that the cost of this can be measured in monetary terms, as represented by the rising marginal damage cost schedule MDC. This schedule represents the amount that these individuals are willing to pay to have each marginal unit of pollution removed. If it is also assumed that the firm sells its output at a price equal to marginal cost then its marginal profit can be represented by the downward sloping schedule MB. Given that some pollution is bound to take place in an industrialised society, some economists have suggested that in a situation like this X^* is the optimum level of pollution; in other words, pollution should be allowed up to the point where its marginal benefit, measured by the firm's marginal profit, is equal to its marginal cost, measured by what the individuals suffering from it would be prepared to pay

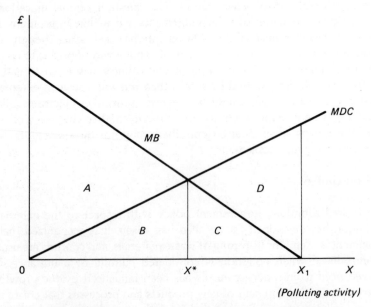

FIGURE 12.6   The optimal level of pollution

---

5.   See Department of the Environment, *Pollution Control in Great Britain: How it Works* (London: HMSO, 1978).

to have it stopped. This solution can be criticised from a number of stances, however. Some of these criticisms are related to the different methods by which it may be achieved, as explained below.

If there were no controls on pollution then the firm would produce at X_1, that is, it would expand output as long as the contribution to profit was positive. Now consider what would happen if the government conferred the right to the environment that is being polluted to the individuals affected and ruled that the firm would have to pay compensation for any suffering caused by the pollution. The firm would then only expand output as long as the extra profit obtained exceeded the compensation that would have to be paid and it would therefore operate at X^*, the suggested optimum. On the other hand, suppose that the property right to the environment that is being polluted is given to the firm. If it was possible to get together and bargain, those affected by the pollution could bribe the firm to reduce its output level. They would again end up at X^* because below this output level the lost profit that they would have to compensate the firm for would be greater than their valuation of the suffering caused, and hence the amount that they would be willing to pay to have the pollution stopped.

In theory, then, whichever party is allocated the property rights the same 'optimum' pollution level X^* will be achieved. Some economists have gone so far as to say that it does not matter who gets the property rights and that all that matters is that they are allocated to one party or the other so that the process of payments and bargaining can ensure that society's optimum pollution level is achieved. This 'solution' to the problem of pollution can be criticised on a number of counts, both normative and practical.

Considering first the normative question of who is allocated the property rights, the distributional effects of the different policies can be assessed by considering the areas A, B, C and D in Figure 12.6. If, in the absence of any controls, the firm operates at X_1, its total profits will be represented by the total area under the MB schedule, that is, $A + B + C$, and the individuals' losses will be represented by the area under the MDC schedule, $B + C + D$.

If the firm has to pay compensation for the damage caused by the pollution it will operate at X^*. Thus the individuals affected will gain

$C + D$ by the reduction of pollution from X_1 to X^*, and
B as compensation for the pollution that still takes place.

On the other hand the firm loses

C in lost profit due to reduced output, and
B in compensation payments.

Thus the individuals gain $(B + C + D)$ and the firm loses $(B + C)$ and so there is a net gain to society equal to area D.

If the individuals have to bribe the firm to reduce output they will pay out C to gain $C + D$, and will still suffer B. The firm is fully compensated for the lost profit C and so neither loses nor gains. Thus there is again a net gain to society of area D.

Although these different solutions result in the same net gain to society, in distributional terms they obviously have different effects and so opinions will differ as to the desirability of the different policies. Another possibility, which is nearer to what happens in practice, is that the government rules that pollution above X^* is illegal but below this level no compensation need be paid. In this case the individuals would gain $C + D$ and the firm would lose C.

The criticism that willingness to pay is not necessarily the best way of measuring welfare has already been considered, but a particular problem with respect to pollution is that its effects can build up over a long time period and may not be immediately noticeable. Thus those individuals who are affected may not recognise the effects and so will not accurately assess the damage that it causes.

From a practical viewpoint the suggestion that those suffering from the pollution should bribe the firm to reduce its output by compensating for its lost profits is totally impractical in most actual cases. Aside from moral objections to this approach, it is difficult enough for one individual accurately to assess the detrimental effects of any pollution that they are suffering from and so the problem is compounded when a large number of individuals are affected. Even if everyone could accurately assess the damage caused by the pollution, the cleaner environment that would result from a reduction in pollution would be a public good and so the 'free rider' problem would arise. Individuals would be reluctant to disclose the full benefits that pollution reduction would bring them if they knew that they would be asked to pay a charge related to these benefits, given that they would still enjoy the benefits of this reduction regardless of what they paid.

If individuals were to be compensated then the reverse problem would arise. If people were told that they were to be paid compensation for the pollution in relation to the amount of suffering caused then they would tend to overstate their claims for compensation. Even if the damage caused by the pollution could be accurately assessed there would still be the problem of getting firms actually to pay out compensation. When only one firm is involved it is likely that it will contest any claims for damages and those pressing for compensation may have trouble in proving the extent of any suffering caused by the pollution. If there are several firms involved it may make it impossible accurately to attribute pollution damage, and hence a bill for compensation, to each one.

Even if the individuals concerned were able to band together and fight a joint legal action the costs of doing so could possibly exceed any damages they might be awarded and the only people to gain would be the lawyers involved in the case. This sort of bargaining without state intervention is usually feasible only in one-to-one situations. For example, if one neighbour annoys another by burning rubbish in the garden they could possibly come to some form of arrangement whereby the neighbour suffering from the smoke is compensated or, alternatively, the one who is prevented from burning rubbish, and has to pay to have it disposed of in some other way, is compensated.

Because of these problems pollution policy in the United Kingdom, as already explained, usually imposes pollution standards rather than attempting to 'price' pollution. There is, however, a certain amount of flexibility in some of these standards and controls which can go some way towards balancing the costs and benefits of pollution. Most dangerous types of pollution have strictly controlled limits, but with 'nuisance' pollution discretion is sometimes given to local authorities to take into account local circumstances when laying down pollution standards. For example, if a company provides a large number of jobs in an area of very high unemployment and any extra expenditure on pollution controls would force it to close down, then it might be treated more leniently than a firm situated in an area of low unemployment. Firms are also frequently instructed to use the 'best practical means' to reduce pollution, which effectively means only those methods that the firm can afford to use without being forced into bankruptcy.

As a final word on the suggestion that pollution can be efficiently controlled by putting a price on it, it has to be said that if it was so simple to let the market system deal with externalities then there would not be an externality problem in the first place. It is only because the market cannot cope with externalities that this problem requires special policy measures.

PUBLIC GOODS

A good is a public good if it is (a) non-excludable (that is, one cannot stop different people consuming it), and (b) non-rival (that is, one person consuming the good will not affect the satisfaction that another person derives from it.)

An example of a public good is street lighting. Many people can enjoy its benefits without affecting others' enjoyment, and it is difficult to stop people 'using' street lighting. Private goods, on the other hand, are excludable and rival. For example, if one person buys and eats an apple then this obviously precludes anyone else from consuming it. This definition of a public good should not be confused with the normal usage of the term 'public good'. Education, for example, is not a public good according to the economist's definition, because it is possible to exclude people from classes, even if education is provided by the state.

'Pure' public goods that always satisfy the conditions above are rare, but there exist many 'quasi' public goods. For example, roads usually satisfy the definition of a public good, although when a road becomes congested extra people using it will affect the benefit derived from it by others.

In a free market economy public goods will either not be provided or the amount provided will be below the optimal level. This is explained using the example illustrated in Figure 12.7. Assume that there are two individuals whose demand schedules for public good X are shown by D_1 and D_2. If X was provided in a competitive free market then the amount X_0 would be produced and would be paid for by individual 1, even though individual 2 would still enjoy the benefits of this amount of X.

To discover the optimum amount of X that should be provided (based on the consumer surplus principle) it must be recognised that the total benefit accruing from any one unit of X is the sum of the benefits enjoyed by the two individuals. This can be determined for any given amount of X by vertically summing the two demand schedules, given that each consumer's

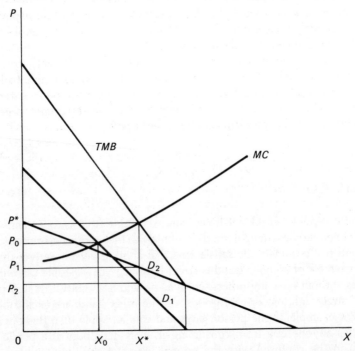

FIGURE 12.7   Optimal production and pricing of a public good

benefit from each unit of X is assumed to be measurable in terms of what they are willing to pay for it. The resulting total marginal benefit schedule TMB cuts the marginal cost curve MC at an output of X^*. This is the optimum amount of X because the total marginal benefit to consumers equals the marginal cost of providing it.

The optimum method of financing a public good is for each individual to pay according to the benefit that he or she receives. Thus in this example individuals 1 and 2 should pay prices P_1 and P_2, respectively. By definition P_1 plus P_2 equals P^* and hence equals the marginal cost of providing X^* units of this public good. In practice, however, it is difficult to discover individual demand schedules for a public good, and funding usually comes from general taxation where individuals' payments are not related to the benefit that they receive.

Even if individuals were able accurately to assess the value to them of different amounts of a public good, it would be difficult to discover these assessments because of the 'free rider' problem. If a public good is provided one cannot, by definition, stop people enjoying its benefits. Thus, if people are asked to place a value on the amount of a public good that is provided on the understanding that they will pay a charge based on this valuation, they will tend to understate their valuation of the benefit they derive. Because they will enjoy its benefits regardless of what they pay, human nature will cause many individuals to give misleading answers in order to save themselves money.

CONCLUSIONS

This chapter has considered some of the ideas that have been put forward as guidelines for economic policy and how they relate to certain specific areas of microeconomic policy. Only a few actual policy applications have been considered, and only the basic problems involved have been discussed, the main concern being the examination of the basic principles on which these policies are based. Criticisms can be classified into two broad categories. Firstly, not all the effects of economic policies are taken into account by the welfare indicators that have been considered. Secondly, one can disagree with the value-judgements on which these welfare indicators are based.

Economists have recognised that there may be certain reservations about some of the basic principles upon which welfare economics is based, but it is easier to criticise than to suggest an alternative set of proposals. Rather than giving up the problem because there is no perfect solution, economists have developed a set of policy guidelines based on what they consider to be the most appropriate set of principles. It is then up to the government to decide whether or not to use these guidelines, bearing in mind both the shortcomings of these guidelines and the lack of any alternative proposals.

Appendix

PARETO OPTIMALITY

Assume that:

1. there are two resources, L and K, and a limited amount of both is available for use in production;
2. there are two goods, X and Y, whose production requires the use of the resources K and L as inputs;
3. there are two consumers, A and B, whose utility depends on the amounts of the goods X and Y that they consume.

PARETO EFFICIENCY IN PRODUCTION

The Pareto efficient combinations of the two resources K and L can be determined using an Edgeworth box diagram, which is a graphical construction used to analyse the case of limited resources. Assume that the maximum amounts of K and L available are 52 and 60 units, respectively. This is illustrated in Figure 12A.1 by the vertical and horizontal axes radiating from the origin O_X having limited lengths, corresponding to these specified quantities of K and L, respectively. The set of isoquants I_{10}^X, I_{34}^X, I_{53}^X, representing output levels of 10, 34 and 53 units, respectively, of good X, are drawn in the usual way, with isoquants further away from origin O_X representing higher levels of output.

To explain how the rest of the diagram is constructed, consider what would happen if some specific amounts of K and L were used in the production of good X. For example, suppose that 34 units of X are produced using 13 units of K and 31 units of L. This production mix, shown by point P, means that 39 units of K and 29 units of L can be used in the production of good Y. The amounts of K and L that are available for use in the production of good Y can be measured along the axes radiating from origin O_Y, in the top right-hand corner of the diagram. Given that the same maximum available quantities of the resources apply, then these axes will measure in the opposite direction, but have the

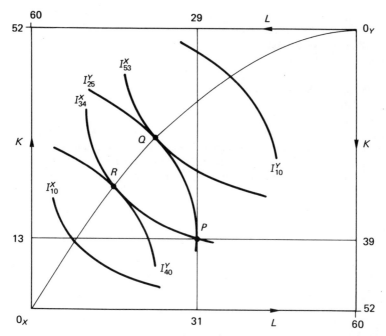

FIGURE 12A.1 Pareto efficiency in production

same lengths, as the axes radiating from O_X. Thus the two sets of axes together form a rectangle.

Given that the quantities of K and L available for use in the production of good Y are measured from O_Y, then the isoquants, I_{10}^Y, I_{25}^Y, I_{40}^Y, representing output levels of 10, 25 and 40 units of Y, respectively, are drawn such that the isoquants further away from O_Y represent higher levels of production. (If this is not obvious, turn the page upside down and the isoquant map for the production of Y can be seen to take the usual format.)

Pareto optimal input combinations are those where it is impossible to reorganise production so that the output of at least one good is increased without the output level of the other good falling. Thus combination P is not Pareto optimal. It is possible, for example, to move from P to Q, which would involve an increase in the production of X, from 34 to 53 units, while the output of Y remained at 25 units, in other words, a Pareto improvement. Alternatively, there could be a move to R, where production of Y is increased while the output level of X remains constant, or to anywhere between points Q and R, where the output of both X and Y would be higher than at P.

Points such as Q and R, where the X and Y isoquants are tangent to each other, are Pareto optimal. If one starts with these combinations then it is only possible to produce more of one good by producing less of the other one.

The line O_XO_Y, that joins all the Pareto optimal input combinations in Figure 12A.1, that is, all the points where the X and Y isoquants are tangent, is known as the *contract curve*. Any input combination not on this line must by definition be Pareto inefficient. Since the negative of the slope of an isoquant is equal to the $MRTS_{KL}$, and all Pareto optimal input combinations involve tangency of X and Y isoquants (that is, their slopes are equal) then the condition necessary for Pareto optimality in production is

$$MRTS_{KL}^X = MRTS_{KL}^Y. \tag{1}$$

This result will be used later.

The production possibility frontier (*PPF*) corresponding to the production possibilities in Figure 12A.1 is illustrated in Figure 12A.2. Pareto efficient combinations such as Q and R correspond to the points Q' and R' which are on the frontier, while Pareto inefficient combinations, such as P, correspond to points inside the frontier, such as P'.

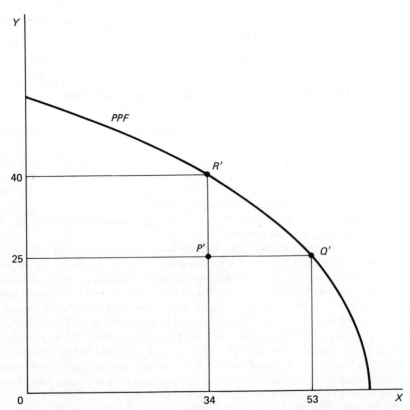

FIGURE 12A.2   The production possibility frontier and Pareto efficiency

PARETO EFFICIENCY IN DISTRIBUTION

It can be seen from Figure 12A.1 that there are numerous possible Pareto optimal combinations of X and Y. Whichever combination is actually produced, there still remains the problem of ensuring that the distribution of these goods between the two consumers A and B is Pareto optimal. To show how this can be achieved, assume that the Pareto efficient combination of 34 units of X and 40 units of Y (corresponding to point R in Figure 12A.1, above) is produced. An Edgeworth box diagram is, again, used but this time the axes represent these given amounts of the two goods X and Y (see Figure 12A.3). The indifference map representing the utility function of the consumer A is shown in the usual format with indifference curves further away from the origin O_A representing higher levels of utility. The amounts of the goods X and Y that are consumed by B are measured along the axes radiating from the origin O_B, and B's indifference curve map is also drawn with reference to this origin.

Consider now the distribution of X and Y represented by point C. This shows that A consumes 16 units of X and 9 units of Y. Thus 18 units of X and 31 units of Y are available for consumer B. Point C does not represent a Pareto optimal distribution, however. It is possible, for example, to move from C to D, which involves A moving

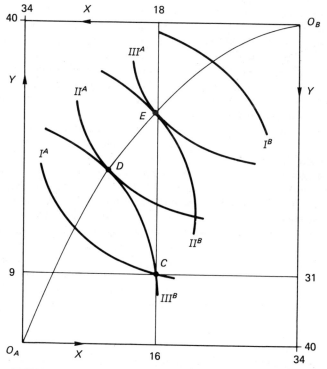

FIGURE 12A.3   Pareto efficiency in distribution

to a higher indifference curve while leaving B's utility level unchanged. The distribution patterns represented by points such as D and E, where A's and B's indifference curves are tangent to each other, are Pareto optimal because they do not allow any further improvement in one consumer's utility without a deterioration in the other's.

All Pareto optimal distribution organisations involve tangency of the two consumers' indifference curves, and are joined by the contract curve $O_A O_B$. Given that the negative of the slope of an indifference curve equals a consumer's MRS_{YX} between the two goods, then the condition for Pareto optimality in distribution can be specified as

$$MRS_{YX}^A = MRS_{YX}^B \tag{2}$$

PARETO EFFICIENCY IN PRODUCTION AND DISTRIBUTION

From the preceding analysis it would appear that there exist an infinite number of Pareto optimal production combinations, and an infinite number of Pareto optimal ways in which any one of these production mixes may be distributed. A Pareto optimal organisation of an economic system, however, requires the satisfaction of a third condition, which relates production to distribution patterns.

In Figure 12A.4, assume that the production levels of X and Y are represented by point R, which is on the production possibility frontier PPF and, therefore, Pareto efficient with respect to production. In the corresponding Edgeworth box, $OY_1 RX_1$, the Pareto efficient ways of distributing this production mix are shown by the contract curve OR. For Pareto optimality in both production and distribution it is necessary for the rate at which consumers are willing to exchange good Y for good X (that is, the MRS_{YX}) to be equal to the rate at which good Y can be substituted for good X in terms of production levels.

This latter ratio is called the marginal rate of transformation from X to Y (MRT_{XY}) and at any point on the production possibility frontier it is equivalent to the negative of the slope of the frontier. To understand the rationale for this condition, consider a situation where, for both consumers A and B, the MRS_{YX} is 0.5, and production of X and Y is such that the MRT_{XY} is 1. This means that consumers would require 0.5 of a unit of Y to compensate for the loss of one unit of X and that if production of X was reduced by one unit then production of Y could be increased by one unit. If this production reorganisation did take place, then half of the extra production of Y could be used to compensate consumers for the loss of one unit of X, and the rest could be distributed so as to increase the utility level of one, or both, consumers. If such a Pareto improvement is possible then it must mean that the original situation was not Pareto optimal. Thus for there to be Pareto optimality in both production and distribution

$$MRS_{YX}^{A,B} = MRT_{XY}. \tag{3}$$

Returning to Figure 12A.4, it can be seen that only at point R' on the contract curve OR are the slopes of the indifference curves equal to the slope of the PPF at R.

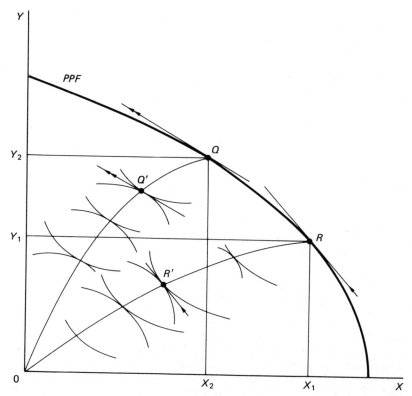

FIGURE 12A.4   Pareto efficiency in production and distribution

Similarly, on the contract curve OQ only the distribution allocation represented by Q' satisfies condition (3) above.

THE UTILITY POSSIBILITY FRONTIER

At R in Figure 12A.4, above, B consumes nothing, and thus has a zero utility level, while A's utility is at a maximum, given this particular output combination. Moving along the contract curve towards O, B's utility increases and A's diminishes until, at O, A's utility is zero and B's is at a maximum. This change in the utility levels of A and B is traced out by the line U_1U_1' in Figure 12A.5. This line is known as a utility possibility frontier, and it links together distribution allocations of a given production mix that satisfy the Pareto optimality condition (2). Only the utility combination shown by R'', which corresponds to point R' in Figure 12A.4, also satisfies condition (3), however. Similarly, on the utility possibility frontier U_2U_2', which corresponds to the production mix shown by Q in Figure 12A.4, the allocation that satisfies the production and exchange condition (3) is Q'', corresponding to Q' in Figure 12A.4.

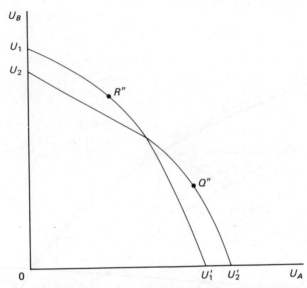

FIGURE 12A.5   Utility possibility frontiers

Given that along the *PPF* in Figure 12A.4 there are an infinite number of possible Pareto optimal production combinations then there are also an infinite number of corresponding utility possibility frontiers. Although these may intersect, they trace out an outer envelope known as the grand utility possibility frontier (*GUPF*). This *GUPF* joins up all the points that satisfy Pareto optimality condition (3), including *R"* and *Q"*, as shown in Figure 12A.6.

Along the *GUPF* there are an infinite number of utility combinations and so the problem of which one to choose still remains. If a particular utility combination could be identified as being preferable to all the others then by working backwards the corresponding output combination and the most efficient input mixes to produce these output levels could be identified.

THE SOCIAL WELFARE FUNCTION

One method of finding this 'best' solution is to suppose that society has a social welfare function (*SWF*) that can be represented by a series of indifference curves over different values of *A*'s and *B*'s utility, such as those shown by W_1, W_2, W_3 in Figure 12A.7. These show that the most preferred utility distribution is represented by *M*. With this knowledge the optimal production and input combinations, and the best method of distributing output, can be worked out.

The form that any such *SWF* might take is based on value-judgements and there is no way of objectively determining it. Arrow[1] demonstrated that such a preference

---

1. K. J. Arrow, 'A Difficulty in the Concept of Social Welfare', *Journal of Political Economy*, vol. 58 (1950), pp. 328–46.

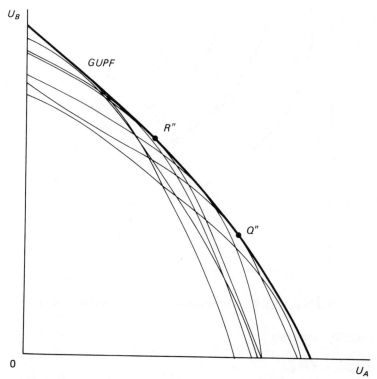

FIGURE 12A.6   The grand utility possibility frontier

ordering could not be determined by voting, but that is only one way in which a government might try to determine society's preferences for different policies. In any case, this is a theoretical model that bears no resemblance to the way policy objectives are specified in reality and there is not much point in pursuing further the question of how this sort of *SWF* could be derived. As pointed out in the main section of this chapter, the unrealistic assumptions cannot be justified on the usual methodological grounds used in positive economics because nothing is being predicted.

The main argument arising from this analysis that has some relevance to actual policy decisions is the question of whether or not perfect competition in all markets will ensure a Pareto optimal allocation of resources in the economy. The question of whether or not this might be the 'best' Pareto optimum allocation remains unanswered, given that the *SWF* cannot be unambiguously defined.

PERFECT COMPETITION AND PARETO OPTIMALITY

It can be shown that perfect competition satisfies the three conditions necessary for Pareto optimality, namely:

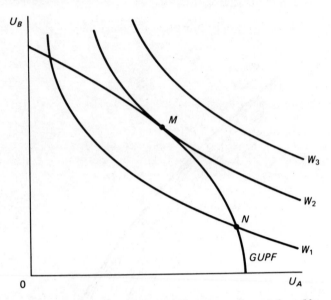

FIGURE 12A.7   The maximisation of social welfare

$$MRTS_{KL}^X = MRTS_{KL}^Y \tag{1}$$

$$MRS_{YX}^A = MRS_{YX}^B \tag{2}$$

$$MRS_{YX}^{A,B} = MRT_{XY} \tag{3}$$

Firms minimise the cost of any given output by adjusting the usage of inputs until the budget line representing the given price ratio is tangent to the relevant isoquant, that is,

$$MRTS_{KL} = P_L / P_K.$$

As all firms in perfect competition face the same set of prices, P_K and P_L, for inputs K and L, respectively, then it must be the case that

$$MRTS_{KL}^X = P_L / P_K = MRTS_{KL}^Y.$$

Thus condition (1) for Pareto optimality is met.

Consumers maximise utility subject to the budget constraint that they face when the slope of the highest attainable indifference curve is tangent to the slope of their budget constraint, that is,

$$MRS_{YX} = P_X / P_Y.$$

Since in perfect competition all consumers face the same set of prices, P_X and P_Y, for goods X and Y, respectively, then it must be the case that

$$MRS_{YX}^A = P_X/P_Y = MRS_{YX}^B$$

Thus condition (2) for Pareto optimality is met.

The satisfaction of the third condition for Pareto optimality requires rather more explanation. With reference to Figure 12A.8, starting at R, consider a small increase, ΔX, in the output of good X. The cost of this increase will be the change in X multiplied by the marginal cost of X, that is, $\Delta X.MC_X$. To remain on the *PPF*, the production of Y must be reduced to compensate for this increased output of X. The cost saved by reducing production of Y by ΔY will be $\Delta Y.MC_Y$, and this must be equal to the extra cost incurred by expanding production of X, given that on the *PPF* production is Pareto efficient and all resources are used up.

Thus $\Delta X.MC_X = -\Delta Y.MC_Y$, since ΔY itself is negative

and so $\Delta Y/\Delta X = MC_X/MC_Y$

The ratio $\Delta Y/\Delta X$ is also the negative of the slope of the *PPF* and thus equal to the MRT_{XY}. Therefore

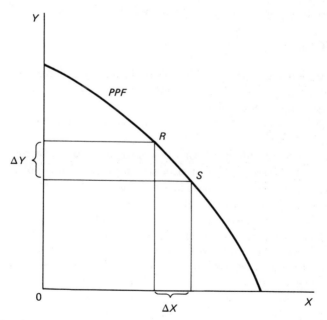

FIGURE 12A.8   The rate of change of the production possibility frontier

$$MRT_{XY} = -\Delta Y/\Delta X = MC_X/MC_Y.$$

In perfect competition price equals marginal cost and so

$$P_X = MC_X \quad \text{and} \quad P_Y = MC_Y.$$

Therefore $MRT_{XY} = MC_X/MC_Y = P_X/P_Y$.

It has already been shown above that

$$P_X/P_Y = MRS^A_{YX} = MRS^B_{YX}$$

and so

$$MRT_{XY} = P_X/P_Y = MRS^A_{YX} = MRS^B_{YX}.$$

Thus condition (3) for Pareto optimality is met under perfect competition.

Although it has been demonstrated that if there exists a state of perfect competition in all markets then all the necessary conditions for Pareto optimality are satisfied, this does not mean that it has been 'proved' that perfect competition yields the 'best' allocation of resources. One obvious possibility, which can be seen from Figure 12A.7, is that perfect competition may achieve a position on the *GUPF* such as N, which is not the most preferred Pareto optimal organisation of the economy. Some other criticisms of the Pareto optimality are explained in the main body of this chapter.

QUESTIONS

1. What is the difference between welfare economics and positive economics?
2. What value-judgements are implicitly made if Pareto optimality is used as the criterion for making social policy decisions?
3. What criticisms might be raised at the use of Pareto optimality in actual policy decisions?
4. What price would the theory of consumer surplus recommend for a nationalised industry? What criticisms are there of this policy, (a) from a practical viewpoint in these industries and (b) due to the shortcomings of consumer surplus as a welfare indicator?
5. How have economists suggested that the optimum level of an externality, such as pollution, can be determined? What criticisms can be made of this approach?
6. 'The purpose of introducing cable TV is that broadcasting companies can stop people viewing programmes that they could watch if they were broadcast from a transmitter.' Comment, with respect to the distinction between private and public goods.
7. Does the provision of a public good necessarily mean that it is produced by the state? Are all state-produced goods public goods?

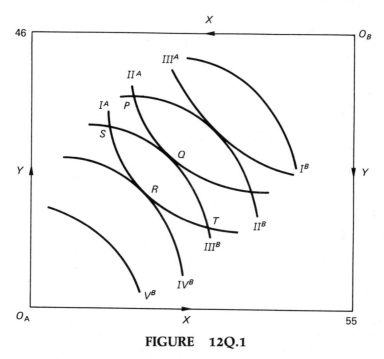

FIGURE 12Q.1

8. When will the 'free rider' problem occur?

9. If there are two markets in an economy, and in one $P = MC$ and in the other $P = KMC$, where $K > 1$ and cannot be altered, which good should be taxed to bring about a 'second best' solution?

10. What are the three sets of marginal conditions necessary for the efficient allocation of resources?

   Is a state of perfect competition in all markets necessary and sufficient to ensure a Pareto optimal allocation of resources? Assuming that a social welfare function can be imposed, is perfect competition both necessary and sufficient to achieve the allocation of resources that maximises social welfare?

11. Assume an economy has limited amounts of two resources, K and L, which are used to produce two goods, X and Y, and these are consumed by the two consumers, A and B. In Figure 12Q.1 the indifference maps of A and B are shown in an Edgeworth box diagram for given amounts of X and Y. Are the following changes in the distribution of goods improvements according to the Pareto criteria: (i) from P to Q; (ii) from R to Q; (iii) from S to T; (iv) from R to S? What price ratio for the two goods is compatible with distribution Q? What position would correspond to the maximum utility for consumer A?

Index